Corporate Strategies to Internationalise the Cost of Capital

Corporate Strategies to Internationalise the Cost of Capital

Lars Oxelheim, Arthur Stonehill,
Trond Randøy, Kaisa Vikkula,
Kåre B. Dullum and Karl-Markus Modén

With contribution by:

Eva Liljeblom
Anders Löflund
Svante Krokfors

HANDELSHØJSKOLENS FORLAG
Copenhagen Business School Press

© Handelshøjskolens Forlag, *Copenhagen Business School Press*, 1998

Printed in Denmark 1998
Set in Plantin and printed by AKA-PRINT A/S, Århus
Cover designed by Kontrapunkt
Book designed by Jørn Ekstrøm
ISBN 87-16-13271-8

Series A
Copenhagen Studies in Economics
and Management, No. 12

Distribution

Scandinavia:
Munksgaard/DBK, Siljangade 2-8, P.O. Box 1731
DK-2300 Copenhagen S, Denmark
phone +45 3269 7788, fax: +45 3269 7789

North America:
Global Management, LLC, Book Service, 2564 Branch Street, B2
Middleton, WI 53562, USA
phone +1 608 836 0088, fax: +1 608 836 0087
E-mail: 102135.2151@compuserve.com

Rest of the World:
Marston Book Service, P.O. Box 269,
Abington, Oxfordshire, OX14 4YN, UK
phone +44 (0) 1235 465500, fax: +44 (0) 1235 465555
E-mail Direct Customers: direct.order@marston.co.uk
E-mail Booksellers: trade.order@marston.co.uk

Preface

Lars Oxelheim, Arthur Stonehill and Trond Randøy

The genesis of this book sprang from the relationships first established at the Danish Summer Research Institute (DSRI) at Gilleleje, Denmark during three two-week research summer workshops in 1990, 1991, and 1992. The DSRI was organised by Lauge Stetting, Chairman of the Institute of International Economics and Management at the Copenhagen Business School. The workshops were funded primarily by grants from the Danish Academy of Science and several non-profit funds (Danish Social Science Research Council, The Research Academy, the Danish Society for the Advancement of Business Education, the Danish Central Bank Foundation, the J. Lauritzen Foundation, Hedorf's Foundation, and the Krista and Viggo Petersen Foundation). The theme of the workshops was preparation for an integrated single market within the European Economic Community (now European Union) in 1992.

Each summer 25 senior scholars and 35 junior scholars (mainly doctoral students) were invited to attend DSRI free of charge in order to discuss research papers prepared by the participants and to establish future research networks. Participants were mainly from Europe and North America but included a few participants from Japan and Israel.

One network that grew out of these workshops focused on issues related to corporate efforts to internationalise the cost of capital. A sub-group of this network then decided to put the country-wise experience as regards institutional changes and corporate strategies impacting the internationalisation together in a publication; actually the current book. The sub-group comprises three senior scholars (Kåre B. Dullum, Lars Oxelheim and Arthur Stonehill), two of the junior scholars (dr. Trond Randøy and dr. Kaisa Vikkula) and one researcher who joined later (dr. Karl-Markus Modén). This network met numerous times after the DSRI during the period 1993-1997. In 1996, to secure the perspective of the investors, dr. Eva Liljeblom, dr. Anders Löflund and dr. Svante Krokfors were invited to submit a contribution which became Chapter 3. The different sections of the manuscript were finally completed during intensive three week workshops conducted at the University of Hawaii at Manoa in February-March 1996 and 1997. We are greatly indebted for the editorial assistance of Liv M. Borgen and Karin Roland both from Agder College, Norway.

A regional approach is adopted in the book. The region studied is the Nordic one meaning that companies based in Denmark, Finland, Norway and Sweden have been under investigation. All four Nordic equity markets have transformed themselves from illiquid, segmented equity markets during the post-World War II period to more liquid, nearly unsegmented markets at present. The regional approach provides excellent opportunities for comparisons of many relevant dimensions of this transformation process, while having most other aspects matched and without losing in terms of generality. The joint experience as described and analysed in this book should be of great importance to policy-makers in countries where capital markets are still to some extent segmented or illiquid. The same is true for corporate managers trying to capture an understanding of the role of segmented markets on the competitiveness of their own company.

Plan of this Book

In Chapter 1, Lars Oxelheim presents some of the main elements of the transformation of national equity markets into well-integrated parts of a global equity market. He emphasises the role of regulators, corporate managers and investors in this process. In Chapter 2, Oxelheim provides background data necessary for a better understanding of the role of each of these participants in the internationalisation of the cost of capital. Key dates as regards introduction and dismantling of regulations are provided together with descriptions of take-over defences practised by companies in the Nordic region. Time series data on cross-border equity-related activities are also given in this chapter.

In Chapter 3 Eva Liljeblom, Anders Löflund and Svante Krokfors provide a closer look at Nordic equities from the perspective of investors. The chapter identifies the magnitude of the benefits from international diversification from a Nordic point of view.

In Chapter 4, Karl-Markus Modén and Lars Oxelheim measure the transformation from segmented to integrated equity markets by means of statistical event studies. They compare the response of the domestic equity market to the announcement of the undertaking of a domestic equity issue as opposed to an issue directed to investors abroad. Differences in the responses are then interpreted in terms of segmentation.

Chapter 5 contains a presentation by Arthur Stonehill and Kåre B. Dullum on the different strategies used by companies to even out unfavourable – in an international perspective – differences in their cost of capital. They give a corporate explanation of why the transformation was both necessary and desirable. They also chronicle the gradual transition from selling directed share issues in specific foreign markets to the present mode of selling Euroequity issues simultaneously in many markets.

Chapters 6 to 17 present individual case studies of Nordic firms that have issued equity abroad. Corporate strategies are the key issue in these chapters. Chapters 6-8, covering strategies by Danish companies, have been written by Arthur Stonehill and Kåre B. Dullum, Chapters 9-11 about Finnish companies by Kaisa Vikkula, Chapters 12-14 about Norwegian companies by Trond Randøy and, finally, Chapters 15-17 about Swedish companies by Lars Oxelheim and Arthur Stonehill.

Table of contents

Summary

Lars Oxelheim, Arthur Stonehill and Trond Randøy

The focus of this book is on the transformation process of capital markets – from segmentation to integration. We are especially emphasising the role of corporate strategies in the internationalisation of the cost of capital. The empirical analysis is regional in scope and involves the four major Nordic countries. The Nordic region is characterised by having been severely regulated in the post-WWII period. By using this region as an example, the current book provides a chart of almost all imaginable barriers and inefficiencies that affect internationalisation of capital.

In Chapter 1 Lars Oxelheim points out that the internationalisation of the cost of capital should be seen as a process with three stakeholders; managers, regulators, and investors. On the one hand regulators pursue policies that are aimed at insulating the domestic market from the global one, and on the other hand managers strive to eliminate disadvantages by trying to circumvent barriers and restrictions imposed by regulators. Finally, investors are characterised by an endless search for new profit opportunities and portfolio risk reduction created by the interplay between these two forces.

In the 1980s one major venue for companies to escape a "thin", inefficient and regulated domestic market was to place an equity issue on a foreign "prestigious" capital market. A successful issue was supposed to render the company benefits from a higher price/earnings (P/E) ratio abroad as compared to the one at home.

According to Oxelheim, the internationalisation of the cost of capital can, at the macro level, be divided into four stages with relevance for the analysis put forward in this book.

In Chapter 2 Oxelheim points out that during the early 1980s a gradual liberalisation came about in the Nordic countries that was not expressed in terms of an explicit deregulation. Rather, it was reflected in a more relaxed attitude by central bankers in dealing with authorisation issues. Oxelheim illustrates in this chapter in details all dimensions of the Nordic deregulation process. Oxelheim argues that even if the deregulation process has proceeded at a high pace, there is still lots of room for corporate managers to maintain control and resist takeovers.

In Chapter 3 Liljeblom, Löflund, and Krokfors investigate the magnitude of the benefits from international diversification from a Nordic perspective. One question of special interest is whether potentially increased co-movement of stock markets, together with more volatile Nordic currencies, have resulted in decreased benefits from international diversification towards the end of the 1980s. They find significant increases in stock market co-movement. In spite of that, when *ex ante* investment strategies are investigated, substantial benefits from international diversification are revealed for the Nordic countries. While the *ex ante* global minimum variance portfolio generally outperforms the other strategies, quite good results are also obtained for a simple equally weighted Nordic portfolio.

In Chapter 4, Modén and Oxelheim discuss how large Nordic companies in the early 1980s started to go abroad to tap foreign sources of capital. This was concurrent with the revival of the Nordic stock markets as sources of new risk capital. Their hypothesis is that the stock price reaction to an announcement about a foreign equity issue should differ depending on whether the issuing company was previously traded on a segmented capital market only, or if it was traded on a stock market that is integrated with the rest of the world. The chapter shows how foreign equity issues by Nordic companies in the pre-deregulation period produced positive abnormal returns. Modén and Oxelheim conclude that there seems to be a lack of perfect international integration of Nordic equity markets in the period 1981-1986. However, the analysis of the next period (1987-1993) indicates an increasing integration of these markets.

Chapter 5 explains why and how Nordic firms have reacted and responded to the opportunities presented by increased investor demand for equities originating in foreign countries and currencies. Corporate management resident in both Nordic and non-Nordic equity markets have had to devise strategies to overcome the root causes of market segmentation. This chapter discusses the alternative paths for a firm to internationalise its cost and availability of capital. Stonehill and Dullum describe the reasons why firms crosslist their shares abroad, which are broader than merely escaping a segmented and illiquid home equity market. Furthermore they discuss the three main instruments used to tap foreign equity markets; directed issues, Euroequity issues, and strategic alliances. Barriers and costs associated with listing and selling equities abroad are emphasized.

In Part IV the trilogy of Danish cases written by Stonehill and Dullum illustrate three different scenarios for raising equity capital internationally. Chapter 6 illustrates how Novo Industri A/S (NOVO) performed a directed share issue. In Chapter 7, Tele Danmark A/S is an example of a modern Euroequity issue motivated by a desire to privatise. In Chapter 8, Bang & Olufsen A/S shows how a firm can raise equity capital on favourable terms through a strategic alliance when a public issue would not generate an acceptable revenue.

The Novo case describes the path taken by Novo to internationalise its cost of capital and the obstacles it faced along the way. The Novo case was very significant for Nordic companies because it was the first Nordic company to float a convertible bond issue in the Eurobond market (1978) accompanied by a listing on the London Stock Exchange. It was also the first Nordic Firm since World War II to float a successful public stock issue in the United States and to list on NASDAQ and subsequently on the New York Stock Exchange (1981).

The Tele Danmark case unfolds in April 1994, long after the Danish and other Nordic equity markets had become deregulated. The path to its Euroequity issue was also made much easier by the many successful privatisation issues by other (non-Danish) companies during the 1980s and the early 1990s. In fact, its USD 2.9 billion issue was not at all unusual for the modern Euroequity market, but it was by far the largest Danish equity issue ever floated.

The Bang & Olufsen strategic alliance with Philips NV shows that a company does not need a sparkling stock market track record in order to attract foreign investors. Both Bang & Olufsen and Philips NV recognised the synergies that might be obtained through a strategic alliance, with an equity infusion by Philips into Bang & Olufsen. Philips was even willing to pay a 30% premium over Bang & Olufsen's stock market price to capture anticipated operating as well as other synergies.

In Part V Vikkula presents three cases which illustrate the transition of the Finnish equity market from segmentation to integration with global capital markets. Many of the first international equity issues of Finnish companies in the early 1980s were directed issues in a single foreign market. Foreign investors saw at the outset of deregulation the capital gains opportunity in the Finnish stock market. During the transition period in the 1980s stock market reactions to international equity issues were mainly positive. Companies were able to issue new equity at attractive prices while the stock market was going up. In the early 1990s Finnish capital markets became more efficient and well integrated with the global capital markets. In the 1990s, stock market reactions to new issue announcements were mainly negative, with the exception of high-tech companies that were enjoying the investor rally.

In Chapter 9 the Amer case illustrates the whole corporate and capital market transition process with different types of equity issues designed to seize opportunities in the prevailing market conditions. In Chapter 10 the Nokia case demonstrates how a fast growing global company from a small domestic capital market can reduce its cost of capital to the level of its large global competitors by globalising its capital sourcing. In Chapter 11 Vikkula shows how the Huhtamaki case represents a strategic alliance with a foreign partner, where the foreign partner supplied capital, but the controlling interest remained with the old Finnish shareholders.

Chapter 9 covers three international equity issues by Amer: A directed issue in 1984, a private placement in 1986 and an Euroequity issue in 1989. In the early 1980's Amer, a diversified Finnish company, was ready for a major new acquisition. The company realised that it was about to outgrow the Finnish market and should start to look for new growth opportunities abroad. In May 1984 Amer was listed on the London Stock Exchange. At the same time a new equity issue was targeted to British and US institutional investors. The purpose of the London listing was not to raise capital, but to establish Amer's name internationally and to enhance company reliability for future international acquisitions. When foreign investors became aware of the strong economic growth and domestic consumer demand in Finland in the mid-1980's, Amer became their favourite stock. In 1987 Amer established a sponsored American Depositary Receipt (ADR) facility with Citibank N.A. in New York, but the facility remained passive. US institutional investors developed a knowledge about European equities and preferred trading in Europe where the liquidity and the knowledge of the local stock market was better.

In Chapter 10 Vikkula shows how Nokia's debut on Wall Street with a FIM 2.5 billion (USD 484 million) stock issue was an immediate hit. The issue was oversubscribed. Nokia, a leading telecommunication company, became the first Finnish company to be listed on the New York Stock Exchange. Nokia was the first Finnish company to price the issue without any discount, at the closing price of the Helsinki Stock Exchange on July 1, 1994. Nokia's rapid growth in telecommunications not only astonished the securities markets, but also far exceeded the most revolutionary thoughts of Nokia's management. Nokia's finance strategy has been closely linked to the corporate strategy. Nokia wanted to internationalise its cost and availability of capital and to reduce its dependence on traditional bank loans. Nokia was among the first Finnish companies to launch a USD 300 million Eurocommercial paper (ECP) program in 1988. An announcement of a FIM 2.5 billion issue and NYSE listing was published May 25, 1994. The share price of the preference share fell from FIM 438 to FIM 410, but the turnover peaked from 89,000 to 198,000 shares that one day. The share price started to rise steadily from June 14, 1994 onwards. Within three months Nokia's shares had surged 45% vs. a 2% gain for the NYSE composite index (Exhibit 10.5). The price formation had clearly shifted from the Helsinki Stock Exchange to New York. Nokia had name recognition as one of the world's leading telecommunication companies. Its stock was priced comparably to its peers, Ericsson and Motorola. Nokia's ownership structure changed dramatically. In the mid-1990s, a total of 61.4% of the shares were held by foreigners, mainly by U.S. investors.

In Chapter 11 Vikkula discusses the strategic alliance between Huhtamaki and Procordia's United Brands confectionery business. The other part of the Procordia/Huhtamaki alliance was the establishment of a joint venture between Procordia's pharmaceutical company, Kabi Pharmacia, and Huhtamaki's pharmaceuticals division (Leiras) in January 1994. In 1993, Huhtamaki was a Finnish-based consumer products group with worldwide operations. The financing of Huhtamaki's acquisition of Procordia's confectionery business was done through a targeted share issue. Procordia paid a premium of some 10%. The stock market's reaction to the announced alliance and agreed transactions between Huhtamaki and Procordia was positive.

In Part VI Randøy investigates three Norwegian companies that illustrate some of the financial innovations that companies took in order to succeed in the international marketplace. Companies, such as Norsk Data (Chapter 12) and Hafslund Nycomed (Chapter 13), understood the necessity of accessing internationally-priced equity. The three cases show that the different financial strategies promoted the overall internationalisation of these companies. The Norsk Data case is an example of internationalising capital in the early 1980s, whereas, the Elektrisk Bureau (Chapter 14) case is from the mid-1980s, and the Hafslund Nycomed case from the early 1990s.

In Chapter 12 Norsk Data provides an interesting illustration of how sourcing international capital made this company able to compete head-on with large U.S. or European rivals. At a higher P/E-ratio than on the domestic equity market, Norsk Data was able to sell its shares and at a similar P/E-ratio to other comparable American computer companies. In July 1981 Norsk Data listed on the London Stock Exchange. During 1981 the stock price increased by 700%. In March 1982 Norsk Data made its first foreign equity issue in London, providing the company with NOK 100 million. A second successful issue was made in September 1984 in the United States, providing the company with NOK 396 million.

In Chapter 13 Randøy argues that by the end of the 1980s the degree of market segmentation in Norway had decreased substantially. However, Hafslund Nycomed's large market capitalisation relative to the Norwegian equity market, made the company less attractive to domestic investors. Another important fact was that the U.S. equity market was much more experienced in assessing pharmaceutical companies. Hafslund's two successful international stock issues, one on June 22, 1989 in London, and the second one in New York on June 22, 1992, are discussed.

Chapter 14 shows how Elektrisk Bureau was able to make a strategic alliance with ASEA, later known as ABB. Through a 20% targeted issue towards ASEA in September 1986, Elektrisk Bureau was able to obtain NOK 370.5 million in new equity. Elektrisk Bureau's stock price increased 18% within two weeks after the announcement of the strategic alliance.

In Part VII Oxelheim and Stonehill discuss the internationalisation of the cost of capital as it relates to Swedish companies. Three Swedish cases – Fortia, L M Ericsson and Electrolux – were chosen from a much larger sample of cases (see Chapter 4) in order to illustrate typical directed share issues prior to deregulation, as well as a post-deregulation Euroequity issue. All three cases reinforce our earlier findings in Chapter 5 that Nordic companies sell equity issues abroad not only because of the potential for higher share prices and liquidity, but also to enhance the company's image with customers, suppliers, the news media, and the financial community.

The Fortia case (Chapter 15) was a significant case of internationalisation of capital because in November 1981 Sweden was still a very segmented equity market. Fortia followed in the footsteps of Novo Industri (Chapter 6) with similar favourable results for its share price. Apart from enjoying the share price premium abroad, Fortia's equity issue was motivated by a desire to gain more credibility in the worldwide pharmaceutical industry to help market its products.

L.M. Ericsson´s (Chapter 16) internationalisation of capital was partly motivated by a desire to increase its credibility and image as a technology leader. It felt that success with the U.S. news media and financial community would enhance its worldwide reputation. Further motivation came from the need to improve its debt ratio, provide funds for expansion, and fund an expected increase in working capital requirements. Although the large initial equity issue was sold out, many of the shares flew back to Stockholm, a segmented and illiquid home market. The result was a drop of 32% in the unrestricted share price by March 1984. This illustrates the potential downside of a foreign equity issue.

In Chapter 17 the AB Electrolux Euroequity issue of $275 million in June 1986 illustrates what could happen after Sweden had almost deregulated its equity market. Unlike Fortia and L.M. Ericsson, the shares of AB Electrolux were not undervalued by world standards. Since AB Electrolux pursued a growth-by-acquisition strategy, it became necessary eventually to undertake a foreign equity issue to meet foreign exchange restrictions. The acquisitions of Zanussi in Italy and White in the United States were financed in part by an unusually high level of debt. An equity issue was necessary to lower the resulting debt ratio. The Swedish equity market was too small and illiquid to provide the equivalent of $275,000,000, the amount raised by the Euroequity issue. Similar to Fortia and L.M. Ericsson, AB Electrolux Euroequity issue was also motivated by a desire to enhance the company's corporate image and credibility with customers, suppliers, and the worldwide financial community.

Part I

Nordic Equity Markets
In Transition

1. From Market Segmentation to Market Integration

Lars Oxelheim

1.1. Introduction

During the last two decades corporate managers have had to learn how to cope with dramatic changes in the structure and functioning of national financial markets and the financial service industries. In those days ignorance had a high price in terms of deteriorating competitiveness. In the mid-1990s the price has decreased since differences between national financial markets have vanished and these markets have become more or less perfectly integrated parts of a global financial market. However, contrary to this commonly held view the description applies only to some parts of the global financial system; i.e. to a large extent to credit markets of some developed countries when measured in a capital flow perspective (Oxelheim 1996). For the case of equity markets the integration process has been slower and a large number of "barriers" to perfect integration does still exist in many developed countries. The way the transformation process – from segmented to integrated capital markets – has proceeded will be discussed in this book with special emphasis on the role of corporate strategies in the internationalisation of the cost of capital.

The internationalisation of the cost of capital should be seen as a process with three stakeholders; managers, regulators, and investors. In the battle between these forces the regulators for different reasons pursue policies that are aimed at insulating the domestic market from the global one. As regards the cost of capital, managers on the other pole strive to eliminate disadvantages by trying to circumvent barriers and restrictions imposed by regulators. In between these two poles the investors are characterised by an endless search for new profit opportunities and portfolio risk reduction. The "drivers" are inefficiencies created by the regulators and other inefficiencies, such as general market inefficiency, asymmetric information or tax wedges.

In a competitive environment the drive for profits generates financial and organisational innovations. The successful ones have been emulated by other actors, with the resulting erosion of profits to be made from them. In the case of cost of capital this will mean an equalisation. The emergence of the "information age" paved the way for the development of highly sophisticated financial engineering systems, such as the swap market in the 1970s and the subsequent development of markets for options and futures. Once financial engineering was established, the likelihood increased for new solutions to bypass every new regulation imposed. This is the process of combined innovation and "creative destruction" which Schumpeter (1943) identified as the driving force of a capitalist economy. Since the 1970s this process seems to have become increasingly typical of financial markets and should be seen as a major component in the internationalisation of the cost of capital.

The role played by companies in the equalisation of the cost of capital while maintaining control is the key issue of this study. In the 1980s and beginning of the 1990s one major venue for companies to escape a "thin", inefficient and heavily regulated domestic market was to place an equity issue on a foreign "prestigious" market. In order to make such an issue successful companies often had to proceed stepwise; to start with a less "prestigious" market, with a listing or a bond issue to get increased global recognition. A successful issue was supposed to render the company benefits from a higher price/earnings (P/E) ratio abroad as compared to the one at home. In Chapter 5 the benefits will be discussed in greater details. Over time there have also been other reasons, beside the purely financial ones, for issuing abroad. One such reason relates to the marketing of the company and its products.

1.2. On the Analysis of the Cost of Capital

The cost of capital encompasses debt and equity costs. The expected cost of capital is determined by the rate of return required by investors to purchase and hold equity and debt instruments. The corporate cost of capital will be equalised across countries on an ex ante, after-tax and risk-adjusted basis, provided efficiency exists and there are no major distortional costs. Hence, the complete equalisation means perfect international capital market integration.

Barriers to perfect integration can be raised by regulators at the border of a country; e.g. in the shape of capital controls (external regulations) or on the domestic market (internal regulation); e.g. in the shape of ownership control. However, barriers can also be raised by the companies themselves in order to maintain corporate control (corporate take-over defences). A number of take-over defences will be highlighted in the next chapter. Without preempting that discussion we can pinpoint one such measure that has become a hotly debated issue in the mid-1990s; the corporate use of shares with different voting power. The "one share-one vote" issue is currently on the desk of the European Union regulators.

In this book we will concentrate on the cost of equity. The cost of debt has been previously investigated in Oxelheim (1996). In the Modigliani-Miller (1958) world there would be no argument in favour of either of the two forms at the expense of the other. In the real world, however, the relative importance of the two will to a large extent be influenced by politicians and their actions; predominantly fiscal policy measures. Tax policies and interest deductibility have worked in favour of debt financing of corporations in most countries.

Even in the case of perfect financial integration from a capital flow view point segmentation may prevail as regards the corporate cost of capital.[1] Segmentation may be caused by differences as regards credit risk assessment in the case of credit market integration and as regards paradigms for assessing corporate profit prospects in the case of capital market integration. A case for segmentation may be found in the home country of a company. Small country companies may have an information disadvantage compared to large-country-based companies.

A high *relative* cost of capital will mean that the sustainable profits out of two companies similar in terms of project risk will differ and that the company with the higher cost of capital (lower sustainable profits) will be outcompeted by the other company. At an aggregated level this will mean a deteriorating competitiveness for an entire industry or of a whole nation. Moreover, additional long-run implications for the economy will appear due to differences in cost of capital. Real investments that have a positive net present value when undertaken in one country will have a negative present value in the other country and, hence, will not be undertaken. Consequently, an understanding of the relative cost of capital should be of crucial importance not only to managers aiming at corporate or shareholder wealth maximisation but to all politicians interested in economic growth and welfare enhancing activities.

---

1. With a capital flow perspective means that changes in the risk adjusted differences between government securities will give rise to capital flows.

Many studies have claimed that a low Japanese cost of capital as compared to the US has rendered Japan a competitive advantage over the US.[2] However, in these studies, like most focusing on the cost of capital, the calculations have turned out to be very tricky; providing many degrees of freedom in the interpretations.

1.3. Does a Global Market Exist?

It should also be emphasised at this early stage that the global market we will be referring to in the book is nothing but a network of national financial markets. In the absence of a global central bank and global institutions, the creation of a truly global market has to be assessed in terms of the closeness of links between national markets, i.e. how high is the level of international financial integration. This integration is often measured in terms of capital flows, which take place through the foreign exchange market and the market for various financial assets. Among these assets we can distinguish between the market for intermediates and the market for securities. In the first of these, claims are transferred via financial intermediaries, while in the second market liquid claims such as equity, various fixed income securities and derivatives are transferred directly between issuers and investors. This book will be focusing on aspects of integration related to equity transfer.

1.4. The Case for a Regional Approach

The empirical analysis will be regional in scope and involve the four major Nordic countries.[3] The Nordic region is characterised by having been severely regulated in the post-WWII period. By using this region as an example the current book will provide a chart of almost all imaginable barriers to circumvent and inefficiencies to cope with at the corporate strategic level. This is offered without any loss in generality.

Moreover, by adopting a regional approach several factors can be matched across countries leaving room for an in-depth analysis of other relevant aspects. As the Nordic region consists of a group of countries singularly free from intra-regional barriers, its high degree of transparency

2.   See e.g. Kester (1986), Meerschwan (1989), Hoshi et al. (1989), McCauley and Zimmer (1989) and French and Poterba (1991).
3.   Because of its relative size, the fifth Nordic country, Iceland, has been excluded. Moreover, its capital market is very young and immature.

allows us to concentrate on differences in the transformation of their national capital markets without having to control for differences in language, accounting principles, and disclosure norms.

The Nordic countries constitute a very homogenous region in many respects, with close-knit economic relations, similar levels of welfare (and high taxes), and a common cultural and social background. Despite these similarities, there are also some major differences between the countries, which suggests that the deregulation process may have proceeded differently in terms of both speed and outcome. Some major differences may be mentioned already here. One regards the membership in the EC and later the EU. The Danish membership dates back to 1973, while Sweden and Finland joined as late as 1995. Norway remains outside despite two referendums.

Another dimension of relevance to a study of equity markets appears in the structure of the manufacturing industry. The role of large multinationals has traditionally been important in Sweden, while small and medium size companies have been prominent in the other Nordic countries. Among the top 1,000 global publicly-traded companies, according to market values as of May 1992 we find twenty-one Nordic companies: four Danish, no Finnish, two Norwegian and fifteen Swedish.[4] In terms of the number of multinational companies per capita, Sweden occupies a top position in a European ranking together with the Netherlands and Switzerland.

Moreover, the internationalisation of the manufacturing industries of all four countries is continuously increasing.[5] In terms of net flows of FDI as a percentage of GDP, Sweden exhibits a special feature. It had the highest gap (1986-90) between outward and inward investment (3.44 percent outward and 0.56 percent inward) of any OECD country. Finland also exhibited a big gap, 1.5 percent, whereas Denmark and Norway showed a tiny average net outflow of half a percentage point.[6]

1.5. Market-based Versus Bank-based Economies

Since the book emphasises only the equity part of capital cost the relation between equity markets and other parts of the financial markets should be addressed at this early stage of the presentation. As a general phenomenon

---

4. Business Week, July 13, 1992.
5. See Oxelheim and Gärtner (1994).
6. See OECD (1992).

the distinction between equity and debt has become blurred over time due to financial engineering. The problems may be illustrated by falling debt ratios in French companies as a result of an increase in equity financing by share issues giving limited or zero voting rights.

National financial systems can be classified according to the basic setup of financial and supervisory institutions. A common way is to classify the systems into two major cases: a market-based system with little government influence, and a bank-based system with heavy government influence. As a general rule the deregulation appears to have pushed national financial systems in the direction of market-based national systems. In the mid-1990s the UK system provides an excellent example of a European market-based system, while Germany exemplifies the opposite, i.e. a bank-based system with heavy government influence on the allocation of capital.

In any analysis of the financial market structure, the close involvement of industry in the development and transformation of national financial systems has to be emphasised. The financial systems differ across countries in that respect. For instance, there is no direct equivalent in the United States of the German system whereby the lead bank acts as equity holder and management supervisor, or of the Japanese Keiretsu system. Such differences in market structure have to be considered whenever comparisons of cost of capital are made. For example, identical leverage ratios may imply different levels of risk in the different countries. If they do, what light does this shed on cost-of-capital induced differences in competitiveness between countries?

In countries like France and Japan governments have owned the most substantial fraction of their respective financial systems. The governments of these countries have also used their ownership as a channel for providing assistance to companies through soft loans, subsidised credits, and government guarantees. The governments of the highly leveraged G-7 countries have tended to hinder securitized channels for debt financing.

The Nordic financial systems can be classified as bank-based systems. The Danish market comes closest to a market-based system with a credit market structure similar to that of the United States.[7] However, the 50% share of the credit stock held by the bond market is of different character in the two countries. In Denmark, as opposed to the US, the bond issues are more or less entirely made by the government or by mortgage insti-

---

7.   See Oxelheim (1996).

tutes. Hence, the Danish bond market has only offered cash management opportunities to Danish companies. However, indirectly they may have benefited by being able to borrow funds raised by mortgage institutes. In the other Nordic countries the share held by the bond market is fairly small and resembling that of the German and Japanese markets.

When it comes to debt ratios of non-financial companies, Finnish, Norwegian and Swedish companies are highly leveraged (above 60 percent), while Danish companies are parked some 5 to 10 percentage points lower. Many reasons for the high Nordic leverage can be found. Fairly close relationship between banks and non-financial companies is one reason for the Nordic companies' position in the upper part of the OECD leverage spectrum. However, since banks have only recently been allowed to own shares in these companies the relationship is not as strong as they are in Germany and Japan, for instance. In Germany, banks directly own almost 10 percent of the stock of shares. As a result of shares held in custody, they influence another 40%. In Japan, banks hold directly about one-fifth of total shareholding, while corporations have about one-third. The intermediaries' simultaneous holding of equity and debt claims provides an environment more favourable to leverage by reducing the agency cost of conflict between shareholders and debtholders.

As opposed to debt ratios of other OECD countries, the average debt ratio of US firms increased substantially in the 1980s. One reason for increased debt ratios in the United States was that equity was being bought back – an operation for which there is little evidence in the Nordic region. Taxation and "thin" national equity markets have also favoured a debt approach by Nordic companies.

1.6. External Regulation and Capital Controls

Capital controls have been directed predominantly at capital outflows, usually with a view to preserving scarce domestic savings for domestic use and reducing the risk of capital flight during periods of exchange rate pressure or balance-of-payments weakness. Restrictions on the inflow of capital from abroad have been imposed mainly for reasons of monetary control or for non-economic reasons, as in the case of foreign acquisitions of domestic business or investment in real estate. Some OECD countries have operated comprehensive exchange control regimes involving restrictions on capital outflows and inflows, thereby attempting to isolate their domestic financial markets from external influences. According to OECD

(1990) the most restrictive measures throughout the post-WWII period have concerned the admission of foreign securities into domestic capital markets. Whereas some form of control has been considered necessary by most countries because of the size of potential foreign placements relative to the absorption capacity of the domestic market, restrictions on domestic companies and institutions in issuing securities abroad have been much less pronounced.

Liberalisation of capital controls started to accelerate in the 1970s, gained momentum in the 1980s, and by the mid-1990s was nearly complete. In a global perspective, however, there is an alarming inconsistency in the policy path, as most countries implement further liberalisation on the tariff side, while at the same time increase the use of non-tariff barriers and measures that are incompatible with "fair" competition. Regulators are also beginning to realise that economic problems which appeared in the late 1980s were almost as much of a regulatory debacle as a financial one.

As a general feature the efficiency of external controls is a prerequisite for the efficiency of internal controls. The shelter provided by capital controls paves the way for politicians to create opportunities for rent-seeking. Companies benefiting from these opportunities may try to preserve the existing structure. Banks have for long periods in most countries benefited from ownership regulations providing them a franchise. Consequently they have not acted too eagerly to reduce the efficiency of parts of the regulatory body with relevance to this issue.

At the macro level, considering the efficiency of capital controls, the internationalisation of cost of capital can be divided into four stages. The first stage comprises the periods when capital controls were efficient; preventing crossborder equity transactions – issue or trade – to take place. The second stage applies to periods when capital controls have become inefficient (i.e. become *de facto* deregulated) or formally abolished (i.e. exposed to a de jure deregulation), but inefficiencies still remain as regards differences in cost of capital. The inefficiencies may reflect remaining internal regulations or tax wedges. The third stage involves periods when markets contain no formal barriers, but segmentation prevails at the company level, i.e. crossborder information asymmetries or information costs related to individual companies cause differences in capital costs. Finally, the fourth stage is reached when all inefficiencies in the market as well as at the corporate level have vanished and the national equity market has become an integrated part of the global equity market.

In the case of the Nordic countries, severe exchange controls were in force for many years in the post-WWII period. The Danish exchange rate regulation that dates back to 1931, was abolished in October 1988. The Finnish exchange control was reintroduced in the autumn of 1939 and remained in force until October 1991. In Norway, the exchange regulations were introduced in July 1950 and formally abolished in July 1990. Finally, in the case of Sweden, the foreign exchange controls were put in force in 1939 and dismantled in July 1989. However, the efficiency of the exchange controls of these countries was eroded long before the formal dismantling came about. Based on studies of bond rates, the Nordic exchange controls were inefficient as early as 1982, except possibly the Finnish *de facto* integration.[8] Capital controls that have applied specifically to Nordic equity markets will be discussed in greater details in Chapter 2.

1.7. The Internationalised Cost of Capital – Prospects for the Future

What might happen to the cost of capital in the next decade? Will total deregulation be the end-station? In the mid-1990s there are many signs that history might repeat itself.

The role of regulations can always be disputed and this is reflected in the many schools of thought on the subject. History shows that periods of war and general distress are followed by periods of extensive regulations. The "creative destruction" already mentioned, forces authorities to acknowledge the inefficiency of regulations by formal abolition, or by imposing new regulations. Hence, the pendulum swings around a set of regulations that can be seen as the minimum regulations required to guarantee the infrastructure of the financial markets. This is a set of regulations that promotes the soundness of a financial market and guarantees competition. By aiming for this set of regulations, national authorities should improve the general confidence of the market.

However, once national financial markets are approaching perfect global integration, there is a risk of policy-makers starting to compete in attracting investment in the financial industry, by adopting a "looser" interpretation of the content of this minimum set of regulations in the national regulatory body. Thus, they are potentially triggering a wave of re-regulation and by that a new segmentation of the cost of capital.

8. See Oxelheim (1996).

The high unemployment rates of the mid-1990s signal the kind of distress that may trigger such a wave. It has already triggered a race between countries to attract direct investments from abroad in order to create more jobs.[9] In a globalized world, however, the freedom for policy-makers to accomplish anything within the limits of their short political mandates and using devices compatible with fair competition is much restricted. The temptation to use the economic equivalent of a dose of anabolic steroids just to make the investment opportunities look attractive very quickly, may be too strong. The "steroids" comprising subsidies, soft loans, grants, equity participation on lower than market requirements, tax advantages, etc. will insert a wedge between domestic and foreign cost of capital and reverse the trend towards an internationalised cost of capital. The race will produce losers; countries in which the politicians will be inclined to listen to lobbyists recommending them to close the borders in order to reduce the outflow of foreign direct investments. There is thus a non-negligible likelihood that a period of global efforts to control capital flows may ensue. Although some elements in the liberalisation may be seen as irreversible others may still lend themselves to re-regulation. This would engender a great leap backwards in global welfare and a return from the "global factory" to multidomestic companies.

9.   See Oxelheim (1993).

References

French, K.M. and J.M. Poterba, 1991: "Were Japanese Stock Prices Too High?" *Journal of Financial Economics,* Vol.29, No.2, October, pp. 337-63.

Hoshi, T., A. Kashyap and D.Scharfstein, 1989: "Bank Monitoring and Investment: Evidence from the Changing Structure of Japanese Corporate Banking Relationship" in Hubbard, R.G. (ed): *Asymmetric Information, Corporate Finance and Investment.* Chicago: University of Chicago Press.

Kester, W. C.: "Capital and Ownership Structure: A Comparison of United States and Japanese Manufacturing Corporations". *Financial Management,* Spring 1986, pp. 5-16.

McCauley, R. and S. Zimmer, 1989: "Explaining Differences in the Cost of Capital". *Federal Reserve Bank of New York Quarterly Review,* Summer, pp. 7-28.

Meerschwan, D., 1989: "The Japanese financial System and the Cost of Capital" in Krugman, P. (ed.): *The US and Japan in the '90s: Trade and Investment.* Chicago: University of Chicago Press.

Modigliani, F. and M. Miller, 1958: "The Cost of Capital, Corporation Finance, and the Theory of Investment". *American Economic Review,* 48, pp. 261-97.

OECD, 1990: *Liberalisation of Capital Movements and Financial Services in the OECD Area.* Paris: OECD.

OECD, 1992: *National Accounts,* Vol 1, Paris: OECD.

Oxelheim, L., 1996: *Financial Markets in Transition – Globalization, Investment and Economic Growth.* London and New York: Routledge.

Oxelheim, L., 1993: "Foreign Direct Investment and the Liberalisation of Capital Movements" in Oxelheim, L. (ed.): *The Global Race for Foreign Direct Investment: Prospects for the Future.* Heidelberg: Springer Verlag.

Oxelheim, L. and R. Gärtner, 1994: "Small Country Manufacturing Industries in Transition – the Case of the Nordic Region". *Management International Review,* Vol. 34, No.4, pp. 351-70.

Schumpeter, J., 1943: *Capitalism, Socialism and Democracy,* (republished 1987 in London: Unwin paperbacks.).

2. Regulations, Institutions and Corporate Efforts – the Nordic Environment

Lars Oxelheim

2.1. Introduction

In this chapter we discuss the struggle between politicians trying to retain control over capital flows, regulators trying to achieve a sound and safe financial infrastructure, investors searching for profit opportunities and managers trying to internationalise the cost of capital while maintaining control. The discussion about how the battle has developed is organised as follows. In Section 2.2 a brief description is provided as regards the structure of Nordic equity markets and the role these markets have played in supplying corporations with risk capital. The relative role of individual Nordic national equity markets – in terms of the size of international equity issues by domestic firms as compared with their issues in the home equity market – is also emphasised here. Hence, this section paves the way for putting emphasis in the remainder of the chapter on the environment for internationalising the cost of capital in general and on the equity perspective in particular.

Section 2.3 deals with external deregulation together with institutional and regulatory changes in domestic equity markets with relevance for the internationalisation. Section 2.4 emphasises the efforts of corporations to maintain control at the same time as the cost of capital is internationalised. Section 2.5 illustrates at the corporate level the internationalisation process by a discussion about foreign listing practice of Nordic firms and their propensity to raise capital in foreign equity markets through equity issues. In Section 2.6 the major findings are summarised.

2.2. Nordic Equity Markets and Their Role as Risk Capital Suppliers

All Nordic equity markets – except the Danish one – were heavily regulated up to the mid-1980s. However, during the early 1980s a gradual liberalisation came about that was not expressed in terms of an explicit deregulation but rather in a more relaxed attitude by central bankers in dealing with authorisation issues. In the first part of the 1990s, the Nordic markets were then all made part of the global market place as regards the regulators' efforts. The changed attitude of policy makers and regulators was to some extent an acknowledgement by them that existing regulations had eroded and had become inefficient. But the liberalisation and relaxed attitude was also an expression of a change in the philosophy underlying national economic policies in the 1980s, reflecting a growing recognition that excessive controls are not compatible with efficient resource allocation and solid and balanced economic growth. In the 1980s it became increasingly evident that controls discourage financial savings, distort investment decisions and render the intermediation between savers and investors ineffective.

In the mid-1990s, in a global perspective the market capitalisation of Nordic equity markets is small. The market value of domestic companies traded in the Swedish market (the Stockholm Stock Exchange) – which is the biggest Nordic market – amounts to just about 4-5 percent of the market value of shares traded at the New York Stock Exchange. Taken together the market value of the Danish, Finnish and Norwegian markets is smaller than that of the Swedish equity market. As shown by Exhibit 2.1 the local currency turnover as well as the market capitalisation have increased dramatically since the mid-1970s. This is also true in real terms. However, the turnover has increased more than the market capitalisation implying an increased turnover velocity of domestic shares. Although increasing, in the mid-1990s the velocity is still lower than on most major markets with the exception of the Tokyo Stock Exchange. The low figures for the 1970s and 1980s for all the Nordic markets reflect to a large extent successful efforts by regulators and policy makers to keep markets in a shape that best fits their own purposes.

The change of attitude of Nordic policy makers and regulators together with the ongoing globalisation of equity markets has given rise to a debate about letting the Nordic national markets form a common Nordic market

Exhibit 2.1:   Key Features of Nordic Equity Markets in an International Perspective.

Market value of trading volume in shares, Billions of local currencies				
	1976	1981	1986	1991	1996*
Denmark	0.375	0.417	15.0	59.4	218
Finland	0.1533	0.3549	9.5	6.3	101
Norway	0.249	0.5775	29.9	75.5	235
Sweden	2.146	18.58	141.3	124.3	937
London	14.1	16.2	90.6	178.8	895
NYSE	165.7	389.2	1389.0	1432.2	4063
Germany	24.9	30.9	294.7	629.6	1233
Tokyo	23662.3	49364.6	159836.0	110897.5	129928

Market value of shares of domestic companies at year-end, Billions of local currencies				
	1976	1981	1986	1991	1996*
Denmark	27.6	45.2	127.5	265.2	494
Finland	na	9.9	56.1	58.8	285
Norway	9.6	19.4	74.9	131.7	367
Sweden	43.8	95.9	432.0	539.1	1649
London	40.9	99.4	320.7	522.0	1010
NYSE	858.3	1098.6	2128.0	3484.4	6842
Germany	125.9	141.1	500.1	563.3	1034
Tokyo	52987.7	91905.7	285471.5	391956.3	634865

Turnover velocity of domestic shares in percent				
	1976	1981	1986	1991	1996*
Denmark	1.4	0.9	10.3	22.4	44
Finland	na	3.6	16.9	10.7	35
Norway	2.6	3.0	39.9	52.3	64
Sweden	4.9	19.4	32.7	23.1	57
London	34.5	16.3	28.3	34.3	89
NYSE	19.3	35.4	65.3	41.1	59
Germany	19.8	21.9	58.9	111.8	119
Tokyo	44.7	53.7	56.0	28.3	20

Note: * Estimations.
Source: FIBV, *Annual report*, various issues; Copenhagen Stock Exchange, *Database*; Unitas, *Pörsin Avain*, 1976; Oslo Stock Exchange, *Annual report*, various issues; Stockholm Stock Exchange, *Annual report, 1976.*

or letting them take part in the creation of an EU market place. A joint Nordic market place would constitute Europe's fourth biggest by market capitalisation. A first step in the direction of cooperation was taken in 1990 with the establishment of NORDQUOTE, which collects and dissemi-nates via satellite real time information from each of the four Nordic exchanges.

2.2.1. General Features of Nordic Equity Markets

The embryo to the Nordic national equity markets all date way back. They started as informal market places that were later embellished by extensive regulations. The transformation of the Nordic national equity markets has been triggered by some common forces and some country specific. Among the common ones are the tax relaxation on unit trust savings and/or tax relaxation on dividends and capital income. Also a more positive attitude towards equity financing and savings in shares was expressed by politicians who allowed an entry of foreign investors into the business community.

The Danish Stock Market

The Danish stock exchange – actually the Copenhagen Stock Exchange – can be traced back to the end of the 17th-century. However, in the 19th-century it became more closely organised. In 1808, as one of the first markets in the world, it began regulation of trade and broker conditions. It then continued to function as an independent market place under the supervision of the Wholesaler Association (Grosshandlarsociteten). The first modern law for the Stock Exchange appeared in 1919. In 1987 this was replaced by a new law. The Copenhagen Stock Exchange (the only Danish market place) is an autonomous, non-profit institution with a monopoly position as regards trading in shares.

For the period under investigation, substantial changes came about as regards the organization and regulation of the Danish security markets. In 1983, a central register for all securities ("dematerialization of securities") was introduced (Act on Securities Registration). To begin with, the register involved only bonds. In 1988, however, also shares were included in the register. In 1986 a computerised trading system with decentralised location of dealers was introduced. Reporting of all transactions in securities included in the central register became mandatory the same year. There was also an introduction of corporate membership with banks and other financial institutions being allowed to take participation in existing, or to set up new, stock broker firms.

On the supervisory side, in January 1988 Finanstillsynet (the Danish Financial Supervisory Authority) was established as an amalgamation of the former supervisory authorities for banks, insurance and securities. In September 1988, the official financial futures and options market at the Copenhagen Stock Exchange started operating. A Guarantee Fund administers the system and functions as an intermediary between creditors and debtors. In January 1989, the futures and options market was fully computerised.

The Finnish Stock Market

The Finnish Stock Exchange can be dated back to the "Russian" period. It was initially based on self-regulation and gentlemen agreements. In August 1989 a law was introduced implying that the Stock Exchange came under the supervision of a public authority. The Finnish stock market is built around a number of market places. However, the Helsinki Stock Exchange is the dominating one.

A major reorganisation of the Helsinki Stock Exchange came about during the second part of the 1980s. In 1987 a law on unit trusts (mutual funds) passed. The derivative market started in September the same year. According to a law passed in 1988, activities of corporations engaged in options and futures trading became subject to authorisation and control by the authorities.

The supervision of the securities business was included among the tasks of the Bankinspektionen from 1 November 1988 for the option market and from 1 August 1989 for the trade of securities in general. On 1 October 1993, Bankinspektionen changed its name to Finansinpektionen. In 1988, proposals for a securities market law and for a law on securities firms were put forward. The proposals were rich and included in the case of the security law provisions on many issues. They required firms and the industry to provide information on secondary markets, on the marketing and issues of securities offered for public subscription, public quotations of securities, authorisation of stock exchange trading, insider trading and responsibilities of securities dealers. As regards the law on securities firms, the law encompassed provisions on authorisation and control of operations, permitted activities of securities firms, the extent of securities trading in an agency's own name, and solvency issues. In 1988-89, the Helsinki Stock Exchange gradually changed over to computer-based trading.

The Norwegian Stock Market

The first signs of a Norwegian Stock Exchange can be traced to the 18th century. However, the Stock Exchange Regulation (Børsloven) from June 1931 should be seen as the starting point of a market of the kind we see today. The market was fundamentally reorganised in 1988 implying a closer link to the central government. A new Stock Exchange Act came into force the same year meaning a closer regulation of the activities on the stock

market. Since 1991, Norway has only one stock exchange, the Oslo Stock
Exchange. Prior to that there were also two regional exchanges; in Bergen
and in Trondheim. The new single market place was the result of a merger.

The major reorganisation of the Norwegian Stock Exchange came
about by the mid-1980s. In 1985-86 comprehensive reforms of the regulatory and supervisory framework applying to securities markets and intermediaries were introduced. The Securities Trading Act of 1985 included
regulation of the issue of securities and derivative products, definition and
regulation of securities market intermediaries, and regulation of insider
trading and other violations of securities legislation. As in the case of Denmark a central register was introduced that year. The Act on the Norwegian Registry of Securities introduced a computerised book-entry system
for the mandatory registration of all bonds and quoted shares. The Norwegian Kredittilsynet (The Norwegian Banking, Insurance and Securities
Commission) was established in 1986 as a merger between the Banking
Commission and the Insurance Commission. Although it was formally
established on 24 March 1986 it was not fully operative until mid-1987. By
1 April 1991 a substantial reorganisation of Kredittilsynet was completed.

In 1988, an electronic trading system was introduced with information
conveyed in real time. In May 1990 a Norwegian derivative market was
launched.

The Swedish Stock Market

The Swedish stock market dates back to February 1863. The first regulation
of the stock activities on the Stockholm Stock Exchange appeared in January
1868. A stock market of the type we see today was constituted in 1901. After
a very calm period for decades, the introduction of tax-subsidised investment
funds in the Autumn 1978 meant a restart to the development of the only
equity market place in Sweden, the Stockholm Stock Exchange.

The creation of a regulated Swedish options and futures market came
about in 1985-86. The market place was privately owned outside the
Stockholm Stock Exchange. In 1987 a commission was formed with the
task of reforming company law, the equity market and the Stock
Exchange. The task encompassed a modernisation of the Stock Exchange
(automation, review of practices), protection of small shareholders, regulation of majority shareholders, regulation of insider trading, supervision of
price manipulation and a revision of the existing takeover code of 1971.
The result of the commission's work was seen at the beginning of the
1990s. In May 1990, the old call-over trading system in Stockholm was

replaced by the Stockholm Automated Exchange (SAX) electronic trading system. In February 1991, a new insider trading law came into force.

Finansinspektionen (the Financial Supervisory Board) was established in July 1991 as a merger between the Banking (supervising banks and security operations) and Insurance Commissions. The regulatory body that was established in 1991 for the activities of the Finansinspektionen included the supervision of some thirty laws dating from 1934 onwards. A new law came into force in April 1992.

2.2.2. The Supply of Risk Capital in Nordic Equity Markets

In the mid-1990s much attention is paid to equity markets and their role as risk capital supplier. The equity market is one of several sources from which a firm can acquire its financing. Research in this area points to the fact that irrespective of the size of country or nationality, internally generated funds have been by far the most important source. This is a pattern that may very much reflect the influence from governments and central banks. With the completion of national and international financial liberalisation, the source of finance chosen will increasingly depend on the cost and availability of funds. These reflect a number of different, but interrelated, factors such as the interest rate, expectations about exchange rate and political stability on the macro level, expectations about future profits and growth, and strategies on the corporate level.

We will here only address the task of supplying new risk capital and of allocating the resources in an efficient way so that new and profitable companies are able to attract resources. This disregards the other main tasks of an equity market, such as being an indicator of market values of firms, and a location to contest the market for corporate control.

The importance of the Nordic equity markets as suppliers of risk capital has varied considerably over time. After a period with low activity the amounts of equity issues began to increase in the mid-1980s. Exhibits 2.2 and 2.3 provide a historical perspective on the relative size of that increase using Sweden as an illustration. Exhibit 2.2 shows the volume of new equity issues on the Stockholm Stock Exchange between 1915 and 1992 in real terms (in fixed 1979 SEK). Except for the booming interest in new issues in the period immediately preceding the crash of 1929, for the whole period 1915-92 there is nothing similar to the high issuing activity 1985-92. However, as Exhibit 2.3 shows, the relative importance of stock markets as suppliers (equity issues in percent of GDP) of new capital increased

only slightly during that period. Considering changes in relative importance, one may fruitfully divide the observation period into three parts:
1915-1929, 1930-1979 and 1980-1992. The average yearly equity issues (in
percent of GDP) for these periods were: 1.13%, 0.17% and 0.39%, respectively. Although the relative measure for the last period is far below that of
the first, it still indicates a significant increase compared to the period in
the middle, which was characterised by heavy regulation. Hence, we can
see that new equity issues as a source of financing increased in importance.

Exhibits 2.2 and 2.3 also support a further division of the period 1980-
1992 into two parts; 1980-85 and 1986-92. In the case of Sweden, such a
division shows that the average yearly equity issues increased between the
two periods from 0.17% (of GDP) to 0.56%. Similar patterns can be found
for the other Nordic countries for the same two sub-periods. For example,
average equity issues in Denmark went from 0.33% to 1.07% (of GDP), in
Finland from 0.38% to 0.95%, and in Norway from 0.42% to 0.55%.

To provide an idea of the incidence of equity issues abroad by Nordic
companies Exhibit 2.4 shows the total amount of such issues, as well as their
percentage of total issues in each country. It should be noted and taken as a
word of caution that an analysis of the relative importance of equity issues

*Exhibit 2.2:   Equity Issues on the Stockholm Stock Exchange in Fixed Prices
(1979 SEK) 1915-1992.*

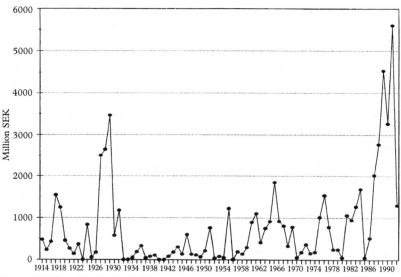

Source: Modén and Oxelheim (1995).

Exhibit 2.3: *Equity Issues on the Stockholm Stock Exchange in Percent of GDP, 1915-1992.*

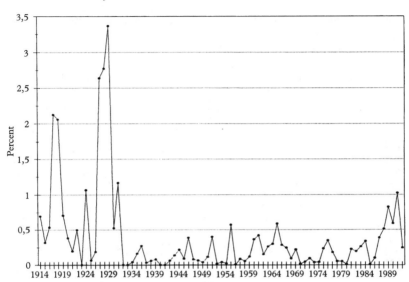

Source: Modén and Oxelheim (1995).

abroad is for different reasons connected with severe data problems. For a country like Denmark the data gathering boils down to a search in annual reports for such issues. Danish authorities have shown no particular interest in regulating, and, hence, registering cross border issues. For the other countries some aggregated data can be found. However, the mode of reporting differs across the countries.

What is found in Exhibit 2.4 is an effort to capture the total amount of capital raised through equity issues directed to foreign investors. By total amount is also meant that no distinction between public issues and issues directed to one or a couple of investors has been possible to make. Convertible bond issues are excluded. A further registration problem is the appearance of Euroequity issues and the fact that *directed* issues are getting increasingly blurred and harder to identify. One reason is that the foreign investors' rate of return requirement and savings can be obtained already in the home market. Hence, the opening up of Nordic national equity markets to foreign investors should have reduced the need for issues abroad directed to that category for pure capital market reasons. The entrance of foreign investors should work as a catalyst in the process of making the national equity market a part of the "global" equity market. Eventually, in

*Exhibit 2.4:   Amounts of Capital Raised through New Equity Issues Directed
to Foreign Investors.*

Nominal amount in local currency and as a percentage of total capital raised from new
equity issues.

	Denmark		Finland		Norway		Sweden	
	Raised by Danish firms abroad (million DKK)	Percentage of total capital raised from new equity issues	Raised by Finnish firms abroad (million FIM)	Percentage of total capital raised from new equity issues	Raised by Norwegian firms abroad (million NOK)	Percentage of total capital raised from new equity issues	Raised by Swedish firms abroad (million SEK)	Percentage of total capital raised from new equity issues
1981	450	78.9	na	na	0	0	798	28.2
1982	0	0	34	3.7	20	1.9	150	6.5
1983	966	33.7	370	29.6	217	7.6	3904	40.8
1984	0	0	635	21.8	646	21.4	371	5.6
1985	115	2.5	182	13.1	123	3.5	547	19.3
1986	232	2.5	996	28.6	1027	32.5	2366	55.2
1987	407	11.4	601	11.4	4	0.2	42	0.6
1988	698	14.0	231	2.7	6	0.1	0	0
1989	615	4.7	419	4.9	1924	26.4	250	3.0
1990	237	3.5	499	29.7	2708	40.3	2441	24.6
1991	na	na	5	0.1	650	22.3	0	0
1992	na	na	0	0	458	8.1	710	17.1
1993	na	na	4188	42.8	na	na	870	3.2
1994	na	na	7701[1]	69.8	na	na	194	0.5
1995	na	na	2727[1]	89.5	na	na	193	0.7

[1] Estimated value

the case of perfect equity market integration, directed issues with the aim
of internationalising the cost of capital should of course come to zero.
However, other reasons for equity issues abroad exist.

The general picture for Swedish firms is that issues abroad lost their
relative importance after 1986, whereas for Finnish and Norwegian firms
they have kept their relative importance in the first half of the 1990s. In
terms of the amount of capital raised (both in nominal, as shown in Exhibit
2.4, and in real terms) Swedish companies' interest peaked in 1983, Norwegian companies in 1990 and Finnish companies in 1993. As regards
Danish companies the importance of issues abroad has been insignificant
for the entire period under observation. One company, Novo, (the Danish
biotechnical and pharmaceutical), accounted for the whole amount raised
in 1981 and 1983.

The pattern shown by the use of issues directed to investors abroad very
much correspond to the common view on how the de facto integration has
proceeded. The eventual (de jure) deregulation that came about fairly late

in the Nordic countries was then just an acknowledgement by authorities that existing regulations had eroded and had become ineffective.

2.3. Restrictions on Equity Trade and Issues

Regulators and policy-makers have exerted a major influence on national equity markets for long periods. Their objectives have varied over time. The regulatory devices can be divided into two kinds, namely external and internal regulations. External regulations refer to measures such as capital controls and exchange rate regulations and involve national controls on cross-border activities as a support for the efficiency of many internal regulations. In the latter category are found regulations controlling the supply of products/services, participation of financial institutions in domestic markets, activities of individual households, non-financial companies and local governments, etc. Among the internal devices are also found rules governing tax obligations.

At a global scale a shift of opinion in favour of greater freedom for cross-border capital transactions appeared in the 1950s, manifesting itself for example in OECD's adoption of a Code of Liberalisation of Capital Movements in 1961. Nonetheless, international deregulation remained fairly modest, and even suffered a setback in the 1960s due to balance-of-payment problems. Liberalisation started to accelerate in the 1970s, fuelled by the OECD Declaration and Decision on International Investment and Multinational Enterprises in 1976. It gained momentum in the 1980s, and by the mid-1990s, was nearing completion.

2.3.1. Restrictions on Crossborder Equity Activities

The Second World War was followed by a period when policy-makers believed that the best way to heal the economic wounds of the war was to impose various forms of internal and external regulations on the financial markets. In this way the authorities did their best to create cheap domestic financing in order to boost the economic recovery. By imposing external regulations they paved the way for the use of internal controls of different kinds.

The regulatory body applying to cross-border equity transactions has for the Nordic countries been severe for long periods. As was mentioned in Chapter 1 capital flows over the borders have been under the control of governments for most of the post-WWII period. Prior to World War II, at least some Nordic companies were traded on foreign stock markets. Among those early traded companies we find Unibank, GN Store Nord and ÖK Holding from Denmark, Norsk Hydro from Norway and Alfa Laval, Electrolux, SKF and Swedish Match from Sweden. These companies also issued new equity directed toward foreign investors concurrently with their introduction abroad. Finnish companies did not appear in this respect until the 1980s. This early episode came to an abrupt halt at the time of the stock market crash of 1929. The depression following the crash implied that the demand for new capital was very low, and by the time the demand might have picked up, the outbreak of World War II led to the institution of extensive capital controls.

In Sweden, for instance, the capital controls of 1939 made it illegal to sell Swedish securities to foreigners, as well as for Swedes to buy foreign securities. A couple of exceptions applied. For example, Swedish and foreign securities which were in foreign and Swedish hands, respectively, in February 1940, could be sold. This gave the seller a so-called "switch right," which was a right to buy a foreign security. The switch rights were themselves tradable. During the 1970s the capital controls on security trading started to be loosened somewhat. In 1974 Volvo was granted permission to export shares of common stock abroad; between 1975 and 1981 half a dozen additional companies received such export permits (see Stjernborg 1987). However, no companies issued new equity abroad, but rather created markets with existing stocks on foreign exchanges. As we will show below, export activity took off in earnest after 1982, with companies being granted permission to export shares on a routine basis (as long as they were listed on the Stock Exchange). A further liberalisation was undertaken in 1986 when the Central Bank officially stated that permission to export shares would "normally" be given to all officially listed stocks, OTC-stocks, and under certain circumstances for other stocks as well. In 1989 the remainder of this regulation was abandoned. Norway and Finland subscribed to systems similar to the Swedish "switch" system.

Exhibit 2.5 provides a framework for analysing the time table of Nordic regulation/deregulation of cross-border equity activities. Many of the combinations covered by the exhibit are regulated by the Exchange Controls, but a large number are subject to changes in practice by the Central Bank and to changes of other law bodies like Concessions Acts and Acquisition laws. In Finland, Norway and Sweden, the exchange regulations normally controlled the maximum amounts traded in a particular share, whereas the Concession Acts dictated maximum limits for foreign investors in equity of individual companies. The limits differed across countries as well as industries. In addition to this, it was then open to the firm to further reduce the proportion of shares available to foreigners by a provision in the Articles of Association. A number of companies gave foreign investors no chance at all.

In Exhibit 2.5 the years given under "Introduced" indicate when the current period of regulation started. The identification of this date as well as most of the dates given in the exhibit involve some discretion. In most of the cases the year given is the year of introduction of exchange controls. After that year the regulation/deregulation pendulum may have swung back and forth a couple of times until a steady route to deregulation was embarked upon. The years given under "Eased" are supposed to be key-dates on the way to a deregulated market. However, sometimes it is not possible to identify an individual year but just a period under which policy-makers or central bankers have started to show a more relaxed attitude towards cross-border equity activities. In such a case a period rather than an individual year is given in the exhibit. Finally, the years given under "Abolished" can also be questioned. The years given are those when restrictions on the right to carry out an activity were abolished. After that date some restrictions may remain as regards how the activity is conducted. A frequent remaining restriction after the dates of abolition given in the exhibit was the restriction that acquisition of foreign shares by domestic investors go through a domestic broker and that the shares should be kept in domestic custody.

The pattern provided by Exhibit 2.5 is that Danish regulators have been very liberal in their attitude towards cross-border equity activities as indicated by their embarkment at an early time on the road to equity market integration and an internationalised cost of equity. The same observation was reported in Oxelheim (1986) as regards the cost of debt. However, this fact can explain only part of the low interest of Danish firms in equity issues directed to international investors. Another important explanatory factor is the Danish size-distribution of firms; a distribution dominated by small and medium-sized firms. Hence, the low number of firms that can afford an international issue may to a large extent explain the low frequency of international equity issues by Danish firms.

In Finland, Norway and Sweden, the *de jure* deregulation started in the mid-1980s. Differences across these countries as regards the corporate use of international issues after that starting point, as was shown in Exhibit 2.4, may reflect differences in the size-distribution of firms. In the 1980s a

Exhibit 2.5:   Regulations of Nordic Crossborder Equity Activities.

| | Dates for institutional changes. | | | | | |
| | Denmark | | | Finland | | |
	Introduced	*Eased*	*Abolished*	*Introduced*	*Eased*	*Abolished*
Listings and Issues						
Restrictions on listings abroad	—	—	—	—	—	—
Restrictions on listings of foreign companies on the domestic equity market	—	—	—	Sep 1941	June 1985	Jan 1994
Restrictions on equity issues directed to foreign investors	1931	Dec 1972	Jan 1984	Sep 1941	During the 1980s	Feb 1990
Restrictions on foreign equity issues on the domestic market	1931	Dec 1972	Oct 1988	Sep 1941	Apr 1985	Feb 1990
Investments						
Restrictions on the acquisitions of foreign shares by domestic investors: – listed shares	1931	—	Jan 1984	Sep 1941	Jan 1986, 1987, 1988	Sep 1989, July 1990[1]
–non listed shares	1932	June 1985	July 1986	Sep 1941	—	Sep 1989, July 1990[1]
Restrictions on the acquisitions of domestic shares by foreign investors: – listed shares:	1932	—	Dec 1972	July 1939	May 1959	Jan 1993
– non-listed shares:	1932	—	May 1983	July 1939	Jan 1973, Feb 1990	Jan 1993
– shares of national strategic value (e.g. defence)	1937	1990	—	July 1939	Jan 1993	—

[1] Abolished for companies in September 1989, for private individuals in July 1990.

Nordic top-twenty list of companies contained 16 to 18 Swedish companies depending on which variable was used for the ranking (market value,
value added, or turnover). The larger Swedish companies were better
equipped with knowledge about financial markets and about how to deal
with international financial issues than other Nordic companies. This fact

Exhibit 2.5   (continued).

Dates for institutional changes.

	Norway			Sweden		
	Introduced	*Eased*	*Abolished*	*Introduced*	*Eased*	*Abolished*
Listings and Issues						
Restrictions on listings abroad	—	—	—	—	—	—
Restrictions on listings of foreign companies on the domestic equity market	1950	During the 1980s	Jan 1994	Feb 1940	Jan 1980, Apr 1982, Jan 1983	Jan 1989
Restrictions on equity issues directed to foreign investors	1950	Early 1980s	July 1990	Feb 1940	Early 1970s, 1975,1979	Jan 1989
Restrictions on foreign equity issues on the domestic market	1950	1989	1992	Feb 1940	—	Jan 1989
Investments						
Restrictions on the acquisitions of foreign shares by domestic investors: – listed shares	1950	June 1984	July 1990	Feb 1940	1979[a], Feb 1980[b], 1982[b], Aug 1987[c], Feb 1988 Central Bank practice[e]	Jan 1989
–non listed shares	1950	June 1984	July 1990	Feb 1940	Central Bank practice[e]	Jan 1989
Restrictions on the acquisitions of domestic shares by foreign investors: – listed shares: Consessions acts	1917	1972, 1974, 1988	Jan 1994	1916	Jan 1983[d]	Jan 1992, Jan 1994
Exchange controls	1950	1979, 1982	July 1990	Feb 1940	Central Bank practice[e] 1979	Jan 1989
– non-listed shares: Consessions acts	1917	1972, 1974, 1988	Jan 1994	1916	Jan 1983[d]	Jan 1992, Jan 1994
Exchange controls	1950	1979, 1982	July 1990	Feb 1940	Central Bank practice[f] 1979	Jan 1989
– shares of national strategic value (e.g. defence) Consessions acts	1917	1972, 1974, 1988	Jan 1994	1916	Jan 1983[d]	Jan 1994
Exchange controls	1950	1979, 1982	July 1990	Feb 1940	Central Bank practice[e]	Jan 1989

a) The general permission for insurance companies to acquire foreign shares.
b) Foreign companies operating together with Swedish industry are under some conditions given the permission to sell shares to Swedish investors.
c) Employees in Swedish subsidiaries of foreign companies are allowed to buy shares in the foreign company as part of a company program directed towards them.
d) Law of 1982.
e) In the practice of the central bank in the 1970s (insurance companies)
f) In the practice of the central bank in the early 1980s (applications to the Central bank)

Source: Oxelheim (1997)

may explain why issues abroad by Swedish firms peaked early as compared to the peak of Finnish and Norwegian firms. The pace with which the rules were relaxed may also have contributed to that difference.

A restriction that remained in most of the Nordic countries, even after the lifting of capital controls, was the restriction on foreigners' acquisition of shares of firms possessing national strategic values. As shown by Exhibit 2.5, until the 1980s foreign investors were to a very limited extent welcome – with the exception of Danish firms – to take stakes in Nordic firms. Restricted shares existed in all the Nordic countries. Foreign investors could only buy non-restricted shares. The company laws were for long periods defining an upper limit for foreign ownership. In the 1980s, 20 per cent was often used as an upper limit. The articles of association of many companies were also prohibiting any foreign ownership at all. For instance, in 1988 listed Finnish industrial companies had only about 10 per cent non-restricted shares and listed trade and transportation companies about 3 per cent.

The attitude towards foreign ownership and the size-distribution of firms is reflected in the development shown in Exhibit 2.6. At the end of the 1980s the share of foreign ownership was the highest in Norway, 27

Exhibit 2.6:   Share of Foreign Ownership of Stocks Listed on Nordic Stock Exchanges 1987-1996.

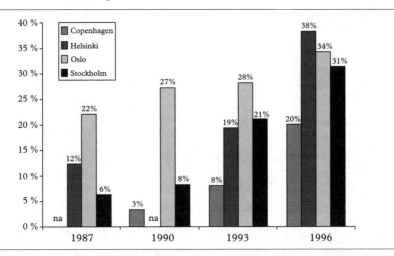

Source: Copenhagen Stock Exchange, *The Nordic Securities Market Quarterly Statistics* 2/95, *Supplement*; Copenhagen Stock Exchange, *Database;* Helsinki Stock Exchange, *Database;* Oslo Stock Exchange, *Database;* Stockholm Stock Exchange, *Database* and *own estimates.*

Exhibit 2.7: Number of Companies Listed on the Nordic Stock exchanges 1980-1995.

| Year end | Denmark | | | Finland | | | Norway | | | Sweden | | |
	Total	Do-mestic	For-eign	Total	Do-mestic	For-eign	Total	Do-mestic	For-eign	Total	Do-mes-tic*	For-eign
1980	222	218	4	50	50	0	124	117	7	103	103	0
1981	214	210	4	50	50	0	115	109	6	130	130	0
1982	210	206	4	49	49	0	118	112	6	139	138	1
1983	210	206	4	48	48	0	119	113	6	150	145	5
1984	236	231	5	52	52	0	148	140	8	165	159	6
1985	249	243	6	51	50	1	163	156	7	171	164	7
1986	281	274	7	52	49	3	154	147	7	233	226	7
1987	277	269	9	52	49	3	139	149	10	230	223	7
1988	267	260	7	69	66	3	134	128	6	226	217	9
1989	265	257	8	82	78	4	129	122	7	266	256	10
1990	268	258	10	77	73	4	121	112	9	258	243	15
1991	272	261	11	65	63	2	116	107	9	230	217	13
1992	268	257	11	63	62	1	127	119	8	205	192	13
1993	257	246	11	58	58	0	135	124	11	205	195	10
1994	253	243	10	65	65	0	146	132	14	228	217	11
1995	252	242	10	73	73	0	165	151	14	223	212	11

Note: * A-list 1980-1985 and Total list 1986-1995 (including from 1986 the OTC-list and from 1989 the O-list).

per cent (up from 15 per cent in 1985) and the lowest in Denmark, 3 per cent. One firm, Novo Nordisk, accounted for about half the Danish figure. In January 1994 the European Economic Area Treaty made all the Nordic equity markets become part of the "European" equity market. This meant the end to the use of restricted shares. In 1996 about 1/3 of the shares in Finnish, Norwegian and Swedish firms are owned by foreigners. Despite the open attitude towards foreign ownership shown by Danish authorities at an earlier time than by the authorities in the other Nordic countries, the Danish figure is substantially lower.

The positive attitude shown by policy-makers towards equity made also foreign companies willing to list their shares on the Nordic stock exchanges. Exhibit 2.7 shows that the Danish, Norwegian and Swedish markets experienced substantial increases in foreign listings from 1987. Four companies (Swedish) were listed on the Finnish stock exchange in 1989. Four years later no company remained on the list. The reasons for a listing on the fairly small Nordic stock exchanges were others than direct capital cost reasons. One plausible reason was to facilitate trading for employees in subsidiaries that had received equity interest through company programs.

2.3.2. Internal Regulations and Institutional Changes

The internal regulatory bodies of Nordic countries contain one very important law. It is the taxation law covering capital gains taxes, wealth taxes, taxes on dividends and taxes on securities in trade. Government policy has also played a major role, through a variety of channels, in influencing the development of Nordic debt/equity ratios. In addition to taxation, the regulation of the operations of the financial system has been important. Three factors which favour debt financing can be distinguished: impediments to the development of stock markets, the extent to which financial and non-financial companies are owned by the government, and the granting of financial assistance to companies in the way of various subsidised credit facilities.

A typical way the Nordic authorities have influenced the balance between different sources of capital is through tax policies. Equity financing has for most of the post-WWII period been more expensive for a company than credit financing. To be able to pay a dividend a company must show a profit on which a tax is payable, whereas the costs of credit financing are tax-deductible. Considering that the countries in the Nordic region are all to be classified as "political economies" with extremely high tax burdens it is easy to understand that the interest tax shield has been very attractive for long periods after World War II. The debt ratios in two of the Nordic countries – Finland and Norway – were at the beginning of the 1980s close to Japanese levels whereas in the other two countries the levels were slightly above the European standard. However, in the mid-1990 the ratios of all the Nordic countries have converged to an "OECD" standard (See Oxelheim 1996).

As pointed out in OECD (1991), at the beginning of the 1990s all the Nordic countries showed tax wedges, when both company and personal income taxes were considered, that were above the EU average, and, except for Sweden, above the OECD average as well. During the 1980s Nordic policy-makers attempted gradually to eliminate incentives that favored loans rather than equity. The double taxation of dividends was abolished in all the Nordic countries in the early 1990s; in Denmark 1991, in Finland 1990, in Norway 1991 and in Sweden 1994. In 1995, however, with a new government installed the double taxation was reintroduced in Sweden.

The equity euphoria at the end of the 1980s made some governments place new tax burdens on equity. In 1988 a one per cent turnover tax on equity trading was introduced in Norway. The tax was very shortlived and was lifted at the end of the year. In the other Nordic countries similar efforts were more long-lasting. In Denmark under some conditions a fee of 1 per cent of the market value of traded shares was charged by the authorities. Finland imposed a tax of 1 per cent on the amount traded at the stock exchange and 1.6 per cent on the amount traded outside. In addition there was also a stock exchange fee of .05 per cent; (maximum FIM 500). In Sweden both buyers and sellers had to pay a tax of .5 per cent of the amount traded.

In addition to the tax laws there are other internal measures of importance to the functioning of equity markets. As is shown in Exhibit 2.8 there are regulations controlling competition and monopolies, restrictions for companies to buy back their own shares, and obligations to announce (to flag) major increases in stakes of a company. In the case of Sweden, restrictions were placed on the number of shares that can be voted. Under debate today is also the EU proposal of "one share – one vote". In the mid-1990s shares with different voting power exist in all the Nordic countries. In Finland there is a maximum spread of 20 votes (A-shares) against one (B-shares) set by the authorities. Companies cover the whole spectrum. In Denmark and Sweden shares traded on the stock exchanges are mostly carrying 10 votes for A-shares to 1 vote for B-shares. In Norway B-shares have sometimes no voting rights at all.

Finally, on the internal side there are also the laws previously mentioned; stock exchange laws, securities laws and laws about supervision. As was noted earlier a merger of different national supervisory institutions into one for each country came about in the Nordic countries at the beginning of the 1990s. This was to avoid conflict situations and to eliminate arbitrage opportunities emanating from different supervisory systems inside a country.

2.4. Corporate Efforts to Maintain Control

Even if the deregulation process has proceeded at a high pace the last decade there is lots of room for manoeuvring for corporate managers to maintain control. Exhibit 2.8 shows the most important measures employed by Nordic firms. Hostile takeovers are still unlikely to play an important role in the restructuring process triggered by the regionalization on a global scale. In this respect there are obvious indications that the conclusions made by Dullum and Stonehill (1990) for a number of OECD countries at

Exhibit 2.8:   General Takeover Defences Practised or in Force in the Nordic Equity Markets in the Mid-1990s.

	Denmark	**Finland**	**Norway**	**Sweden**
1. Restrictions on the number of shares that can be voted	Commonly used	In some companies	In some companies	Regulated by law
2. Restrictions on foreign ownership of shares	No restrictions (restricted shares no longer allowed)	No restrictions (restricted shares no longer allowed)	No restrictions (restricted shares no longer allowed)	No restrictions (restricted shares no longer allowed)
3. Dual classes of stock	Commonly used but declining	Commonly used but declining	Commonly used but declining	Commonly used but declining
4. Provisions in the corporate charter that might require a supermajority vote on a takeover bid	Not commonly used	Not commonly used	Not commonly used	Not commonly used
5. Selling a special issue of voting shares or convertibles to "stable" or "friendly" investors	Not commonly used	Not commonly used (if approved by the general meeting of shareholders)	Not commonly used	Not commonly used
6. Finding a "white knight"	Not commonly used	Possible (but no case yet)	Not commonly used	Not commonly used
7. Control by a foundation	Commonly used	Commonly used	Not commonly used	Commonly used
8. Forming a strategic alliance and/or interlocking boards of directors	Not commonly used	Not commonly used	Commonly used	Commonly used but declining
9. Relying on a network of close personal relationship (i.e. belonging to "the establishment")	Not commonly used	Commonly used but declining	Commonly used	Commonly used but declining
10. Government regulations controlling competition and monopolies	Yes, in force	Yes, in force	Yes, in force	Yes, in force
11. Buy own shares	Restricted by law to max 10% of shares outstanding	Possible within the limits of free equity capital	Not allowed (restricted by law)	Not allowed (restricted by law)
12. Obligations for investors to disclose ownership increases	Yes (mandatory by law for prespecified increases of ownership)	Yes (mandatory by law for prespecified increases of ownership)	Yes (mandatory by law for prespecified increases of ownership)	Yes (mandatory by law for prespecified increases of ownership)

the end of the 1980s should still be valid in the mid-1990s in an all-Nordic context. However, signs of a trend towards decreased use of takeover defences can be found. Many defences that were widely used 10 years ago are not practised any longer.

Dullum and Stonehill (1990) report findings from an analysis of takeover defences used in the restructuring of global industries as a result of a conflict between two paradigms; the Corporate Wealth Maximization framework (Donaldson and Lorsch, 1983) and the Shareholder Wealth Maximization framework. They found a number of takeover defences being used in the Anglo-American markets. Among the most used measures were 1) going private through leveraged buyout; 2) finding a "white" knight; 3) creating a "poison pill"; 4) granting "golden parachutes" to existing management; 5) changing a firm's corporate charter to require qualified voting on mergers and staggered elections for the board of directors; 6) accusing the takeover entity with anti-trust violations or a breach of the securities laws; 7) paying "greenmail"; and 8) proposing a plan for voluntary restructuring to be carried out by existing management.

When the findings in Exhibit 2.8 are compared with those for seven Non-Anglo-American countries as reported in Dullum and Stonehill (1990), there are some differences to be emphasised. As a general feature of the markets covered in their study, banks and insurances companies can and do heavily invest in corporate equities. That is not the case in Sweden, for instance, where banks and insurance companies have not been allowed to hold equity in other companies except for emergency cases. Another difference is that the debt/total capitalisation ratios decreased in the 1980s. Moreover, governments no longer regulate the ownership-sensitive industries like defence, banking, insurance, newspaper, television, telecommunication, shipping and aviation. This means that a larger number of firms are open for takeovers, especially by foreign firms.

A comparison with the results of Dullum and Stonehill (1990) shows that the most frequently used (i.e. in all 7 studied countries) defence in their study – relying on a network of close personal relationships – is losing its importance. The second most frequently used measures (used in 6 of 7 countries) in their study were the use of dual classes of voting stocks and selling a special issue of voting shares or convertibles to "stable" or "friendly" investors. The first of these two defences is still commonly used but declining in importance in all the Nordic countries, whereas the second is not commonly used. Forming a strategic alliance and/or having interlocking boards of directors (used in 5 of 7 countries) is frequently used in Norway and Sweden, but not commonly used in the other two countries. Stronger defences are found in the Nordic countries as regards the number of shares that can be voted. Another defence that has grown stronger due to regulation is, as was mentioned above, the obligation for investors to disclose ownership increases that means a major stake in a

Exhibit 2.9: Nordic Listings on International Stock Exchanges – Prior to 1980.

Danish listings on international stock exchanges prior to 1980	
Novo Nordisk	London (1978)
Unibank	Amsterdam (1899) (formerly Privatbanken)
GN Store Nord	London (1869), Paris (1924)
ÖK Holding	Paris (1909)

Finnish listings on international stock exchanges prior to 1980
No companies were listed abroad

Norwegian listings on international stock exchanges prior to 1980	
Norsk Hydro	Geneva (1909), Paris (1909), London (1972), Düsseldorf (1975), Hamburg (1975), Basel (1976), Zurich (1976)

Swedish listings on international stock exchanges prior to 1980	
AGA	London (1979)
Alfa Laval	London (1928), Geneva (1928), Amsterdam (1928)
Asea	London (1969)
Atlas Copco	Frankfurt (1970), Hamburg (1970), Düsseldorf (1970)
Electrolux	London (1928), Geneva (1955)
Ericsson	London (1960), Paris (1960), Frankfurt (1961), US Nasdaq (1962), Düsseldorf (1964), Hamburg (1964), Oslo (1972), Geneva (1973), Basel (1973), Brussels (1973), Zurich (1973)
Esselte	London (1979)
Sandvik	London (1977)
SKF	London (1928), Paris (1929), Geneva (1935)
Swedish Match	London (1922), Geneva (1925), Amsterdam (1927), Basel (1927), Bern (1927), Lausanne (1927), Zurich (1927), Paris (1928), Antwerpen (1928), Brussels (1930)
Volvo	London (1972), Frankfurt (1974), Hamburg (1974), Düsseldorf (1974), Oslo (1979)

Source: Corporate annual reports; Stockholm Stock Exchange, *Database* and *interview data.*

company. Levels at which the disclosure should take place are specified in legislation.

2.5. Corporate Efforts to Internationalise the Cost of Capital

Corporate effort to internationalise the cost of capital can be combined into many different strategies. However, the main ingredients are to list the company's shares at one or more foreign stock exchanges or to direct equity issues to investors in one or more foreign countries. Although, these are often combined in practice, they are discussed below under two different headings.

2.5.1. Listing of Nordic Companies Abroad

Prior to 1980 no Finnish companies were listed abroad, whereas 4 Danish companies, 1 Norwegian and 11 Swedish companies were listed on inter-

Exhibit 2.10: Listing of Nordic Companies on Different Stock Exchanges Abroad 1980-1996.

Companies from	Year	Nordic Markets				Other European Markets							Non-European Markets			
		Denmark	Finland	Norway	Sweden	Belgium	France	Germany	Italy	Netherland	Switzerland	UK	US NASDAQ	NYSE	US Pink Sheet	Japan
Denmark	1980	–	0	0	0	0	2	0	0	1	0	2	0	0	0	0
	1985	–	0	0	0	0	2	0	0	1	0	2	0	1	0	0
	1991	–	0	1	0	0	2	5	0	1	2	6	0	1	0	0
	1996	–	0	0	0	0	0	1	0	0	2	5	0	3	0	0
Finland	1980	0	–	0	0	0	0	0	0	0	0	0	0	0	0	0
	1985	0	–	0	3	0	0	0	0	0	0	3	1	0	0	0
	1991	0	–	0	2	0	1	1	0	0	0	10	1	2	0	0
	1996[1]	0	–	0	1	0	1	1	0	0	0	2	4	3	0	0
Norway	1980	0	0	–	0	0	1	1	0	0	1	1	0	0	0	0
	1985	0	0	–	2	0	1	3	0	0	1	3	1	0	0	0
	1991	1	0	–	1	0	1	4	1	1	1	13	1	1	0	0
	1996[2]	2	0	–	2	0	1	2	0	1	1	5	4	6	0	0
Sweden	1980	0	0	2	–	2	3	3	0	2	5	10	1	0	0	0
	1985	2	1	4	–	2	5	3	0	2	5	18	6	0	4	0
	1991	6	3	4	–	1	5	6	0	1	6	15	7	0	3	2
	1996[3]	4	0	2	–	1	5	7	0	0	5	15	8	2	4	2

[1] In addition 25 Finnish companies can be traded on SEAQ INTERNATIONAL, and also on US PORTAL SYSTEM.
[2] In addition 13 Norwegian companies can be traded on SEAQ INTERNATIONAL.
[3] In addition 14 Swedish companies can be traded on SEAQ INTERNATIONAL.

national stock markets. (see Exhibit 2.9). The practice differed between countries. Danish companies were predominantly listed on only one market. Ericsson, with a listing on 11 markets, and Swedish Match were the Swedish shares represented on most exchanges. Of the 11 markets for Ericsson, three were in Switzerland. Swedish Match was represented on five exchanges in Switzerland. Norsk Hydro was listed on eight markets, of which three were in Switzerland.

During the period 1980-1996, a large number of Nordic firms listed on stock exchanges abroad, both with and without simultaneous equity issues. This is illustrated in Exhibit 2.10. Exactly which companies were listed is detailed in the Appendix to this chapter. The motives for listing are explained in Chapter 5.

After having had a peak in 1991, the number of Danish companies listed abroad is back to five. A listing in the UK or the US seems to be what the large Danish firms opt for.

The Finnish companies started to list abroad at the beginning of the 1980s. In 1985, there were six listings abroad by Finnish companies, three of them in Stockholm. In 1985, in addition to Stockholm, Finnish firms opted for London. In 1991, 10 firms were listed in London; a number that was reduced to two in 1996. The reason may have been the high cost and the fact that the companies can be traded on SEAQ international once three markets-makers are willing to back up the company. In 1996, all the seven listed Finnish companies had opted for a presence on the US market.

Norway is the Nordic country that shows the best internationalisation efforts by its firms as regards listing practice. From only one firm listed abroad in 1980 there were 14 listings in 1991. All of them except Freia had a presence in the UK. In 1996 many Norwegian firms were traded on SEAQ International without listing on the London Stock Exchange. Norwegian firms also increased their presence in the US markets.

About 20 Swedish firms have been listed abroad in the period 1985-1996. The new pattern is that by 1996 Swedish companies were listed on the New York Stock Exchange for the first time (Astra and Scania). 14 companies were traded on SEAQ International as an alternative to a listing on the London Stock Exchange.

Roughly speaking, the take-off as regards foreign listing of Nordic companies in the post-World War II period came about at the end of the 1980s. The London Stock Exchange (LSE) was at that time the most popular market place for that activity. In the mid-1990s, the US markets (NASDAQ and New York Stock Exchange) have passed LSE as the most popular choice of markets for a listing.

2.5.2. Nordic Equity Issues on Foreign Markets

Exhibit 2.4 has previously shown our estimate of the aggregate amount of Nordic equity issues directed to foreign investors. It is worth repeating that figures regarding corporate international issues are hard to capture for many reasons. The task of collecting data about them is getting increasingly difficult in an integrated world where authorities are no longer interested in registering crossborder financial activities. The behaviour of firms has also changed. In the 1990s issues directed to a specific market have been replaced by Euroequity issues with tranches aimed for the domestic as well as for several foreign markets.

2.5.3. Danish Firms

Danish firms have shown relatively little interest in international equity issues. In a Nordic comparison they were early in being granted the opportunity to raise capital abroad. Consequently, the first Nordic issue in the post World War II period was made by a Danish firm; Novo Industri A/S (Novo Nordisk). However, besides the interest shown by Novo (1981 and 1983) issuing activities abroad were carried out by only a handful of companies. In the 1980s, these companies were ÖK Holding (1985), Uni-Danmark (1986 and 1987), Baltica Holding (1988), ISS (1988) and Top-Denmark.

In the 1990s, Euroequity issues have been used. The international part of the typical Danish issue of DKK 2-400 million has been 10-20 per cent. Three big privatisation projects were launched in 1993 and 1994. When the Girobank was privatised in 1993, 2,300,000 shares were offered publicly (in addition 250,000 were offered to employees). Of these, 950,000 shares were offered internationally. Another 500,000 shares were aimed for Danish investors. In addition Danish institutional investors were guaranteed 850,000 shares. Individual Nordic investors were guaranteed by a Danish Guarantee Consortia. Hence, at the time of introduction the proportion of international risk capital should have been somewhere between 41 and 63 percent. When Copenhagen Airport was privatised in 1994, 2,450,000 shares were offered in two tranches; one for the Danish market (20 percent of the shares) and one for the international market aimed for international and Danish institutional investors (80 per cent of the shares). With that formulation of the prospectus the proportion of international risk capital at the time of introduction could have landed somewhere between 0 and 80 percent.

The third big privatisation, TeleDanmark in 1994, contained a tranche directed to a particular market, the New York Stock Exchange. In addition to the Copenhagen Stock Exchange and the NYSE, the shares were also aimed at being traded on the SEAQ International System of the International Stock Exchange of the United Kingdom and the Republic of Ireland Limited. The following tranches were offered: 25,919,770 B-shares in the United States and 37,310,000 B-shares outside the United States. The latter tranche contained some sub-tranches in terms of 8,850,000 shares offered in Europe, 12,650,000 shares in the Nordic region, 5,690,000 shares in the "rest of the world", and 10,120,000 shares in the United Kingdom. Danish investors were included in the sub-tranche aimed for the Nordic market. Hence, in this case more than 80 percent of the risk capital was supposed to come from international markets. It should be emphasised, however, that clauses about the right to redistribute between tranches are always attached to the prospectus making an estimate of the share of international risk capital a delicate task. Still, considering all uncertainty about figures, by 1993 risk capital raised abroad seems to have increased its relative importance. The way the three companies were privatised increased substantially the share of foreign ownership of Danish listed companies.

2.5.4. Finnish Firms

The first post-World War II issue abroad by a Finnish company was undertaken in 1982. The issuer was Kone and the issue of FIM 21.1 million nominal value brought in FIM 33.4 million. The issue was directed to the Swedish market. The choice of market was based on other reasons than cost of capital arguments.

Sweden continued to be the most popular market for Finnish equity issues abroad. Also in 1983, Kone, Nokia, and Wärtsilä directed issues to the Swedish market. However, the two biggest issues that year were an Euroequity issue (Finnish Sugar) and an issue directed to the US market (Instrumentarium). In terms of amounts raised through international equity issues 1984 and 1986 were the peak years of the 1980s. Pohjola (FIM 280 mill.) and Wärtsilä (FIM 201.5 million) were the two biggest issuers in 1984. Wärtsilä and the third biggest issuer, Amer (FIM 78 million), directed their issues to the UK market, whereas the Pohjola issue was an international issue of Euroequity kind. In 1986 Nokia directed an issue to the UK and US markets which gave the company an infusion of FIM 295 million of new risk capital. The second biggest issuer that year was Pohjola (FIM 247.5 million).

Banks started to show interest in raising capital abroad through directed equity issues in 1985. Union Bank of Finland raised FIM 182.4 million from Sweden. New issues abroad by the same bank followed in 1986. FIM 246.2 million was raised through an Euroequity issue. In 1988 the KOP-bank raised capital through two issues directed to institutional foreign investors (Nippon Life, Japan and Proventus, Sweden, respectively).

By 1987, the big paper and pulp companies started to issue abroad. That year Kymmene (Finland's most important export company at the time) and United Paper Mill raised FIM 282 million and FIM 315 million, respectively. In 1988, Enso-Gutzeit raised FIM 224 million through an Euroequity issue.

In the period 1989-1992, the use of issues directed to foreign investors was low. However, the lifting of restrictions on foreign ownership of Finnish companies, effective from 1 January 1993, triggered a revival of this way to raise capital. In 1993, Nokia raised FIM 954 million through an issue directed to major financial centers. Huhtamäki managed to get FIM 980 million through two issues. The KOP-bank, Metsä-Serla and Outo-kumpu were other major issuers on foreign markets that year. The peak came in 1994, with eight issues ranging from FIM 83 million to FIM 2592 million. Nokia (the biggest issue) and Outokumpu (second biggest issue) were out again. Among the major newcomers were Kemira (FIM 1273 million), Rautaruukki (FIM 828 million), Valmet (FIM 671 million) and Finnlines (FIM 385 million). The activity decreased in 1995 with only four issues abroad. Two issues (Rauma, FIM 1109 million and Neste, FIM 1039 million) accounted for 80 percent of the capital raised this way.

2.5.5. Norwegian Firms

Norwegian companies have by Nordic standards had a high share of for-eign ownership since the mid-1980s. Actually, a virtual takeoff as regards foreigners' acquisition of Norwegian shares came about in the period 1982-1984. The takeoff coincided with the lifting of restrictions on the amount of Norwegian shares a foreign investor was allowed to acquire. However, there were still restrictions on the proportion of shares in each company that foreigners were allowed to hold. Among Norwegian compa-nies interest in international issues boomed in 1989-1990. In 1989, Hafs-lund Nycomed (now Nycomed) raised NOK 796.5 million through an issue targeted to international institutional investors in London. Later that year Orkla Borregaard raised NOK 529 million through an issue directed to the UK market. Storli raised NOK 400 million through an Euroequity issue.

In 1990, Kværner turned to international investors with an Euroequity issue. Aker followed later that year with an Euroequity issue bringing in net funds of NOK 656.6 million. In 1992, Hafslund Nycomed placed an issue in the United States and listed on the New York Stock Exchange. This issue was directed towards American investors and resulted in a gross capital contribution of NOK 458 mill.

2.5.6. Swedish Firms

When Swedish companies began to approach foreign equity markets, it was not done through flotation of new equity. A major break in this pat-tern took place in 1981 when the pharmaceutical company Fortia/Pharmacia was introduced on the NASDAQ market in the United States, together with a large (compared to the size of its market capitalisation) issue of new shares. Over the period 1981-1993 a total of 30 issues directed to foreign investors were offered by Swedish companies.(See Chapter 4). The peak as regards the amount raised (in real as well as in nominal terms) through equity issues abroad occurred in 1983. Nine issues were directed to foreign investors that year. After one issue 1981 and one more in 1982 (Cardo), Ericsson was out as number 3 (announced in February 1983) with at the time the biggest foreign issue in the US market. The issue brought in five times more capital than the second biggest that year (Pharmacia). The capital raised corresponded to about 15 percent of the market value of the company. Pharmacia went for a second round in 1983, trying to copy the success made by Novo. The other companies that raised capital from international investors that year were Gambro, Perstorp, Volvo, PLM, Alfa Laval, Sonesson and Aga.

After the peak in 1983 followed a period of two years with a different pattern of issues. In February 1984 two small issues directed to a foreign market were announced. Then followed six issues directed toward private investors in exchange for the whole, or part, of the equity of another company (in chronological order Esab, Fermenta, Fermenta, Volvo, IDK Data and Fermenta). Except for an issue by Electrolux in 1986 the interest by Swedish firms in international issues was low until 1990. The amount of capital raised by Electrolux (SEK 2918 million) was the biggest in nominal as well as real terms as seen over the entire period under investigation. However, compared to the Ericsson issue of 1983 (SEK 2906 million) it was only slightly bigger. In 1990 Atlas Copco (SEK 1203 million) and Gambro (SEK 583 million) temporarily broke the trend. The issues thereafter were small and carried out by companies with lower market values than the companies issuing abroad during the first part of the period.

Something seems to have happened in 1986 that made Swedish companies less interested in issues directed to foreign markets. One potential explanation may be the abolition (June 1986) of the provision in the Swedish capital controls that required foreign financing of direct investments abroad. As reported in Oxelheim (1990) management of the 20 largest Swedish multinationals found in 1985 this provision to be a major obstacle.

An interesting feature of the Swedish issuing behaviour is that almost 60 percent of the companies undertook the listing and the issue as a joint project. Among the companies that did not follow that route we find Alfa Laval and Electrolux that were listed abroad already in the 1920s.

2.6. Concluding Remarks

The Nordic equity markets were for the first four decades of the post World War II period segmented markets with low liquidity. Hence, strong arguments existed for companies from the Nordic countries to opt for an internationalisation of their cost of capital. To secure that and to avoid an erosion of the wealth of existing shareholders (in case the issue was placed at thin and inefficient markets) they mostly opted for the US and UK markets once they got started.

From a regulatory point of view, in the mid-1990s the Nordic markets terminated a transition from being heavily regulated markets to becoming integrated parts of the "global" equity market. However, the Swedish equity market lagged somewhat behind the other Nordic markets being at stage Two as mentioned in Chapter 1 as opposed to stage Three for the other Nordic countries. The reason is the tax wedge that was reinserted in 1995 through the decision to reinstitute double taxation of corporate profits.

Though the markets are integrated from a capital flow and regulatory point of view, Nordic companies still have means to withstand hostile takeover efforts from foreign and domestic firms. Regulatory differences across the Nordic countries together with differences as regards the size distribution of firms are major explanatory variables to national differences in issuing behaviour of Nordic firms.

Finally, it should be noted that the deregulation of crossborder equity activities also meant that Nordic companies had to compete for risk capital with foreign companies in their domestic markets. However, very few foreign companies have raised risk capital in these markets. When it occurred, it was motivated by other reasons than pure cost of capital arguments.

References

Dullum K. B and A. Stonehill, 1990: "Corporate Wealth Maximization, Takeovers and The Market for Corporate Control". *Nationalökonomisk Tidsskrift*, No. 1. Copenhagen, pp.79-96.

Modén, K-M and L. Oxelheim, 1995: "Why Issue Equity Abroad – The experience of small country companies" . *Working Paper*, No.13. Lund University: Institute of Economic Research.

Oxelheim, L., 1997: "The routes to equity market integration – the interplay among regulators, investors and managers". *Working Paper*, Lund University: Institute of Economic Research.

Oxelheim, L., 1996: *"Financial Markets in Transition – Globalization, Investment and Economic Growth"*. London and New York: Routledge.

Oxelheim, L., 1990: *"International Financial Integration"*. Berlin: Springer Verlag.

Stjernborg, S., 1987, "Utrikeshandel med svenska aktier". *Kredit och Valutaöversikt, 4,* pp. 27-35, Stockholm.

Appendix 2.1

Exhibit 2.11: Danish Listing on International Stock Exchanges 1985.

| Danish companies | Market | | | | | | | | | |
| | Nordic countries | | | Europe | | | | | Other | |
	Oslo	Stock-holm	Hel-sinki	Great Britain	Ger-many	Swit-zerland	France	Nether-lands	NYSE	US Nasdaq (ADR:s)
UniDanmark								X		
Novo Nordisk				X					X	
Danske Bank		X								
GN Store Nord				X			X			
ÖK Holding							X			
	0	1	0	2	0	0	2	1	1	0

Source: Corporate annual reports.

Exhibit 2.12: Danish Listing on International Stock Exchanges 1991.

| Danish companies | Market | | | | | | | | | |
| | Nordic countries | | | Europe | | | | | Other | |
	Oslo	Stock-holm	Hel-sinki	Great Britain	Ger-many	Swit-zerland	France	Nether-lands	US	US Nasdaq (ADR:s)
UniDanmark					X			X		
Novo Nordisk				X	X	X			X	
TopDenmark				X	X	X				
Hafnia Holding				X	X					
Danske Bank					X					
Baltica Holding				X						
GN Store Nord				X			X			
ISS				X						
B&W Holding	X									
Ø and Ø Holding							X			
	1	0	0	6	5	2	2	1	1	0

Source: Corporate annual reports.

Exhibit 2.13: Danish Listing on International Stock Exchanges 1996.

	Market									
	Nordic countries			Europe					Other	
Danish companies	Stock-holm	Oslo	Hel-sinki	Great Britain	Swit-zerland	Ger-many	France	Nether-lands	US	US Nasdaq (ADR:s)
TopDenmark				X	X*	X				
ISS				X					X	
Novo Nordisk				X	X				X	
Tele Danmark				X					X	
GN Store Nord				X						
	0	0	0	5	2	1	0	0	3	0

Note: *Basel, Genève and Zürich
Source: Corporate annual reports.

Exhibit 2.14: Finnish Listing on International Stock Exchanges 1985.

	Market							
	Nordic countries			Europe			Other	
Finnish companies	Stock-holm	Oslo	Helsinki	Great Britain	Germany	France	US Nasdaq (ADR:s)	US
Amer				X				
Instrumentarium							X	
Kone	X							
Nokia	X							
Rauma-Repola				X				
Wärtsilä	X			X				
	3	0	0	3	0	0	1	0

Source: Helsinki Stock Exchange, *Annual report 1986*; Finnish Foundation for Share Promotion, *Database.*

Exhibit 2.15: Finnish Listing on International Stock Exchanges 1991.

	Market							
	Nordic countries			**Europe**			**Other**	
Finnish companies	Stock-holm	Oslo	Helsinki	Great Britain	Germany	France	US	US Nasdaq (ADR:s)
Amer				X			X	
Enso-Gutzeit				X				
Huhtamäki				X				
KOP				X				
Kone	X							
Kymmene				X				
Unitas				X				
Nokia	X			X	X	X	X	
Metra				X				
Pohjola				X				
Repola				X				
Instrumentarium								X
	2	0	0	10	1	1	2	1

Source: Helsinki Stock Exchange, *Annual report 1992*; Finnish Foundation for Share Promotion, *Database.*

Exhibit 2.16: Finnish Listing on International Stock Exchanges 1996.

	Market							
	Nordic countries			**Europe**			**Other**	
Finnish companies	Stock-holm	Oslo	Helsinki	Great Britain	Germany	France	US Nasdaq (ADR:s)	US
Amer				X			X	
Cultor							X	
Instrumentarium							X	
Metra							X	
Nokia	X			X	X	X		X
Rauma								X
Valmet								X
	1	0	0	2	1	1	4	3

Note: The following Finnish companies can also be traded on SEAQ International:
Aamulehti, Cultor, Enso, Finnair, Finnlines, Kemira, Kesko, Kone, Huhtamäki, Merita, Metra, Metsä-Serla, Neste, Nokian Tyres Ltd, Outokumpu, Pohjola, Polar, Rautaruukki,Rauma, Sampo, Tampella, Tamro, Tietotehdas, UPM-Kymmene, Valmet. Kemira and Huhtamäki were traded on US Portal System. Nokia was listed in Germany on Deutsche Börse Frankfurt and in the US on New York Stock Exchange, American Stock Exchange and Philadelphia Stock Exchange
Source: Helsinki Stock Exchange, *Database*; Finnish Foundation for Share Promotion, *Database*, and *Corporate Annual reports.*

68   *Nordic Equity Markets in Transition*

Exhibit 2.17: Norwegian Listing on International Stock Exchanges 1985.

	Market										
	Nordic countries			Europe						Other	
Norwegian companies	Stock-holm	Copen-hagen	Hel-sinki	Great Britain	Ger-many	Swit-zerland	France	Neth-erlands	Italy	US Nasdaq (ADR:s)	US
Elkem				X	X						
Norsk Data	X			X	X					X	
Norsk Hydro	X			X	X	X	X				
	2	0	0	3	3	1	1	0	0	1	0

Note: DNC was quoted on SEAQ International
Source: Oslo Stock Exchange, *Statistics* 1986.

Exhibit 2.18: Norwegian Listing on International Stock Exchanges 1991.

	Market										
	Nordic countries			Europe						Other	
Norwegian companies	Stock-holm	Copen-hagen	Hel-sinki	Great Britain	Ger-many	Swit-zerland	France	Neth-erlands	Italy	US	US Nasdaq (ADR:s)
Aker				X							
Bergesen				X							
Dyno Industrier				X							
Elkem				X	X						
Freia Marabou	X										
Hafslund Nycomed				X	X				X		
Kreditkassen				X							
Norsk Data		X		X	X						X
Norsk Hydro				X	X	X	X	X		X	
Orkla Borregaard				X							
Saga Petroleum				X							
Storli				X							
Unitor				X							
Vard				X							
	1	1	0	13	4	1	1	1	1	1	1

Source: Oslo Stock Exchange, *Statistics* 1992.

Exhibit 2.19: Norwegian Listing on International Stock Exchanges 1996.

	Market										
	Nordic countries			**Europe**						**Other**	
Norwegian companies	Stock-holm	Copen-hagen	Hel-sinki	Great Britain	Ger-many	Swit-zerland	France	Neth-erlands	Italy	US	US Nasdaq (ADR:s)
Bergesen				X							
DNB										X	
Elkem					X						
Hafslund Nycomed		X		X						X	
Kvaerner	X			X							
Nera											X
Norsk Hydro	X			X	X	X	X	X		X	X
Orkla											X
PGS											X
Saga										X	
Smedvig										X	
Tomra										X	
Unitor											X
	2	1	0	4	2	1	1	1	0	6	4

Note: The following Norwegian companies can also be traded on SEAQ International: Aker, Bergesen, DNB, Dyno, Elkem, Fokus Bank, Kreditkassen, NetCom, Norske Skog, Orkla, Saga Petroleum, Sparbanken NOR, Storli. DNB = US: ADR N.Y., Norsk Hydro = US: New York, ADR N.Y.; Germany: Düsseldorf, Frankfurt am Main, Hamburg; Switzerland: Basel, Genève and Zürich. Nycomed = US: ADR N.Y.; Saga Petroleum = US: New York, Smevig = US: New York (ADS) and ADR N.Y., Tomra = US: New York and ADR Level 1 N.Y.

Source: Oslo Stock Exchange, *Database*, and Corporate Annual reports.

Exhibit 2.20: Swedish Listing on International Stock Exchanges 1985.

Swedish companies	Nordic countries			Europe						Other	
	Oslo	Copen-hagen	Hel-sinki	Great Britain	France	Swit-zerland	Ger-many	Bel-gium	Neth-erlands	US Nasdaq (ADR:s)	US Pink Sheet (ADR:s)
AGA			X	X							O
Alfa-Laval				X		X			X		O
ASEA				X						X	
Astra				X							
Atlas Copco							X				
Investment AB Beijer				X							
Bilspedition		X									
Electrolux	X			X	X	X					O
Ericsson	X			X	X	X	X			X	
Esselte				X							
Fermenta				O							
Gambro				O						X	
Perstorp				X							
Pharmacia										X	
PLM		X		X							O
Sandvik				X							
SCA	X			X						X	
SKF				X	X	X					
Sonesson				X							
Swedish Match				X	X	X		X	X		
Volvo	X			X	X		X	X		X	
	4	2	1	18	5	5	3	2	2	6	4

Note: X = Official listing, O = Unofficial listing
Source: Stockholm Stock Exchange, *Annual report* 1986.

Exhibit 2.21: Swedish Listing on International Stock Exchanges 1991.

	Market											
	Nordic countries			**Europe**						**Other**		
Swedish companies	Copen-hagen	Oslo	Hel-sinki	Great Britain	Ger-many	Swit-zerland	France	Bel-gium	Neth-erlands	US Nasdaq (ADR:s)	US Pink Sheet (ADR:s)	Japan
AGA				X		X			X		X	X
Alfa-Laval				X		X					X	
ASEA	X		X	X	X					X		
Astra				X								
Atlas Copco				X	X							
Bilspedition	X		X									
Electrolux		X		X		X	X			X		
Ericsson		X		X	X	X	X			X		
Esselte				X								
Gambro										X		
Hexagon	X											
Lindab	X											
Nobel	X											
Perstorp				X			X					
Proventus			X									
Sandvik				X							X	
SCA				X	X					X		
Skandia	X	X		X								
SKF				X		X	X			X		
Stora				X	X							
Volvo		X		X	X	X	X	X		X		X
	6	4	3	15	6	6	5	1	1	7	3	2

Source: Stockholm Stock Exchange, Annual report 1992.

Exhibit 2.22: Swedish Listing on International Stock Exchanges 1996.

Swedish companies	Nordic countries			Europe						Other			
	Copen-hagen	Oslo	Hel-sinki	Great Britain	Ger-many	France	Swit-zerland	Bel-gium	Neth-erlands	NYSE	US Nasdaq (ADR:s)	US Pink Sheet (ADR:s)	Japan
AGA				X			X					O	X
ASEA	X			X	O						X		
Astra				X						X			
Atlas Copco				X	X							O	
Bilspedition	X	X											
Electrolux				X	O	X	X				X		
Ericsson				X	X	X	X				X		
Esselte				X									
Gambro											X		
Lindab	X												
Nordbanken				X								O	
Nordström & Thulin		X											
Oxigene				X		X					X		
Perstorp				X		X							
Sandvik				X								O	
Scania										X			
Skandia	X			X									
SKF				X		X	X				X		
Stora				X	X								
SCA				X	X						X		
Volvo				X	X	X	X	X			X		X
	4	2	0	15	7	5	5	1	0	2	8	4	2

Note: X = Official listing, O = Unofficial listing. The following Swedish companies can also be traded on SEAQ International: Autoliv, Avesta Sheffield, Gambro, Hennes & Mauritz, Incentive, Investor, MoDo, S-E-Banken, Securitas, Skåne-Gripen, Stadshypotek, Sv. Handelsbanken, Trelleborg.
Source: Stockholm Stock Exchange, *Database*; Annual reports, various companies.

Part II

The Role of Foreign and Domestic Investors

3. Global Diversification from a Nordic Perspective[1]

Eva Liljeblom, Anders Löflund and Svante Krokfors.

3.1. Introduction

A vast amount of studies for U.S. and other mainly large capital markets have demonstrated that the co–movements between different national stock markets are of a magnitude low enough to induce significant benefits from international portfolio diversification.[2] For a time period ending in 1988 / mid–1989, similar results have been obtained also for the Nordic stock markets in Haavisto and Hansson (1992)[3], and for Finland in Haavisto (1989). In general, the studies show that benefits occur, even in the presence of currency risk, although additional benefits are likely to occur, at least in the case of large foreign holdings, if one hedges for exchange rate risk.[4] In the early studies, the focus was on the performance of ex post efficient portfolios, while in subsequent studies, also the *ex post* performance of portfolios formed on *ex ante* grounds have been investigated, with estimation risk taken into account. In these more refined studies, the conclusion of large benefits as compared to domestic portfolio holdings remains unchanged.

An increase in the co–movement between national stock markets after the crash of 1987 has been reported in many more recent studies, see e.g.

1. This chapter reports part of the results of a study, the complete results of which are published in the *Journal of Banking & Finance*, Vol. 21 (1997), pp. 469-490 by E. Liljeblom, A Löflund and S. Krokfors, "The Benefits from International Diversification for Nordic Investors", @ 1996. It is published here with kind permission from Elsevier Science, NL Sara Burgerhartstraat 25, 1055 Amsterdam, The Netherlands.
2. See e.g. Grubel (1968), Levy and Sarnat (1970), Solnik (1974), Lessard (1973) and (1976), Solnik and Noetzlin (1982), Logue (1982), Jorion (1985), and Grauer and Hakansson (1987).
3. In their paper, only diversification within the Nordic stock markets was investigated.
4. The empirical evidence on the benefits of hedging is, however, mixed. Whereas hedging produced an improvement e.g. in Eun and Resnick (1988) and in Jorion (1989), in Jorion (1991) the improvement was shown to be much more modest for equity portfolios as compared to bond portfolios, and not always statistically significant – perhaps due to the blurring effect of the generally large volatility of stock portfolios. Mixed evidence was also reported in Levy and Lim (1994), and in Eun and Resnick (1994).

Bertero and Mayer (1990), Jeon and von Furstenberg (1990), Le (1991), Arshanapalli and Doukas (1993), and Longin and Solnik (1995). Also on theoretical grounds, a higher degree of international dependence can be expected especially for the Nordic capital markets (Denmark, Finland, Norway and Sweden) because a number of steps towards integration has been taken.

As described in Chapter 2, the Nordic countries (particularly Sweden and Finland) faced severe legal restrictions for capital movements across national borders until the beginning of the 1980s. These restrictions included barriers for corporate international investment as well as for portfolio investments. These restrictions were subsequently removed during the 1980s, a time period during which many Nordic firms also became much more internationalised. By now, many large companies could be regarded as diversified portfolios of international activities through exports and foreign investment. Thus their stock prices should be expected to be more correlated with that of other firms on global equity markets.

An increase in the international stock market co–movement would in turn suggest decreased benefits from international diversification. In addition, increased exchange rate volatility may also have reduced diversification benefits of unhedged international portfolios. The early 1990s was a turbulent period on the markets for foreign exchange, particularly in Finland, Sweden, and Norway, three countries which finally ended with floating exchange rates. On the other hand, if national risks in terms of stock market volatility also have increased in the Nordic countries, the benefits of international diversification may still be reasonably large despite the increased interdependence between different national equity markets.

The main objective of this chapter is to study the magnitude of the benefits from international diversification from a Nordic focus during the time period of 1974–93, and to investigate whether significant changes have occurred in the time period 1987–93, i.e. after the liberalisation of the Nordic capital markets. We extend the work of Haavisto and Hansson (1992) by examining diversification outside of Nordic countries and by evaluating ex ante diversification strategies. Moreover, since the Finnish markka (FIM) started its float towards the end of our study period, we present early evidence of the situation under a free float.

This chapter is organised as follows. In Section 3.2, the data used in the analysis will be described. In Section 3.3, we will study changes in volatility and the correlation structure of both international stock markets as well as currency returns, and the relative contribution of these two sources of risk for Nordic investors. Next, in Section 3.4, *ex post* efficient frontiers for different Nordic countries are computed. In Section 3.5, the *ex post* performance of different *ex ante* strategies are reported for Finnish and other Nordic investors. A summary and a conclusion are given in Section 3.6.

3.2. The Data

The analyses are performed on equity returns in 18 national stock markets using monthly data provided by Morgan Stanley Capital International. The countries include 17 OECD countries plus Hong Kong. The stock market returns include capital gains as well as dividend payments, and are based on value–weighted indices formed from mainly major companies (based on market capitalisation) on the national stock markets.[5]

Descriptive statistics for the different national indexes (in local currencies), reported in Exhibit A1 in Appendix 3.1, reveal negative skewness for all but three cases, and a somewhat high kurtosis. Average monthly logarithmic returns range from 0.007 (Austria) to 0.019 (Hong Kong).

The time period is 1974–1993, thus starting approximately from the collapse of the fixed exchange rate system. Two subperiods, 1974–1986 and 1987–1993, are investigated separately. The cut–off point was selected based on two criteria. First, 1987 was suggested by international evidence of generally increased stock market volatility as well as co–movement after the crash of 1987.[6] Secondly, around that point in time, the capital market restrictions were being removed in Finland, which was the last of the Nordic countries to fully liberalise its capital and foreign exchange markets.[7]

In analyses based on total returns from foreign investment measured in local Nordic currencies, the translation of the international returns have been performed using month–end exchange rates for the different currencies. Returns are measured as logarithmic differences of indexes measuring the stock market returns, or the total foreign portfolio returns.

---

5. For further details of the data set, see e.g. Ferson and Harvey (1994), where a similar data set has been used. The index for Finland has mainly been constructed at the Swedish School of Economics and Business Administration in Helsinki, Finland, and includes all stocks listed on the Helsinki Stock Exchange, with weights corresponding to market capitalisation.
6. See e.g. Bertero and Mayer (1990), Jeon and von Furstenberg (1990), Le (1991), Longin and Solnik (1993), and Arshanapalli and Doukas (1993).
7. Free foreign borrowing and direct investment (for nonfinancial companies) was possible in 1987 and 1988, respectively, whereas virtually unrestricted household foreign investment was allowed as late as in 1990.

3.3. Changes in Risk and Co-movement of Stocks and Currencies

In order to study whether the co–movement between international stock markets (measured in local currency), and foreign exchange rates has increased during the period, correlation coefficients between monthly stock returns during two subperiods 1974–86 and 1987–93, and monthly exchange rate changes during these subperiods were estimated. The stock returns are measured in local currency (i.e. as if all currency risk was eliminated), and the exchange rate changes in FIM. These correlation coefficients are reported in Exhibit 3.1 for stock returns, and Exhibit 3.2 for exchange rate changes.

A comparison of the upper and lower diagonals in Exhibit 3.1 and Exhibit 3.2 indicates an overall increase in both stock market co–movement as well as currency co–movement during the second subperiod. Of the 153 correlation coefficients between local stock markets, and the 136

Exhibit 3.1:   Correlations between Local Stock Market Returns.

September 1974 – December 1986 above diagonal
January 1987 – November 1993 below diagonal

	AUS	AUT	BEL	CAN	DEN	FRA	GER	HK	ITA	JAP	NET	NOR	SPA	SWE	SWI	UK	FIN	US
AUS	—	0.11	0.25	0.56	0.17	0.34	0.20	0.32	0.25	0.11	0.35	0.29	0.18	0.23	0.40	0.40	0.02	0.48
AUT	0.33	—	0.14	0.15	-0.01	0.23	0.27	0.13	0.08	0.07	0.13	0.01	0.05	0.04	0.21	0.06	0.05	0.12
BEL	0.52	0.31	—	0.25	0.21	0.48	0.37	0.20	0.31	0.29	0.49	0.35	0.18	0.23	0.48	0.45	0.20	0.38
CAN	0.72	0.27	0.61	—	0.20	0.42	0.23	0.29	0.22	0.20	0.49	0.26	0.15	0.25	0.46	0.48	0.01	0.66
DEN	0.35	0.33	0.46	0.43	—	0.09	0.21	0.19	0.25	0.14	0.34	0.17	0.04	0.31	0.28	0.28	0.03	0.23
FRA	0.51	0.44	0.69	0.58	0.43	—	0.38	0.23	0.36	0.28	0.43	0.27	0.20	0.16	0.45	0.46	0.14	0.44
GER	0.51	0.65	0.64	0.55	0.58	0.69	—	0.27	0.20	0.34	0.51	0.15	0.20	0.17	0.61	0.35	0.07	0.34
HK	0.68	0.38	0.54	0.66	0.31	0.49	0.50	—	0.29	0.17	0.42	0.24	0.11	0.19	0.39	0.40	-0.01	0.28
ITA	0.37	0.54	0.59	0.43	0.40	0.66	0.63	0.34	—	0.33	0.30	0.05	0.35	0.22	0.25	0.32	0.07	0.25
JAP	0.28	0.08	0.39	0.35	0.28	0.44	0.22	0.30	0.44	—	0.35	0.08	0.25	0.16	0.31	0.25	0.15	0.26
NET	0.67	0.46	0.73	0.75	0.46	0.67	0.74	0.67	0.63	0.33	—	0.32	0.23	0.32	0.62	0.58	0.06	0.56
NOR	0.60	0.46	0.57	0.62	0.49	0.58	0.61	0.57	0.52	0.31	0.73	—	0.02	0.13	0.32	0.23	0.03	0.40
SPA	0.60	0.46	0.56	0.54	0.47	0.57	0.47	0.63	0.52	0.53	0.61	0.54	—	0.24	0.15	0.18	0.13	0.15
SWE	0.52	0.42	0.57	0.43	0.45	0.51	0.63	0.49	0.59	0.43	0.65	0.63	0.64	—	0.34	0.30	0.28	0.36
SWI	0.59	0.49	0.68	0.67	0.49	0.69	0.78	0.61	0.67	0.33	0.81	0.64	0.61	0.64	—	0.55	0.01	0.60
UK	0.66	0.36	0.58	0.73	0.43	0.60	0.59	0.70	0.53	0.33	0.81	0.67	0.62	0.57	0.73	—	-0.00	0.49
FIN	0.29	0.38	0.39	0.36	0.38	0.34	0.35	0.33	0.46	0.26	0.43	0.48	0.48	0.44	0.39	0.37	—	0.01
US	0.63	0.21	0.62	0.82	0.42	0.63	0.54	0.65	0.37	0.34	0.73	0.61	0.58	0.48	0.68	0.80	0.22	—

All 18 countries:	χ^2	d.f.	prob.
Jennrich χ^2-test of equality of correlation matrices:	173.41	153	(0.124)
Jennrich χ^2-test of equality of covariance matrices:	419.39	153	(0.000)

Four Nordic countries only:			
Jennrich χ^2-test of equality of correlation matrices:	25.645	6	(0.000)
Jennrich χ^2-test of equality of covariance matrices:	98.912	6	(0.000)

Exhibit 3.2:   *Correlations between Currency Returns.* (FIM/Foreign currency)

September 1974 – December 1986 above diagonal
January 1987 – November 1993 below diagonal

	AUS	AUT	BEL	CAN	DEN	FRA	GER	HK	ITA	JAP	NET	NOR	SPA	SWE	SWI	UK	US
AUS	—	0.04	0.06	0.57	0.08	0.14	0.04	0.35	0.15	0.28	0.07	0.14	0.14	0.06	0.01	0.23	0.49
AUT	0.32	—	0.75	0.03	0.81	0.71	0.98	-0.10	0.50	0.18	0.94	0.55	0.27	0.14	0.70	0.10	-0.06
BEL	0.33	0.98	—	0.06	0.69	0.58	0.77	-0.09	0.25	0.18	0.76	0.47	0.25	0.09	0.48	0.15	-0.06
CAN	0.82	0.35	0.36	—	0.07	0.10	0.03	0.67	0.27	0.28	0.05	0.14	0.33	0.09	-0.05	0.31	0.88
DEN	0.34	0.95	0.97	0.39	—	0.65	0.80	-0.08	0.51	0.24	0.81	0.51	0.32	0.19	0.56	0.11	-0.01
FRA	0.37	0.97	0.98	0.39	0.97	—	0.69	-0.06	0.61	0.29	0.71	0.44	0.32	0.05	0.51	0.21	0.04
GER	0.32	0.99	0.98	0.34	0.96	0.98	—	-0.09	0.48	0.19	0.95	0.56	0.25	0.15	0.68	0.11	-0.06
HK	0.80	0.44	0.45	0.94	0.46	0.48	0.43	—	0.14	0.26	-0.10	0.02	0.14	0.19	-0.09	0.11	0.78
ITA	0.15	0.63	0.63	0.23	0.63	0.66	0.65	0.25	—	0.28	0.50	0.27	0.36	0.05	0.39	0.21	0.26
JAP	0.56	0.60	0.60	0.56	0.60	0.61	0.60	0.63	0.32	—	0.20	0.21	0.19	0.11	0.29	0.19	0.29
NET	0.31	0.99	0.98	0.34	0.95	0.98	1.00	0.43	0.65	0.60	—	0.56	0.33	0.11	0.65	0.22	-0.05
NOR	0.46	0.88	0.88	0.47	0.87	0.90	0.87	0.55	0.63	0.61	0.88	—	0.31	0.20	0.33	0.19	0.12
SPA	0.29	0.71	0.71	0.29	0.66	0.71	0.71	0.33	0.55	0.37	0.71	0.70	—	0.04	0.16	0.27	0.31
SWE	0.28	0.67	0.67	0.33	0.68	0.67	0.66	0.35	0.54	0.38	0.66	0.68	0.53	—	0.02	0.02	0.08
SWI	0.36	0.86	0.86	0.29	0.84	0.85	0.87	0.41	0.50	0.61	0.86	0.77	0.54	0.63	—	0.09	-0.11
UK	0.31	0.56	0.58	0.19	0.56	0.58	0.58	0.24	0.47	0.52	0.57	0.59	0.59	0.41	0.55	—	0.25
US	0.80	0.43	0.44	0.94	0.45	0.47	0.43	1.00	0.24	0.63	0.43	0.43	0.55	0.32	0.34	0.40	0.24	—

	χ^2	d.f.	prob.
Jennrich χ^2-test of equality of correlation matrices:	204.46	136	(0.000)
Jennrich χ^2-test of equality of covariance matrices:	418.71	136	(0.000)

correlation coefficients for exchange rate changes, only two and five, respectively, are lower during the latter subperiod.[8] The average stock market correlation increases from 0.256 to 0.521 over the two subperiods whereas the average exchange rate correlation increases from 0.280 to 0.594.

We tested the equality of the correlation as well as covariance matrices using the Jennrich (1970) test of equality. The equality between the covariance matrices could be rejected at the 1% level both for local stock markets as well as for currency returns. The equality of the currency correlation matrices could be rejected at the 1% level for currency returns[9], while local stock market correlations were significantly different only at the 15% level. These results suggest reduced benefits from international diversification given unchanged Nordic stock market volatilities.

The increased co-movement between currency returns from the FIM point of view can be attributed to two large devaluations/depreciations of

8. The lower ones for the stock markets measure the co-movement of the Japanese market with either Germany or the Netherlands. The lower ones for currencies are between CAD and the three currencies of ITL, ESP, and GBP, and finally the coefficient between USD and ITL.
9. The same rejection of equality applies for currency correlation matrices measured from the Danish, Norwegian and Swedish point of view (results not reported here but can be obtained from the authors).

FIM in the 1990s, which produced simultaneous increases in all the foreign exchange rates at the same time.[10] A similar explanation is likely also for Sweden and Norway, which too have suffered from large changes in the external value of their currency during the 1990s.[11]

In order to investigate the relative contribution of stock market and currency risk, a decomposition of the volatility of the total return (measured in the domestic currency) from the investment in one single foreign market was performed in a way similar to that in Eun and Resnick (1988).

Assuming a small cross–product between stock return and exchange rate change, the domestic return of a single foreign investment can be approximated by

$$R_{i,dom} = R_i + e_i \tag{3.1}$$

and the variance of the domestic rate of return as

$$Var(R_{i,dom}) = Var\ (R_i) + Var\ (e_i) + 2\ Cov\ (R_i, e_i) \tag{3.2}$$

where Var (R_i) is the variance of the foreign stock market return (i.e. in local currency) and Var (e_i) is the variance of the exchange rate for the country of investment. The decomposition was performed from the perspective of all the four Nordic countries. Detailed results are reported here only from the Finnish perspective for the two subperiods in Exhibit 3.3, panels A and B.

As is clearly shown in Exhibit 3.3, currency risk stands for only a small part of the total risk of a foreign investment. The pure stock market volatility contributes between 60% (Japan) and 98% (Norway) of the total risk during the first subperiod, and between 53% (Canada) and 96% (Sweden) during the second subperiod. On the average, approximately

10. Although several de- and revaluations of FIM also occurred during the first subperiod, the devaluations/ depreciations during the latter subperiod were much larger. When correlation coefficients between FIM and the rest of the currencies are measured using USD as the benchmark, no large change in the correlation structure is detected. The average correlation coefficient is 0.57 for subperiod 1, and 0.59 for subperiod 2, indicating that the larger foreign currency co-movement from the FIM point of view indeed is due to stronger volatility in the external value of the FIM itself.

11. From the USD point of view, no large increase in general foreign currency co-movement has occurred. Only 83 (61%) of the 136 correlation coefficients between pairs of foreign currencies have increased during the latter subperiod.

Exhibit 3.3: Decomposition of Stock Market Returns in FIM.

Panel A: 1974-1986

Stock Market	var(R_i)	var(e_i)	cov(R_i,e_i)	corr(R_i,e_i)	var(R_i)total	var(R_i)	var(e_i)	2cov(R_i,e_i)
Australia	0.41	0.13	0.04	0.18	0.62	66%	20%	13%
Austria	0.14	0.03	0.00	−0.06	0.17	85%	20%	−5%
Belgium	0.21	0.06	0.00	−0.04	0.26	81%	22%	−3%
Canada	0.30	0.08	0.01	0.08	0.41	75%	19%	6%
Denmark	0.20	0.04	−0.01	−0.12	0.22	93%	17%	−10%
France	0.41	0.04	0.01	0.11	0.47	86%	8%	6%
Germany	0.19	0.03	0.00	0.03	0.23	83%	15%	2%
Hongkong	0.93	0.07	0.00	0.01	1.00	93%	7%	0%
Italy	0.58	0.05	0.00	−0.02	0.62	93%	8%	−1%
Japan	0.17	0.08	0.01	0.12	0.28	60%	29%	10%
Netherlands	0.24	0.04	0.00	−0.05	0.27	90%	13%	−3%
Norway	0.85	0.02	0.00	−0.01	0.87	98%	3%	0%
Spain	0.34	0.07	0.02	0.13	0.45	76%	16%	9%
Sweden	0.32	0.02	0.00	0.05	0.35	91%	6%	3%
Switzerland	0.17	0.06	−0.01	−0.09	0.21	79%	30%	−9%
UK	0.47	0.07	0.02	0.12	0.57	81%	11%	7%
Finland	0.13	0.00	0.00	0.00	0.13	100%	0%	0%
USA	0.20	0.07	0.00	−0.02	0.27	74%	27%	−2%
Average						84%	15%	1%

Note: The variances and covariances are on a monthly level and have been multiplied by 10^2.

Panel B: 1987-1993

Stock Market	var(R_i)	var(e_i)	cov(R_i,e_i)	corr(R_i,e_i)	var(R_i)total	var(R_i)	var(e_i)	2cov(R_i,e_i)
Australia	0.57	0.21	0.07	0.22	0.93	61%	23%	16%
Austria	0.71	0.07	0.00	0.01	0.79	91%	9%	0%
Belgium	0.34	0.07	−0.01	−0.05	0.39	87%	17%	−4%
Canada	0.20	0.14	0.02	0.12	0.37	53%	37%	10%
Denmark	0.34	0.07	−0.02	−0.11	0.38	91%	18%	−9%
France	0.39	0.06	0.01	0.05	0.47	83%	14%	3%
Germany	0.50	0.07	0.00	0.03	0.58	87%	12%	2%
Hongkong	0.83	0.14	0.03	0.08	1.03	81%	14%	5%
Italy	0.38	0.04	0.02	0.15	0.45	84%	8%	8%
Japan	0.49	0.13	−0.01	−0.04	0.60	81%	22%	−3%
Netherlands	0.24	0.07	−0.02	−0.17	0.27	91%	26%	−16%
Norway	0.71	0.06	−0.01	−0.05	0.74	95%	7%	−3%
Spain	0.48	0.07	−0.01	−0.05	0.54	90%	14%	−4%
Sweden	0.60	0.06	−0.02	−0.08	0.63	96%	9%	−5%
Switzerland	0.32	0.08	−0.03	−0.16	0.35	92%	22%	−15%
UK	0.35	0.05	−0.01	−0.09	0.37	93%	13%	−6%
Finland	0.60	0.00	0.00	0.00	0.60	100%	0%	0%
USA	0.22	0.14	0.01	0.03	0.37	59%	38%	3%
Average						84%	17%	−1%

Note: The variances and covariances are on a monthly level and have been multiplied by 10^2.

84% of the total risk can be addressed to local stock market volatility during both subperiods. The results are similar for the three other Nordic countries.[12] These results are in contrast to those generally obtained using a USD numeraire[13], and in line with those of Haavisto and Hans-

12. The proportion of the total risk which can be addressed to local stock market volatility is, for sub-periods one and two, 84% and 86% for Danish investors, 83% and 94% for Norwegian investors, and 82% and 86% for Swedish investors.
13. See e.g. Eun and Resnick (1988). In their study, the relative contribution of the stock market risk is approximately 50% or below, and the contribution of exchange rate volatility by itself above 30% for all countries except France and Canada.

son (1994), who concluded that "exchange rate risk was negligible" [14] for all four Nordic countries.

These results are in general in line of what could be expected when using a fixed currency as a unit of measurement instead of a freely floating (and highly volatile) currency such as the U.S. dollar.[15] Especially for investments within Nordic countries, exchange rate risk does not seem to be very important. Stock market volatility stands for most of the volatility of e.g. Finnish investments in the other Nordic countries (between 91% and 98% for investments in Sweden and Norway, respectively, during the first subperiod, and between 91% and 96% for investments in Denmark and Sweden during the second subperiod). However, a separate investigation (not reported here) revealed that the results of the decomposition are dramatically changed by the float of FIM.[16] Also for intra-Nordic investments, the contribution of the local stock market volatility to overall risk goes substantially down during the floating FIM period, to values between 55% and 74% (Finnish investments in Denmark and Sweden, respectively).

Our next focus is on the question of increased risks. Exhibit 3.3 also shows that the stock market volatility has increased in 11 cases out of 18, is approximately equal in one case, and smaller in six cases during the latter subperiod. A non-parametric Wilcoxon signed rank test taking into account both the sign and the magnitude of the difference between the second and the first subperiod stock return volatilities yields an approximately normally distributed test statistic $z = 2.156$, and hence supports the overall increase in stock market volatility on the 5% level of significance. The exchange rate volatility has increased in 14 cases of 17 and is approximately equal in one case (Wilcoxon z-statistic is 3.195 clearly rejecting the null hypothesis of constant currency risk). For the Nordic countries specifically, an increase in both risks has occurred with the exception of stock market volatility for Norway, which in fact was reduced from 0.85 to 0.71 (monthly variances, multiplied by 10^2). Finally, the rela-

---

14. Haavisto and Hansson (1994) made their conclusion on the basis of more indirect evidence (portfolio weights, efficient frontiers).
15. During the investigation period, FIM was mostly fixed with respect to a currency basket of nearly 20 different currencies, with weights based on the countries' share of Finland's foreign trade. A similar system was in use in Norway and Sweden, while Denmark became part of the ERM. Although parity adjustments occurred, the analysis clearly shows that exchange rate risk is not as largely present as for U.S. investors.
16. When a similar decomposition was made for the rather short period of the float of FIM (in September 1992, which leaves us with 15 monthly observations of the float), on the average 44% of the total risk could be addressed to local stock market volatility, 61% to exchange rate volatility, and -5% to the cross component. These results can be obtained from the authors.

tive contribution of exchange rate risk is larger during the latter subperiod in 10 cases out of 17, approximately equally large in one case, and smaller in six cases (Wilcoxon z-statistic between the two sets of relative contributions is 0.853 and hence insignificant).

Summarising, the results reported in this section show significant increases in local stock market covariances during the latter subperiod of 1987–93. Also the co–movement of foreign currencies has significantly increased from the Nordic perspective. These increased co–movements would indicate reduced benefits from international diversification, if not also the risks themselves had increased on the Nordic markets. Since some although weaker evidence of increased stock market risks was also obtained, the total effect remains so far an unsettled issue.

3.4. Ex Post Efficient Frontiers

Using data for the complete time period, as well as for each of the two subperiods, we computed *ex post* efficient frontiers. Separate frontiers were computed using each of the four Nordic currencies as a numeraire currency. The four Nordic stock markets were then superimposed on the plot separately along with an equally weighted Nordic portfolio and the value-weighted market index (from Morgan Stanley Capital International). These frontiers are based on total returns (i.e. no risk–free interest rate is deducted), and a short sale restriction is enforced.

In Exhibit 3.4, these results for the second subperiod 1987–1993 are reported, clearly showing that substantial benefits from international diversification were obtainable also during the second subperiod for all the Nordic countries with the exception of Denmark. The results also show that although the equally weighted Nordic index (EQW Nordic) comes rather close to the world market index (WORLD), some additional benefits (above all during the first subperiod, not reported here) could have been obtained by extended diversification outside the Nordic countries.

A comparison of subperiod results for 1974-86 (not reported here) and 1987-94 reveal that for several Nordic countries, in fact larger benefits from international diversification seems attainable during the latter subperiod in the sense that the countries lie further away from the portfolio frontier, as well as from the simple rather well diversified proxies WORLD and EQW Nordic.

In Exhibit 3.5, we report more detailed results for one Nordic country, Finland, for the latter subperiod of 1987-94, in this case using excess

Exhibit 3.4:   Ex Post Efficient Frontiers January 1987 – November 1993.

Note: Total returns are measured in FIM, SEK, NOK and DKK. The exhibit includes four frontiers (computed for each of the four Nordic numeraire currencies), and includes six benchmark portfolios, i.e. the four Nordic domestics ones, the Nordic equally weighted portfolio, and the value-weighted world market index. Each portfolio is plotted four times (using each of the Nordic currencies as the numeraire currency).

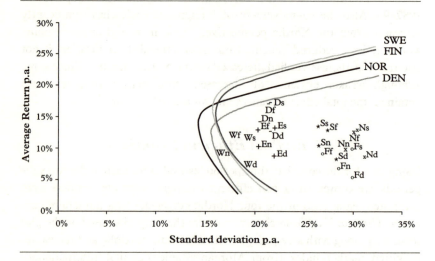

Definitions: **Fn** denotes the stock market index for Finland, as perceived by a Norwegian investor. Correspondingly for all other indexes: N=NORWAY, S=SWEDEN, and D=DENMARK, d=Danish, s=Swedish, f=Finnish investor). **Ed** is the equally weighted Nordic index (EQW Nordic), as seen from the perspective of Danish investors. **Ws** is the value-weighted world market index (WORLD) from a Swedish point.

returns (i.e. with the monthly risk-free interest rate deducted).[17] In relation to many individual local stock market indices, the portfolios of WORLD (value weighted) and especially EQW Nordic (the equally weighted Nordic portfolio) give a better risk-return trade-off.

The results in this section show that at least on an *ex post* basis, there seems to be substantial benefits from international diversification for the Nordic countries. The benefits are, in a relative sense, at least as good during the latter subperiod as compared to the first one. Interestingly, a large part of the benefits can be obtained simply by the use of an equally weighted Nordic portfolio.

---

17. We also computed frontiers based on excess returns for the three other Nordic currencies. These frontiers can be obtained from the authors.

Exhibit 3.5: Ex Post Efficient Frontier January 1987 – December 1993.

(Based on excess returns in FIM).

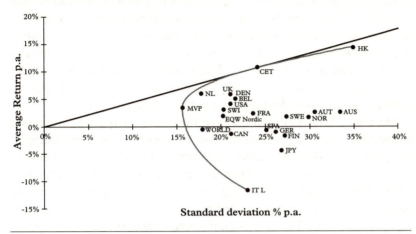

3.5. The Performance of Ex Ante Strategies

Next, we analyse the performance of several *ex ante* investment strategies. These strategies will be analysed from the perspective of both Danish, Finnish, Norwegian, and Swedish investors. The analysis is throughout based on excess returns.[18]

We compare the pure domestic portfolio to several simple proxies: an investment in the U.S. market (USA), an equally weighted Nordic portfolio (EQW Nordic), an investment in the value–weighted world market portfolio (WORLD), and in an equally weighted world market portfolio (EQW World). A fifth strategy is to identify the weights in the *ex post* (historical) tangency portfolio, and to invest in a similar portfolio for the next period. In line with Eun and Resnick (1988), this strategy is called CET or the certainty–equivalence–tangency portfolio strategy, since it assumes no estimation risk. In the sixth strategy, we use the *ex ante* (historical) weights of the minimum variance portfolio (MVP). This strategy assumes that there is no useful asset–specific information in the vector of average returns because it is not required as an input to solve the portfolio problem.[19]

---

18. For the interest rates used when computing excess returns, see Appendix 2.
19. The instability of sample means as compared to variances and covariances has been demonstrated in several studies, e.g. by the striking results in Jorion (1985).

Finally, in line with Jorion (1985, 1986), Eun and Resnick (1988), and others, a Bayes-Stein estimator is implemented. This estimator will take into account the estimation risk involved with historical mean returns, and by the use of a shrinkage factor bringing the elements of the return vector towards the mean return for the *ex post* minimum-variance portfolio MVP. Thereafter, using the conventional unbiased estimator for the inverse of the variance-covariance matrix (see Jobson and Korkie 1981a), the optimal *ex ante* tangency portfolio can be determined. This strategy is called BST. Results for hedged strategies were also performed but are not reported here.[20]

Since the CET, MVP, and BST return strategies require an estimation period, five years are reserved for that. Strategies are then implemented for holding periods of one month. A monthly window is used (next month, new strategies are formed based on an estimation period including the previous 60 months, and executed for the next month). This gives us 171 observations of returns on each investment strategy from September 1979 to November 1993. The out-of-sample performance is measured with the Sharpe ratio which is computed using the average excess return for the monthly strategies, and its time-series standard deviation.

Exhibit 3.6 reports the results for the strategies for all the four Nordic countries for the total time period. In each case, MVP is the best strategy during the overall period, and among the two best strategies during all subperiods[21] but for Denmark, subperiod 2. Two other strategies which frequently occur among the two best are BST and EQW World. These results are consistent with Eun and Resnick (1988) who also find that the two dominating unhedged strategies are the equally weighted world index and the MVP strategy. The value weighted world market portfolio WORLD performs in turn rather badly[22], and is e.g. consistently beaten by CET in the results for the complete time period[23]. All these strategies are, however, seldom significantly better than the domestic portfolio according to the Jobson-Korkie (1981a) z-statistic testing the difference of two Sharpe ratios.[24]

---

20. For results using hedged strategies, see Liljeblom, Löflund, and Krokfors (1997).
21. Subperiod results for Nordic countries other than Finland are not reported here but can be obtained from the authors.
22. In light of results such as those in Harvey (1991), one would expect the value weighted world market portfolio to perform better.
23. In fact, the performance of CET is surprisingly good. Several studies, such as those by Eun and Resnick (1984), Jorion (1985) and (1986), and the domestic (U.S.) based simulations by Jobson and Korkie (1981b), found instead that CET does not perform especially well.
24. However, rejections do occur at the 10% level for Denmark, the 1979–86 subperiod (MVP and EQW World) and for Norway (MVP, EQW World, and EQW Nordic), in the same subperiod.

Exhibit 3.6:　Ex Ante Investment Strategies, All the Nordic Countries.

Panel A. Denmark, September 1979 – November 1993

	mean return	std.dev.	Sharpe ratio	JK z-stat.	(prob.)
CET	6.94	18.12	0.38	0.297	(0.383)
MVP	6.84	13.77	0.50	0.744	(0.229)
BST	7.74	18.83	0.41	0.413	(0.340)
EQW World	6.25	15.45	0.40	0.361	(0.359)
EQW Nordic	6.40	18.26	0.35	0.179	(0.429)
DEN	5.87	19.09	0.31		
USA	6.12	19.43	0.32	0.024	(0.490)
WORLD	5.30	16.43	0.32	0.052	(0.479)

Panel B. Finland, September 1979 – November 1993

	mean return	std.dev.	Sharpe ratio	JK z-stat.	(prob.)
CET	6.24	19.17	0.33	0.286	(0.388)
MVP	6.11	14.10	0.43	0.803	(0.211)
BST	2.70	23.92	0.11	−0.420	(0.663)
EQW World	5.04	15.46	0.33	0.286	(0.387)
EQW Nordic	5.18	17.35	0.30	0.228	(0.410)
FIN	5.14	21.12	0.24		
USA	4.91	19.51	0.25	0.024	(0.490)
WORLD	4.09	16.25	0.25	0.026	(0.490)

Panel C. Norway, September 1979 – November 1993

	mean return	std.dev.	Sharpe ratio	JK z-stat.	(prob.)
CET	4.68	17.84	0.26	0.890	(0.187)
MVP	3.72	13.13	0.28	0.958	(0.169)
BST	3.71	22.44	0.17	0.520	(0.301)
EQW World	3.68	14.41	0.26	0.986	(0.162)
EQW Nordic	3.82	16.71	0.23	1.169	(0.121)
NOR	0.13	32.23	0.00		
USA	3.55	18.51	0.19	0.634	(0.263)
WORLD	2.73	15.49	0.18	0.588	(0.278)

Panel D. Sweden, September 1979 – November 1993

	mean return	std.dev.	Sharpe ratio	JK z-stat.	(prob.)
CET	7.91	17.47	0.45	−0.178	(0.571)
MVP	8.58	14.61	0.59	0.359	(0.360)
BST	8.94	17.31	0.52	0.070	(0.472)
EQW World	7.50	15.14	0.50	−0.011	(0.504)
EQW Nordic	7.65	17.79	0.43	−0.331	(0.630)
SWE	11.90	23.89	0.50		
USA	7.37	19.22	0.38	−0.401	(0.656)
WORLD	6.55	16.34	0.40	−0.374	(0.646)

Note: All returns are expressed as annualised percentages and are in excess of the 1-month domestic interest rate (for interest rate data, see Appendix 3.2). CET is the Certainty Equivalent Tangency portfolio, MVP the Minimum Variance Portfolio, and BST the Bayes-Stein estimation risk adjusted strategy. 60 previous months are used in estimating mean returns and the covariance matrix. EQW World and EQW Nordic stand for equally weighted portfolios of all 18 countries and 4 Nordic countries, respectively. DEN, FIN, NOR, SWE, and USA, represent 100% investment in Denmark, Finland, Norway, Sweden, or the U.S. WORLD, is the Morgan Stanley value-weighted world equity index return. Jobson-Korkie z-statistic (p-value in parenthesis) tests the difference between Sharpe ratios for each strategy against 100% local stock market investment in the domestic country.

The Role of Foreign and Domestic Investors

Exhibit 3.7:   The Subperiod Ex Ante Investment Strategies for Finland.

Panel A. Sample period September 1979 – December 1986

	mean return	std.dev.	Sharpe ratio	JK z-stat.	(prob.)
CET	12.93	18.69	0.69	-0.358	(0.640)
MVP	9.84	9.61	1.02	0.377	(0.353)
BST	4.78	27.28	0.18	-1.326	(0.908)
EQW World	8.06	11.66	0.69	-0.325	(0.627)
EQW Nordic	8.32	13.92	0.60	-0.557	(0.711)
FIN	11.44	13.18	0.87		
USA	5.79	17.92	0.32	-0.930	(0.824)
WORLD	8.31	14.25	0.58	-0.506	(0.693)

Panel B. Sample period January 1987 – November 1993

	mean return	std.dev.	Sharpe ratio	JK z-stat.	(prob.)
CET	-0.85	19.57	-0.04	0.034	(0.487)
MVP	2.15	17.66	0.12	0.520	(0.302)
BST	0.51	19.90	0.03	0.203	(0.420)
EQW World	1.83	18.70	0.10	0.392	(0.347)
EQW Nordic	1.85	20.41	0.09	0.472	(0.319)
FIN	-1.54	27.08	-0.06		
USA	3.97	21.17	0.19	0.525	(0.300)
WORLD	-0.39	18.14	-0.02	0.084	(0.467)

Panel C. Sample period September 1992 – November 1993

	mean return	std.dev.	Sharpe ratio	JK z-stat.	(prob.)
CET	33.26	18.19	1.83	-0.023	(0.509)
MVP	38.37	14.78	2.60	0.341	(0.367)
BST	41.54	21.46	1.94	0.030	(0.488)
EQW World	36.73	15.94	2.30	0.210	(0.417)
EQW Nordic	40.66	17.94	2.27	0.223	(0.412)
FIN	64.66	34.51	1.87		
USA	34.50	18.97	1.82	-0.028	(0.511)
WORLD	28.43	17.30	1.64	-0.125	(0.550)

Note: All returns are expressed as annualised percentages and are in excess of the 1-month domestic, in this case FIM interest rate (for interest rate data, see Appendix 3.2). CET is the Certainty Equivalent Tangency portfolio, MVP the Minimum Variance Portfolio, and BST the Bayes-Stein estimation risk adjusted strategy. 60 previous months are used in estimating mean returns and the covariance matrix. EQW World and EQW Nordic stand for equally weighted portfolios of all 18 countries and 4 Nordic countries, respectively. FIN and USA represent 100% investment in Finland and the U.S., respectively. WORLD is the Morgan Stanley value-weighted world equity index return. Jobson-Korkie z-statistic (p-value in parenthesis) tests the difference between Sharpe ratios for each strategy against 100% local stock market investment in Finland.

The benefits of international diversification for Finland can be studied in more detail in Exhibit 3.7, where results for the two subperiods, and the short period of the float of the FIM, are reported. The results are very much in line with those in Exhibit 3.6 for the complete time period. For example, the performance of the MVP turned out to be quite robust, this strategy being always either the best or the second best strategy. Another observation from these subperiod studies is that the EQW Nordic was always almost as good as the EQW World (their Sharpe ratios differing only some points on the second decimals). The differences between the Sharpe-ratios was again tested using the Jobson-Korkie (1981a) z-statistic (strategies against a 100% holding in domestic stocks), but no significant differences could be detected.

A comparison of the weights (not reported here) for the Finnish investors' certainty-equivalent tangency strategy CET, the minimum variance portfolio MVP, and the Bayes-Stein Tangency Strategy BST during the pre-float period and the float period reveal some rather large differences. Whereas during the pre-float period, Finland and Austria have large overall average weights of 31% and 24% in the MVP, the Netherlands obtains a high post-float weight of 63% on average. In general, besides an investment in the Finnish portfolio, of the Nordic countries only Denmark has a significant weight in the MVP. The BST strategy is the least diversified of the three strategies and obtains extreme weights in both subperiods.

In this section, the *ex post* performance of *ex ante* strategies was investigated. In line with previous research, the historical minimum variance portfolio MVP stands out as one of the best strategies. Surprisingly, the value weighted world market portfolio, which includes 18 countries but admittedly may suffer in stability from not being equally weighted, is outperformed by an equally weighted Nordic index of only four countries. The EQW Nordic was in fact very close to the EQW World during different subperiods. Moreover, this result is not likely to be a consequence of exchange rate risk, since the analysis in Section 3.3 indicated that currency risk generally did not contribute much to the overall portfolio risk for the Nordic countries. These results therefore support intra-Nordic diversification as a first step on the way towards a more diversified portfolio.

3.6. Summary and Conclusions

The main objective of this chapter is to study the magnitude of the benefits from international diversification from a Nordic point of view. Since it is likely that the co–movement of stock markets have increased towards the end of the 1980s, while simultaneously exchange rates for the Nordic countries have become more volatile, it is of interest to investigate whether the relative benefits from unhedged international diversification for these countries would have been reduced. Two subperiods, 1974–86 and 1987–1993 are therefore separately investigated.

We direct a special focus towards the period during which the FIM has floated. Preliminary evidence of how the relative magnitudes of the different risks (local stock market risk, and exchange rate risk) have changed after the float is presented, and the performance of international diversification strategies prior to and after the float of FIM are investigated.

The chapter reports significant increases in stock market co–movement. Only in two cases out of 153 has the pairwise correlation coefficient between two stock market indexes (measured in local currency) been reduced over time. Also the co–movement of foreign currencies has significantly increased for Nordic countries. However, also some weaker evidence of increased stock market volatility was obtained.

The results of *ex post* as well as *ex ante* strategies indicate generally substantial benefits from international diversification for the Nordic countries. The benefits are, in a relative sense, even larger during the latter subperiod. While the value weighted world market portfolio does not demonstrate any especially good performance in the *ex ante* unhedged strategies, equally weighted World and Nordic indexes do rather well, and the global minimum variance strategy MVP shows the overall best performance.

All in all, our results indicate substantial benefits from international diversification for the Nordic countries in spite of significantly increased stock market covariance.

References

Arshanapalli, B. and J. Doukas, 1993: "International Stock Market Linkages: Evidence from the pre- and post-October 1987 Period". *Journal of Banking and Finance, 17,* pp. 193–208.

Bertero, E. and C. Mayer, 1990: "Structure and Performance: Global Interdependence of Stock Markets around the Crash of October 1987". *European Economic Review, 34,* pp. 1155–1180.

Eun, C. S. and B. G. Resnick, 1984: "Estimating the Correlation Structure of International Share Prices". *Journal of Finance, 39,* pp. 1311–1324.

Eun, C. S. and B. G. Resnick, 1988: "Exchange Rate Uncertainty, Forward Contracts, and International Portfolio Selection". *Journal of Finance, 43,* pp. 197–215.

Eun, C. S. and B. G. Resnick, 1994: "International Diversification of Investment Portfolios: U.S. and Japanese Perspectives". *Management Science, 40,* pp. 140–161.

Ferson, W. E. and C. R. Harvey, 1994: "Sources of Risk and Expected Returns in Global Equity Markets". *Journal of Banking and Finance, 18,* pp. 775–803.

Grauer, R. R. and N. H. Hakansson, 1987: "Gains from International Diversification: 1968–85 Returns on Portfolios of Stocks and Bonds". *Journal of Finance, 42,* pp. 721–741.

Grubel, H., 1968: "Internationally Diversified Portfolios: Welfare Gains and Capital Flows". *American Economic Review, 58,* pp. 1299–1314.

Haavisto E., 1989: "Kansainvälisten osakesijoitusten mahdollisuudet" *KOP Taloudellinen katsaus,* pp. 21–29.

Haavisto, T. and B. Hansson, 1992: "Risk Reduction by Diversification in the Nordic Stock Markets". *Scandinavian Journal of Economics, 94,* pp. 581–588.

Harvey, C. R., 1991: "The World Price of Covariance Risk". *Journal of Finance, 46,* pp. 111–157.

Jennrich R.I., 1970: "An Asymptotic χ^2 Test for the Equality of Two Correlation Matrices". *Journal of the American Statistical Association, Volume 65,* pp. 904–912.

Jeon, B. N., and M. von Furstenberg, 1990: "Growing International Comovement in Stock Price Indexes". *Quarterly Review of Economics and Business, 30,* pp. 15–30.

Jobson, J. D., and B. Korkie, 1981a: "Performance Hypothesis Testing with the Sharpe and Treynor Measures". *Journal of Finance, 36,* pp. 889-908.

Jobson, J. D., and B. Korkie, 1981b: "Putting Markowitz Theory to Work". *Journal of Portfolio Management,* 7, pp. 70-74.

Jorion, P., 1985: "International Portfolio Diversification with Estimation Risk". *Journal of Business 58,* pp. 259–278.

Jorion, P., 1986: "Bayes–Stein Estimation for Portfolio Analysis". *Journal of Financial and Quantitative Analysis, 21,* pp. 279–92.

Jorion, P., 1989: "Asset Allocation with Hedged and Unhedged Foreign Stocks and Bonds". *Journal of Portfolio Management,* pp. 49–54.

Jorion, P., 1991: *"Currency Hedging for International Portfolios".* Columbia University Working Paper, pp. 1–22.

Le, S. V., 1991: "International Investment Diversification Before and After the October 19, 1987 Stock Market Crisis". *Journal of Business Research, 22,* pp. 305-310.

Lessard. D., 1973: "International Portfolio Diversification: A Multivariate Analysis for a Group of Latin American Countries". *Journal of Finance, 28,* pp. 619–33.

Lessard, D., 1976: "World, Country, and Industry Relationships in Equity Returns: Implications for Risk reduction through International Diversification". *Financial Analysts Journal, 32,* pp. 32–38.

Levy, H. and M. Sarnat, 1970: "International Diversification of Investment Portfolios". *American Economic Review, 60,* pp. 668–75.

Levy, H. and K. C. Lim, 1994: "Forward Exchange Bias, Hedging and the Gains from International Diversification of Investment Portfolios". *Journal of International Money and Finance, 13,* pp. 159-170.

Liljeblom, E., A. Löflund, and S. Krokfors, 1997: "The Benefits from International Diversification for Nordic Investors", *Journal of Banking and Finance, Vol. 21,* pp. 469-490.

Logue, D., 1982: "An Experiment on International Diversification". *Journal of Portfolio Management, 9,* pp, 22–27.

Longin, F. and B. Solnik, 1995: "Is the Correlation in International Equity Returns Constant: 1960-90?" *The Journal of International Money and Finance, 14,* pp. 3-26.

Solnik, B., 1974: "Why Not Diversify Internationally?" *Financial Analysts Journal, 20,* pp. 48–54.

Solnik, B. and B. Noetzlin, 1982: "Optimal International Asset Allocation". *Journal of Portfolio management, 9,* pp. 11–21.

Appendix 3.1

Exhibit A1: *Descriptive Statistics for Stock Market Returns in Local Currency September 1974 – December 1993.*

	Min.	Max.	Mean	Median	St.dev.	Skewness	Kurtosis
AUS	−0.533	0.228	0.014	0.017	0.068	−2.256	17.512
AUT	−0.266	0.250	0.007	0.001	0.059	0.202	4.988
BEL	−0.259	0.233	0.014	0.011	0.051	−0.014	5.075
CAN	−0.243	0.154	0.010	0.007	0.052	−0.597	3.470
DEN	−0.193	0.139	0.011	0.012	0.050	−0.425	1.345
FRA	−0.245	0.202	0.014	0.018	0.063	−0.416	1.670
GER	−0.256	0.157	0.010	0.010	0.055	−0.951	3.845
HK	−0.571	0.253	0.019	0.023	0.094	−1.417	6.983
ITA	−0.198	0.242	0.011	0.013	0.071	0.199	0.853
JAP	−0.218	0.183	0.008	0.009	0.053	−0.377	2.299
NET	−0.252	0.202	0.013	0.013	0.049	−0.498	4.583
NOR	−0.481	0.395	0.009	0.012	0.089	−0.814	5.456
SPA	−0.292	0.238	0.008	0.007	0.063	−0.247	2.730
SWE	−0.242	0.214	0.015	0.010	0.065	−0.225	1.590
SWI	−0.264	0.204	0.009	0.008	0.047	−0.685	5.780
UK	−0.299	0.436	0.017	0.021	0.065	0.580	9.160
FIN	−0.173	0.272	0.011	0.011	0.055	0.490	3.136
US	−0.239	0.157	0.011	0.012	0.045	−0.560	3.925

Appendix 3.2.

Interest rates are utilised in this study for the computation of excess returns from the perspective of each of the four Nordic countries. We use short-term interest rates, preferably 1 month interest rates (month-end) for the time period 1973-93. If monthly interest rates have not been obtained, the closest possible maturity has been used, and the interest rates are transferred to the monthly level assuming a flat short-end term structure.

The interest rates are obtained from OECD:s Main Economic Indicators (OECD), from the Bank of Finland (BoF), and from the Bank of Norway (BoN). The interest rates (and their sources, in brackets) are: Denmark- Official discount rate 1973-1988 (OECD), 1-month Eurorate 1989-1993 (BoF), Finland- Implicit FIM Eurorate (computed from FIM / USD forward rates assuming covered interest parity) 1973-1986 (BoF), 1-month HELIBOR, i.e. interbank rate 1987-1993 (BoF), Norway-Implicit NOK Eurorate (computed from forward rates) 1973-1988:02 (BoN), 3-month interbank rate 1988:03-1988:12 (BoN), 1-month Eurorate 1989-1993 (BoF) and Sweden- Official discount rate 1973-1981 (OECD), rate on 3-month Treasury discount notes 1982-1988 (OECD), 1-month Eurorate 1989-1993 (BoF).

4. The Stock Markets' View on Corporate Efforts to Internationalise the Cost of Capital

Karl-Markus Modén and Lars Oxelheim

4.1. Introduction

As described in Chapter 2, in the early 1980s, concurrent with the revival of the Nordic stock markets as sources of new risk capital, large companies in these countries started to go abroad to tap foreign sources of capital as well. The increased activity on foreign capital markets raises interesting questions: Why did this latter development take place just as the functioning of local capital markets started to improve? Is, or was, there some significant difference in raising capital abroad as compared to at home? And, if so, has this difference disappeared with deregulation? To answer these questions we study the price reaction on the domestic stock markets to the announcement of equity issues abroad by Nordic companies.

Our hypothesis is that the stock price reaction to such an announcement should differ depending on whether the issuing company was previously traded on a segmented capital market only, or if it was traded on a stock market that is integrated with the rest of the world. The main focus will be on the Swedish experience, the reason for this being the size distribution of firms. The greater number of large firms in Sweden compared to the other Nordic countries explains the higher incidence of Swedish equity issues on foreign capital markets. Although high in comparison to the number of international issues undertaken by firms from the other Nordic countries, the total number of Swedish equity issues on foreign markets was, for the period under investigation 1981-93, still only 30 and hence just at the borderline of a number that, in case of a "super-population" assumption, permits statistical tests of differences in price reactions before and after deregulation. The total number of issues in the other Nordic countries was so small that only tests based on pooled data can be used.

In Section 4.2 the current status is discussed as regards research on initial price reactions to announcement of equity issues. In Section 4.3 the basics of the so-called event study methodology are described. Section 4.4 contains an empirical application of the methodology focusing on the price reaction following the announcement of Swedish domestic and international equity issues. Section 4.5 focuses on the question of whether there is any discernible difference in the price responses to the announcement of international equity issues between periods designated as pre- and post-deregulation. Based on the assumption that such a change would be best reflected by the reaction to announcement by the largest (and most internationalised) companies in the two periods, we here pool the largest Swedish international equity issues with the largest international issues by companies from each of the other Nordic countries. Concluding remarks are given in Section 4.6.

4.2. Price Reactions to International versus Domestic Equity Issues

Studies of reactions of the domestic share price to the announcement of an international public offer have been fairly scarce. The case of Novo, described in Chapter 6, constitutes the pilot study in which a strong positive reaction was found. Novo belongs to the pharmaceutical and biotechnology industry, which during the second half of the 1970s was experiencing a very low price/earnings (P/E) ratio in Denmark as compared to corresponding ratios on the US and UK stock markets. This gap was a result of a "thin" Danish market and of the capital controls and regulations imposed on Danish corporations and investors at that time. Novo's strategy was to be "discovered" by foreign investors, earn a higher (international) P/E, and then to make a public offer in the US market. The higher international P/E-ratio meant an increase in Novo's share price, which would be transmitted to the Danish market.

Much of the previous research has focused on the effects of domestic public offers on share prices[1]. Using the event study methodology, the results convincingly point to a negative reaction, i.e., a decrease in share prices at the time the intention of the public offer is announced. Several

---

1. See among others: Asquith (1986), Hess & Frost (1982), Myers & Majluf (1984), Krasker (1986), Noe (1988), Scholes (1972), Shleifer (1986), Smith (1986), Stulz (1995). For an extensive review see Harris & Raviv (1991).

explanations for this phenomenon are possible, but the logically and empirically most satisfying ones are built on the principal-agent framework. If there is asymmetric information between managers and investors, the latter interpret an equity issue as a signal about the true value of the firm's equity, a fact that is known only to the management. The signal may be interpreted as reflecting either good or bad news. For example, it may be interpreted as good news if managers are assumed to have upgraded their assessment of the future prospects of the firm and decided to start a new investment project on such a big scale that the internally generated cash flow is not sufficient and debt finance will result in too high an overall debt-equity ratio. In this case, investors may value the firm correctly given the available information, but the information on the new prospects for the firm that management just adopted, and which is not yet available to the general investor, calls for an increase in the stock market value.

Alternatively, the issue is bad news to the investors, if the timing of the issue is interpreted as a signal that management finds investors overvaluing the firm's stock, and therefore seizes the opportunity to raise funds "cheaply." If investors are rational they will interpret the announcement of an issue as a confirmation that the firm's stock is indeed overvalued, and the price will drop. It is quite intuitive to assume that management knows about the risk of a drop in price after an issue. Hence, management may try to neutralise the price drop effect by coordinating the timing of the announcement of the issue with the announcement of some good news. In actual practice, new equity issues are often announced together with yearly or quarterly earnings reports. To ensure a strong neutralising effect, other significant announcements, such as major new investment plans or acquisitions, are often made on the same occasion.

Most empirical studies provide support for a negative reaction to the announcement of domestic equity issues. Several characteristics of the negative reaction have been reported. For example, Krasker (1986) studied the relationship between the size of the equity issue and the price reaction, and found that the larger the stock issue, the worse the signal and hence the subsequent fall in the stock price. Another interesting result for our purposes is the finding (Lucas & McDonald 1990) that the announcements of equity issues will tend to cluster after the release of annual reports and earnings announcements, and the stock price drop will be negatively related to the time between the release and the issue announcement. Other studies have also found that, in general, the price drop will be larger, the larger the informational asymmetry (Korajczyk, Lucas & McDonald 1990). Research on purely domestic equity issues has tapered off recently and a consensus about a negative price reaction has developed. For the US case a consensus estimate is a negative price reaction at the announcement date of -2.75% (Stulz 1995).

Recent interest in the information revealed in stock price reactions has turned more towards the domestic price response to the announcement of a listing on a foreign stock exchange. This research is related to ours since it asks the question about the type of signal a company sends with such an announcement. The evidence is mixed regarding the valuation effect of the listing decisions; however, there is a weak tendency toward a positive effect (Marr, Trimble and Varma, 1991 and Sunderman and Logue, 1996).

Segmentation of capital markets generally has a depressing effect on security prices (Marr, Trimble & Varma 1991). In order to prove the usefulness of the domestic market response as an indicator of equity market integration, we analyse the reaction of the Swedish stock markets to international equity issues for the period 1981-1993. This period is split into two sub-periods, one which we have *a priori* reasons to believe can be characterised as more "segmented" (less integrated), and one where the domestic market is more "integrated" (less segmented). In this section, we argue, based on the history of Swedish regulation of international security trade, that the official dismantling of the existing capital controls in July 1989 was merely an acknowledgement of a *de facto* liberalisation that had made capital controls inefficient a long time prior to that date. This conclusion finds additional support in a study of Nordic credit market integration by Oxelheim (1996). He reports that by 1982 the capital controls in all the Nordic countries had, from a general capital flow point of view, become ineffective. However, as was found in Chapter 2, some restrictions remained as regards equity issues and transactions, which motivate us in the case of equity markets to set 1986 as an adequate line of demarcation. In our empirical study we thus designate the 1981-86 period as the "pre-deregulation" period, and 1987-93 as the "post-deregulation" period. As was previously mentioned, we focus on Sweden because the industrial structure there is biased toward capital intensive sectors and is dominated by a few very large companies which are more likely to have a lot to gain from international equity issues. However, when we turn to our study of the pre- and post-deregulation reaction we will pool a collection of Nordic events in order to get an as big as possible large-company sample.

4.3. Event Study Methodology

An event study analyses the price reaction at the time of the announcement of a particular "event," which may be a merger, a takeover, an equity issue, a change in dividend policy, to name a few examples. According to the view that stock market actors are efficient processors of information, the immediate price reaction after the "news" reaches the market will reflect the complete valuation effect of the "news" in question. The basic event study methodology involves studying the stock price reaction around the event date, with a correction for risk.[2] The risk correction is carried out by computing daily excess returns for each company around the event date. The excess, or abnormal, returns are calculated by taking the difference between the actual returns and a control return. The control return is computed by using the so called market model, which is a linear function of the return of a market index:

$$cr_{it} = \alpha_i + \beta_i r_{mt} \tag{4.1}$$

where cr_{it} is the control return for company i in period t, α_i and β_i are estimated parameters, and r_{mt} is the return on a general market index at time t. The coefficient β_i measures the sensitivity of the individual stock with respect to the return of the general market index, and may be thought of as a measure of the "riskiness" of that stock.[3] The excess return at date t of security i is then $e_{it} = r_{it} - cr_{it}$. Where r_{it} is the actual return at date t. The daily excess returns, or residuals from the OLS estimation, are then averaged over each of the n securities included:

$$AAR_t = \sum_{i=1}^{n} \frac{1}{n} e_{it} \tag{4.2}$$

The cumulative average excess (or abnormal) return at time y relative to time x is computed as

$$\sum_{x}^{y} AAR_t = CAR_x^y \tag{4.3}$$

Assuming that the daily excess returns of securities are independently distributed in event time, portfolio daily excess returns approach normal dis-

2. For discussions about the event study methodology in more detail, see for example Jensen & Ruback (1983) and Brown & Warner (1985).
3. According to most asset pricing models, the relevant risk that investors pay to avoid is the "covariance risk," i.e. how the returns are correlated with that of all other assets.

Exhibit 4.1: CAR Around the Date of Announcement for Pharmacia's
International Equity Issue in May 1983.

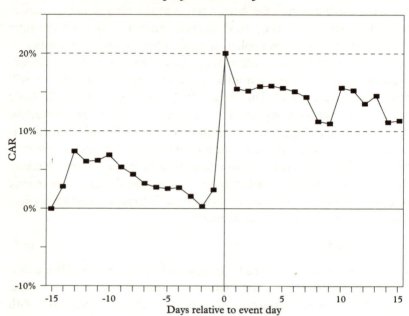

Note: For example two days prior to the announcement date (Day 0) the excess return (AR) was about zero percent. The cumulated excess return (CAR) for day –15 to day 0 is equal to twenty percent, i.e., the sum of the excess returns for the period.

tributions for large samples under the Central Limit Theorem[4]. Conditional on the assumption that we may apply the large sample results from statistical distribution theory, we may perform tests of the event day stock price reaction (AR) and the cumulated average excess returns (CAR) for relevant "event windows."

An example of a response to one individual event, where almost all of the reaction seems to occur at precisely the event date, is given in Exhibit 4.1. This figure illustrates the reaction to an announcement of an international equity issue by Pharmacia in May 1983, showing the cumulated abnormal return from fifteen days before the announcement of the issue to fifteen days after.

4. Brown & Warner (1985) has shown that the daily excess return are not normally distributed and that one needs rather large samples in order for the usual significance test should be applicable. Since we only have a rather small population of events to pick a sample from, this is an important caveat in the interpretation of our results.

4.4. Price Responses to Equity Issues

In this section we study the price response in the Swedish stock market to announcement of issues abroad by Swedish firms. To pave the way for an analysis of the benefits a company may achieve by eliminating the segmentation effect, we also need a reference case; the response to the announcement of domestic equity issues.

4.4.1. Empirical Evidence from Domestic Equity Issues by Swedish Firms

In a separate study of domestic equity issues in a sample including 65 events[5] between 1981 and 1993, we find the price reaction pattern given in Exhibit 4.2. The negative price effect discussed above is verified and sta-

Exhibit 4.2:   CAR Around the Date of Domestic Equity Issue Announcements, 1981-1993.

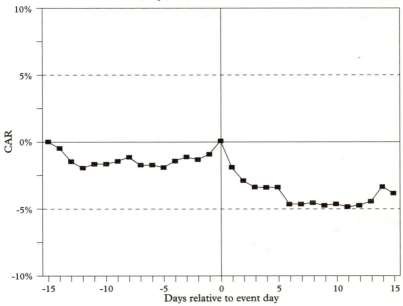

Days relative to event day

5. A list of the sample issues, with the name of the company, issue-size, date and industries, is given in Appendix 4.1. This sample was drawn by identifying the total number of domestic issues over the period and picking out the 100 largest (to exclude very small companies that are substantially different from the larger companies in terms of access to international equity markets). Out of these we were able to identify 65 announcement dates with confidence.

tistically significant; the cumulated average abnormal return from five days before the equity announcement until five days after, CAR_{-5}^{+5} is -2,7%, while the average abnormal return for the day after the announcement is $AR_{+1} = -2.0\%$.

This may seem as a small amount but one should keep in mind that the price decrease as a percentage of the amount raised by the issue is more substantial. The ratio between the issue size and the market value before the issue announcement is 0.18 for the companies in the sample. The average market value was 4,371 MSEK (in 1990 prices) and a price drop of 2.7% implies then that 15% of the new equity raised "disappears". The magnitude of the negative price reaction is also very close to the -2.75% reported by Stulz (1995) from a survey of event studies on US data. One difference between these studies and ours is that the average issue size was twice as big in the Swedish case compared to the one in the US studies.

To control for contaminating announcement timing effects, we divide the sample into two groups of issues: those announced separately from other news and those announced jointly with such news. We then find price-reaction patterns as in Exhibits 4.3 and 4.4. It is obvious from these

Exhibit 4.3: CAR Around the Date of Domestic Equity Issue Announcement Made Separately from other News, 1981-1993.

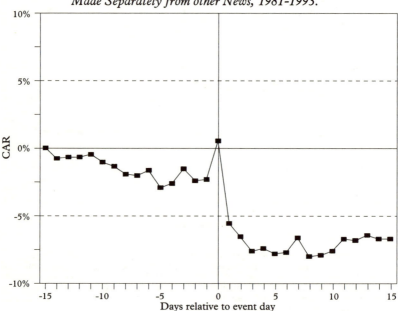

Exhibit 4.4:   *CAR Around the Date of Domestic Equity Issue Announcement Made Jointly with other News, 1981-1993.*

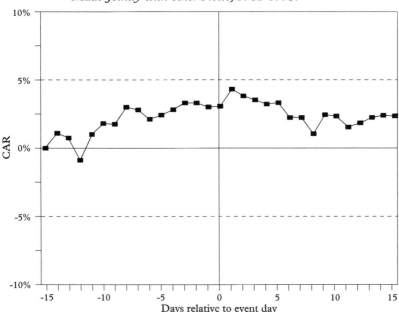

figures that the most negative response is to announcements made separately, which is in line with the arguments made above. CAR_{-5}^{+5} is -6.5%, for separate announcements, while it is +1.1% for joint announcements. In Exhibit 4.3, we do also see positive abnormal returns the days immediately preceding the event date as emphasised by e.g. Lucas and McDonald (1990).

4.4.2. Empirical Evidence from Issues Abroad by Swedish Firms

The results as regards the price reaction to announcements of equity issues abroad by Swedish companies are given in Exhibit 4.5[6]. The reaction patterns are compared to those of domestic issues in Exhibit 4.6. Although the number of observations is small, especially for the post-deregulation period, it is quite clear that the reaction to an equity issue abroad is different from the reaction to a domestic issue. For both periods, and for both

---

6.   Names and features of Swedish companies issues abroad 1981-93 are given in Appendix 4.2.

Exhibit 4.5:   CAR Around the Announcement Date of Foreign Equity Issues by Swedish Firms, 1981-93.

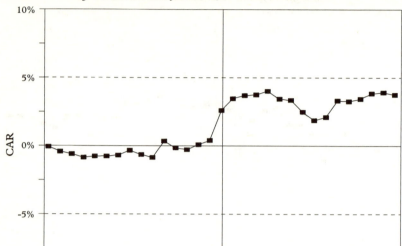

Days relative to event day

separate and joint announcements, the price reactions are positive. The difference between the reactions to foreign and domestic issues is especially pronounced for issues announced separately from other information. It is not meaningful to divide each sub-period with respect to separate or joint announcement since we will end up with very few observations for some of the categories. However, the difference between the price reactions to foreign and domestic issues is found to be statistically significant.

Exhibit 4.6: Cumulated Average Abnormal Returns, CAR_{-5}^{+5}, for Domestic and International Equity Issues.

Feature	Domestic issues (%)	International issues
Pre-integration	-1.14	5.26
Post-integration	-2.46	5.82
Separate announcement	-6.50	7.02
Joint announcement	1.10	2.43

Exhibit 4.7:   Distribution of the Total Amount of New Equity Issues between Domestic and Foreign Issues.

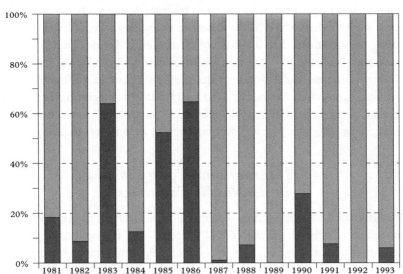

Note: The darker segment is foreign issues

4.4.3. The Swedish Stock Market Response – a Summary

We are not able to establish that the price reaction has changed between 1981-86 and 1987-93, as we would expect when markets go from being segmented to being more integrated. However, as was pointed out above, these are not absolute terms. Even though some legal barriers have been lowered, there remain other significant barriers, especially of an informational nature. Furthermore, if the equity market has become, for all practical purposes, integrated for some firms, for example the large ones, it would not be necessary for these to "seek out" foreign capital directly, because it would flow obediently to them. It would be sufficient to issue equity on one market place only. Exhibit 4.7 shows the proportions of domestic and foreign issues from 1981 to 1993. After 1986, issues directed abroad have exceeded 10% of the total amount in only one year (1991), the average being 6.8%. In the pre-deregulation period the average was 36.5%. The size of the companies issuing equity abroad is also quite different between periods. In fixed 1980 prices, the average size (measured in total sales) in the earlier period was 9.770 MSEK, while it was only 2.512 MSEK in the later period.

It should be noted that there are other reasons for issuing equity abroad than taking advantage of higher valuations elsewhere due to segmentation effects. As will be further discussed in Chapter 5, one such reason is that firms want to attain some media exposure when they enter a product market in a new country. The intention of a listing and offering of a new equity issue may also be to pave the way for future commercial activities in a new country. Whereas the listing provides the bulk of commercial marketing, an issue may sometimes be required to support this marketing effect and to achieve the beneficial financial effects. A "road show" to the benefit of financial investors may be an additional way to accomplish such exposure.

4.5. International Equity Issues in the Nordic Countries

In this section we will focus on a comparison of reactions in pre- and post-deregulation periods. In the case of Sweden we have performed such a comparison by running a regression based on abnormal returns of all issues – domestic as well as foreign – by Swedish companies (Modén and Oxelheim, 1997). Dummies were here used for pre- as opposed to post-deregulation, separate as opposed to joint announcement, and listing prior to the issue as opposed to simultaneous listing and equity offering. We also controlled for size. The only significant result was here found for the difference between the reaction to an announcement of a domestic as opposed to a foreign equity issue. Since we assume that the insignificant outcome of the pre-versus post-deregulation test may reflect the appearance of quite many fairly small companies in the second subperiod of the sample of total abnormal returns that were used, we will here try another avenue and create a sample of only large companies' issues by pooling across the Nordic countries. We argued in the introduction that the four major Nordic countries, Denmark, Finland, Norway and Sweden, all had isolated equity markets up until the 1980s. We also argued that mid-1986 was a good line of demarcation for the transformation of Nordic equity markets. In the pooling procedure, we will hence use the same classification as was used in the case of Sweden as regards pre-deregulation and post-deregulation events.

Chapter 2 provided a basis for a comparison of relative magnitudes of foreign equity issues by companies from the Nordic countries. Roughly speaking the amounts issued by Swedish companies abroad were in the 1980s about twice as big or bigger than the amounts raised by companies from each of the other countries.

Exhibit 4.8:   *CAR Around the Announcement of Equity Issues Abroad for Fourteen Nordic Companies in the Pre-integration Period, 1981-1986.*

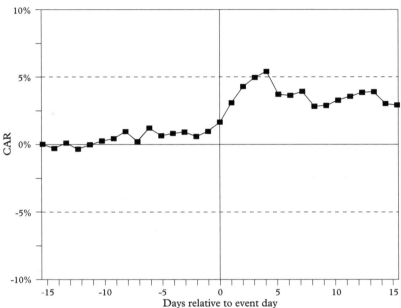

4.5.1. Empirical Evidence from the Nordic Large Company Sample

Our Nordic sample consists of the largest issues from Denmark, Finland, Norway, and Sweden. The cases from Denmark are: Lauritzen (1990), Chr. Hansen (1992), DFDS (1992), D/S 1912 (1989) and Carlsberg (1992); from Finland: Amer (1986), Enso (1988), Huhtamäki (1990), Nokia (1986 and 1993), Pohjola (1986), Huhtamäki (1993), KOP (1993), Metsä-Serla (1993) and Outokumpu (1993); and from Norway: Aker (1990), Hafslund Nycomed (1989), Kværner (1990), Orkla (1989) and Storli (1989). Hence, twenty companies met the common size criterion. To the twenty non-Swedish cases we added the thirteen Swedish cases that met the size criterion, to arrive at a pooled Nordic sample of 33 cases. This sample was then divided up into two groups, a pre-deregulation group containing 14 events and a post-deregulation group containing 19.

Exhibits 4.8 and 4.9 show the cumulative abnormal return for the two subgroups. It is clear from these figures that there seems to be an opposite

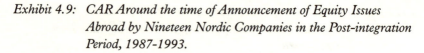

*Exhibit 4.9:   CAR Around the time of Announcement of Equity Issues
            Abroad by Nineteen Nordic Companies in the Post-integration
            Period, 1987-1993.*

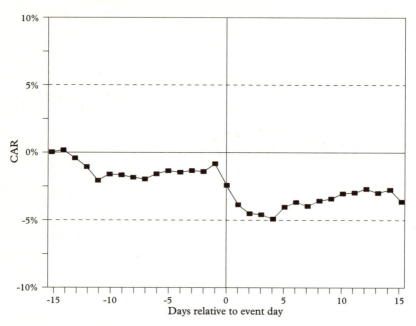

reaction to international equity issues in the two periods. The pre-deregulation period contains eleven Swedish and three Finnish cases, and is
therefore very similar to the Swedish event study discussed above. The
same conclusion remains, i.e., the value of CAR_{-5}^{+5} is positive, and in this
case equal to 2.5%. The post-deregulation period contains five cases from
Denmark and Norway, two from Sweden and seven from Finland. The
results now show a negative CAR_{-5}^{+5} with a value of -2.2%. Since the low
number of observations does not allow further division, we may just conclude that this Nordic pooling seems to add support to the view that the
announcement of equity issues on foreign markets provokes the same reaction as the announcement of a domestic issue does in the post-deregulation
period. Hence, larger companies that have already reaped the benefits of
becoming "international" (being recognised at global financial centres)
have in the post-deregulation period no more to gain from an international
issue in the eyes of the stock market as compared to a domestic issue. For
these companies the domestic market has become just another part of the
global capital market.

4.6. Concluding Remarks

The gap that we recognise between the price reaction to domestic and foreign equity issues by Swedish firms indicates a lack of perfect international integration of the domestic stock market for the period 1980-1993. However, for the period following the *de facto* dismantling of capital controls imposed on the domestic market, the gap has decreased, indicating increased, though not perfect, international integration. The remaining gap in the domestic reaction to the choice of market place for a new equity issue should contain inefficiencies that, for example, are related to prohibitive transaction costs for small and medium-sized firms to use foreign markets rather than wedges created by policymakers. Further research should focus on the gap and the elements that are responsible for it. In other words, are foreign issues essentially different from domestic issues? In such an analysis we should find an answer to the question about potential mismatching. For instance, is it predominantly large firms that issue on international markets and small and medium-sized firms that use the domestic market? If so, the difference in stock market reaction could be explained in terms of transparency; an asymmetric information problem of more serious character may prevail in the small and medium-sized firms.

Another potential explanation that could arise from further analysis of the gap concerns the extent to which a separate announcement of a decision to undertake an equity issue on a foreign market signals new profit opportunities of a commercial character, thereby motivating a more positive reaction than in the case of a domestic issue. This explanation gets some support from our analyses of the Nordic large company sample. For these companies, scrutinised hourly by financial analysts around the world, we found no difference between the stock market reaction to an announcement of a domestic equity issue and an international equity issue in the post-deregulation period. They are truly international and seen by the stock market as already enjoying an international cost of capital.

References

Asquith, P. and D.W. Jr. Mullins, 1986: "Equity Issues and Offering Dilution". *Journal of Financial Economics, 15,* pp. 61-89.

Brown, S. J. and J. B. Warner,1985: "Using Daily Stock Returns – The Case of Event Studies". *Journal of Financial Economics, 14,* pp. 3-31.

Harris, M. and A. Raviv, 1991: "The Theory of Capital Structure". *Journal of Finance, 46, 1,* pp. 297-355.

Hess, A.C. and P.A. Frost, 1982: "Tests for Price Effects of New Issues of Seasoned Securities". *Journal of Finance, 41, 1,* pp. 11-25.

Jensen, M.C. and R. Ruback, 1983: "The Market for Corporate Control: The Scientific Evidence". *Journal of Financial Economics, 11,* pp. 5-50.

Korajczyk, R. A., Lucas, D. and R.L. McDonald, 1990: "Understanding Stock Price Behaviour around the Time of Equity Issues", in: Hubbard, R.G. (ed.). *"Asymmetric Information, Corporate Finance, and Investment".* Chicago: University of Chicago Press.

Krasker, W., 1986: "Stock Price movements in Response to Stock Issues under Asymmetric Information". *Journal of Finance, 41,* pp. 93-105.

Lucas, D. and R.L. McDonald, 1990: "Equity Issues and Stock Price Dynamics". *Journal of Finance, 45,* pp. 1019-1043.

Marr, M.W., Trimble, J.L. and R. Varma, 1991: "On the Integration of International Capital Markets: Evidence From Euroequity Offerings". *Financial Management, Winter.*

Modén K-M. and L. Oxelheim, 1997: "Why Issue Equity Abroad – Corporate Reasons and Stock Market Responses". *Managment International Review,* Vol 37, No 3, pp. 223-241.

Myers, S. and N. Majluf, 1984: "Corporate Financing and Investment Decisions When Firms Have Information That Investors Do Not Have". *Journal of Financial Economics, 13,* pp. 187-221.

Noe, T., 1988: "Capital Structure and Signalling Game Equilibria". *Review of Futures Studies 1,* pp. 331-356.

Oxelheim L. 1990: *"International Financial Integration".* Heidelberg: Springer-Verlag.

Oxelheim L., 1996: *"Financial Markets in Transition – Globalization, Investment and Economic Growth".* London: Routledge.

Scholes, M.S., 1972: "The Market for Securities: Substitution versus Price Pressure and the Effects of Information on Share Prices". *Journal of Business, 45,* pp. 179-211.

Shleifer, A., 1986: "Do Demand Curves for Stocks Slope Down?" *Journal of Finance, 41,* pp. 579-590.

Smith, C.W. 1986: "Investment banking and the Capital Acquisition Process". *Journal of Financial Economics, 15,* pp. 3-29.

Stonehill, A. I. and K.B. Dullum, 1982: *"Internationalizing the Cost of Capital".* New York: John-Wiley & Sons.

Stjernborg, S., 1987: "Utrikeshandeln med svenska aktier". *Kredit- och Valutaöversikt, 4,* pp. 27-35, Stockholm: The Central Bank of Sweden.

Stulz, R.M., 1995: *"Does the cost of capital differ across countries? – An agency perspective".* Mimeo. Keynote address for the fourth meeting of the European Financial Management Association. London.

Sunderman A.K. and D.E. Logue, 1996: "Valuation Effects of Foreign Company Listings on U.S. Exchanges". *Journal of International Business, Studies,* pp. 67-88.

Appendix 4.1

Swedish Companies in the Sample of Domestic Issues, 1981-1993.
All amounts expressed in 1990-prices.

Company	Date	ISIC-code	Relative size	Issue-size	Market value	D2	D3
SAAB	81:02	384	0.067	260	3,889	0	1
SEB	81:02	810	0.062	322	5,150	0	1
SKF	81:02	381	0.119	520	4,366	0	0
Diligentia	81:02	831	0.133	96	722	0	1
Fortia	81:03	352	0.127	283	2,223	0	1
AGA	81:08	351	0.079	270	3,426	0	0
Munksjö	82:01	341	0.143	177	1,241	1	1
Volvo	82:01	384	0.105	988	9,393	0	0
Sonesson	82:02	371	0.142	257	1,808	0	1
Götabanken	82:02	810	0.092	154	1,684	0	1
Esselte	82:07	343	0.120	253	2,104	1	0
Perstorp	83:01	355	0.081	157	1,938	1	0
Incentive	83:02	MF	0.153	200	1,308	0	1
Saab	83:02	384	0.083	914	10,984	0	1
SEB	83:02	810	0.119	1,037	8,723	0	1
Esab	83:02	381	0.060	60	1,002	0	1
Barkman	83:03	MF	0.060	65	1,074	0	1
Skåne Gripen	83:03	MF	0.077	40	523	0	1
Bahco	83:05	381	0.385	145	378	1	1
Fagersta	83:05	371	0.724	246	339	0	1
PLM	83:10	381	0.162	288	1,777	0	0
Aritmos	84:01	MF	0.065	118	1,824	0	1
Broströms	84:02	712	0.560	231	412	1	1
Hexagon	84:02	MF	0.173	213	1,230	0	0
Protorp	84:02	MF	0.245	469	1,912	1	0
Skrinet	84:02	MF	0.213	373	1,755	1	1
Sonesson	84:02	371	0.163	1,026	6,299	0	0
Sydkraft	84:02	410	0.115	612	5,332	1	1
Transatlantic	84:02	712	0.254	225	885	0	1
Kuben	84:03	MF	0.408	147	360	1	1
Modo	84:03	341	0.077	220	2,850	0	1
Bilspedition	85:03	711	0.043	121	2,834	1	0
Pronator	85:10	830	0.153	175	1,142	1	1
Skåne Gripen	86:03	MF	0.136	172	1,260	0	0
Modo	86:04	341	0.144	360	2,493	1	1
Siab	86:04	501	0.180	177	984	0	1
Östgötabanken	86:09	810	0.108	104	958	0	1
Iggesund	86:10	331	0.139	394	2,834	0	1
Nordbanken	87:02	810	0.118	301	2,554	0	1
Cabanco	87:03	810	0.318	131	411	0	1
Holmen	87:03	341	0.101	577	5,401	0	1
Pronator	87:03	830	0.241	349	1,445	0	1
Nobel	87:06	351	0.116	648	5,607	1	1
SCA	87:10	341	0.029	706	24,108	0	1
Trelleborg	87:10	356	0.116	1,199	10,353	1	1
Componenta	88:08	381	0.333	175	525	0	1
Perstorp	88:12	355	0.038	219	5,831	0	0
Bilspedition	89:03	711	0.128	612	4,803	0	0
Sila	89:04	713	0.129	385	2,980	1	1
Esab	89:08	381	0.252	467	1,856	0	1
Argonaut	90:03	712	0.179	519	2,900	1	1
Atlantica	90:03	820	0.087	26	300	0	1
SpectraPhysics	90:07	385	0.406	1,199	2,950	1	1
Bilspedition	90:10	711	0.127	507	4,000	1	0
Nobel	91:08	351	0.283	1,870	6,607	1	1
Nordbanken	91:08	810	0.303	4,799	15,820	0	1
Östgötabanken	91:10	810	0.507	472	931	0	1
Trelleborg	92:03	356	0.130	821	6,297	0	1

Appendix 4.1 (Continued).

Company	Date	ISIC-code	Relative size	Issue-size	Market value	D2	D3
Stena Line	93:03	712	0.598	694	1,161	0	1
Gambro	93:04	385	0.044	379	8,665	1	0
Modo	93:08	341	0.211	1,556	7,384	0	1
SCA	93:08	341	0.061	1,261	20,815	0	1
SEB	93:08	810	0.250	4,707	18,849	0	1
SHB	93:08	810	0.098	2,367	24,120	0	1
Trelleborg	93:08	356	0.166	1,048	6,328	0	1
Bilspedition Sands	93:11	711	0.249	524	2,099	1	1
Petroleum	93:11	220	0.043	48	1,127	0	1

Notes: Relative size = Issue size/Market value; MF = Close end mutual fund; D2 = 1 if the equity announcement was non-contaminated by other significant news (0 otherwise); D3 = 1 if the issuing company was not listed on a foreign stock exchange prior to the issue (0 otherwise).
Source: Stockholm Stock Exchange, *Database* and press releases.

Appendix 4.2

Swedish Companies Issuing Equity on Foreign Stock Markets, 1981-1993.

All amounts expressed in 1990-prices.

Company	Date	ISIC-code	Relative size	Issue-size	Market-value	D2	D3
Fortia	81:08	352	0.311	583	1,877	1	1
Cardo	82:09	MF	0.072	227	3,152	1	1
Ericsson	83:04	383	0.146	2,906	19,869	0	0
Gambro*	83:02						
Perstorp	83:03	351	0.089	165	1,850	1	1
Volvo	83:04	384	0.021	491	22,793	0	0
PLM	83:04	381	0.029	52	1,773	0	1
Alfa Laval	83:04	381	0.066	441	6,704	1	0
Sonesson	83:05	371	0.121	331	2,746	1	1
Pharmacia	83:09	352	0.056	585	10,338	1	0
AGA	83:10	351	0.084	435	5,169	1	0
Skåne Gripen	84:02	MF	0.033	54	1,627	1	1
PLM	84:02	381	0.046	75	1,623	0	0
Volvo**	84:02						
Fermenta**	84:04						
Esab**	85:01						
Fermenta**	85:01						
IDK Data**	85:01						
Fermenta**	85:02						
Bilspedition	85:03	719	0.090	108	1,200	0	1
Electrolux	86:03	381	0.125	2,918	23,357	0	0
Skåne Gripen	86:05	MF	0.090	142	1,575	1	0
Ellos	87:01	623	0.043	52	1,226	0	1
Perstorp	88:12	351	0.050	273	5,458	1	0
Atlas Copco	90:03	381	0.138	1,203	8,700	1	0
Gambro	90:03	382	0.173	583	3,375	0	0
Securitas*	91:12						
Frontline	93:07	712	0.525	378	720	1	1
Svedala	93:03	382	0.138	405	2,923	0	1

Note: Relative size = Issue size/Market value, MF = Close end mutual fund; D2 = 1 if the equity announcement was non-contaminated by other significant news (0 otherwise); D3 = 1 if the issuing company was not listed on a foreign stock exchange prior to the issue (0 otherwise).
* excluded since it was not previously listed on the Stockholm stock exchange.
** excluded since the equity issue was directed toward private investors in exchange for the whole, or part, of stock of shares of another company.
Source: Stockholm Stock Exchange, *Database* and press releases.

Part III

Nordic Strategies to Internationalise the Cost of Capital While Maintaining Control

5. Corporate Strategies: A Conceptual Perspective

Arthur Stonehill and Kåre B. Dullum

5.1. Introduction

The transformation of Nordic equity markets from segmentation to integration with global equity markets has been chronicled in Chapters 1 and 2. The reaction of investors to the increased supply of equities originating from firms located in Nordic markets has been analysed in Chapters 3 and 4. It now remains for Chapter 5 to explain why and how Nordic firms have reacted and responded to the opportunities presented by increased investor demand for equities originating in foreign countries and currencies.

Nordic firms have had to overcome the same segmentation barriers as firms resident in other overregulated and illiquid equity markets. As was shown in Chapter 2, some of these barriers still exist in the Nordic countries. They also exist in non-Nordic countries.

As a result of market segmentation, corporate management resident in both Nordic and non-Nordic equity markets have had to devise strategies to overcome the root causes of market segmentation. These causes are as follows:

- Asymmetric information available to investors resident in different countries. This includes not only financial data on corporations but also the analytic methods used to evaluate the validity of a security's price.
- Different tax regulations, especially with regard to the treatment of capital gains and the double taxation of dividends.
- Regulation of securities markets as described in Chapter 2.
- Alternative sets of optimal portfolios from the perspective of investors resident in one equity market compared to investors resident in other equity markets.
- Different agency costs for firms located in bank-dominated markets compared to firms located in the Anglo-American markets.

- Different levels of financial risk tolerance, such as debt ratios, in different countries.
- Differences in perceived foreign exchange risk, especially with respect to operating and transaction exposures.
- Takeover defences that differ widely between the Anglo-American markets, characterised by one-share-one vote norms, and other markets featuring dual classes of stock and other takeover barriers.
- The level of transaction costs involved in purchasing, selling, and trading securities.
- Political risk such as unpredictable government interference in capital markets and arbitrary changes in rules.

The relative importance of each of these barriers has changed over time and across countries. The Nordic case studies, presented in Parts IV to VII, illustrate the variety of corporate strategies employed to internationalise a firm's cost of capital, as they evolved over time and across countries.

This chapter is organised into seven sections. Section 5.2 describes the alternative paths for a firm to internationalise its cost and availability of capital. Section 5.3 demonstrates graphically the impact on the cost and availability of capital when a firm is able to raise funds outside of its segmented and illiquid home market. Section 5.4 describes the reasons why firms crosslist their shares abroad. The reasons are broader than merely escaping a segmented and illiquid home equity market. Section 5.5 describes the motivations for selling equity abroad. Section 5.6 describes the three main instruments used to tap foreign equity markets. These are directed issues, Euroequity issues, and strategic alliances. Section 5.7 analyses the barriers and costs associated with listing and selling equities abroad. Section 5.8 forecasts the future strategies that might be used to tap global equity markets.

Throughout this chapter reference will be made to the cases described in Parts IV to VII. These cases were chosen because they were typical of a much larger group of cases, which were investigated as part of the background for this book.

5.2. Alternative Paths to Internationalise the Cost and Availability of Capital

Exhibit 5.1 shows the alternative paths available to managers who wish to internationalise their firms' cost and availability of capital. Firms typically maximise their opportunities to raise funds in their domestic financial markets shown at the top of Exhibit 5.1. Ideally, most firms would like to jump from there to the bottom alternative, "Euroequity Issue." This is usually impossible for an average firm because they are not known by the international investment community. Novo Industri was advised by its investment bankers to start with a Eurobond issue and a London crosslisting in 1978.

Normally the path is to start with an international bond issue in a less prestigious market in order to gain experience and to become more visible. If possible, it would be desirable to skip that and go down to the next steps, international bond issue in a liquid target market or a Eurobond issue sold in several markets, such as Novo did. Raising equity requires more commitment to disclosure and investor relations. A firm could start

Exhibit 5.1:   *Alternative Paths to Internationalise the Cost and Availability of Capital.*

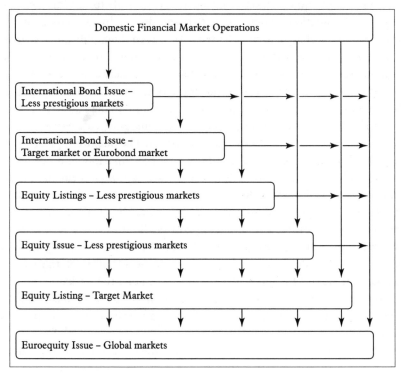

Source: Oxelheim (1997).

by listing and selling an equity in a less prestigious market, i.e. not the United States or the United Kingdom. This is even more costly in time and money than a bond issue, but still less than a full scale listing and equity issue in the United States or the United Kingdom.

The ultimate would be to have an Euroequity issue sold simultaneously in both foreign equity markets and possibly the domestic market. Within the Nordic area Electrolux (1986) was among the first to tap the Euroequity market (see case in Part VII). Euroequity issues are also the path being taken by some of the newly privatised firms such as Tele-Danmark in 1994 (see case study in Part IV).

5.3. Impact on the Cost and Availability of Capital When a Firm is Able to Source its Equity in Global Markets

When a capital market is segmented and illiquid, a firm based in that market is likely to have a higher cost of capital than competitors based in more integrated and liquid markets. However, it is possible for a firm to escape from its dysfunctional home market. It can do this by attracting foreign investors to purchase and hold its securities, even though its home market remains segmented with respect to other firms located there. When a firm escapes from the shackles of its home market, it usually enjoys a lower cost of capital. Exhibit 5.2 illustrates conceptually how a firm's cost of capital is lowered by escaping from a segmented and illiquid home market.

In Exhibit 5.2 the line SS_D represents the marginal cost of capital of a firm in a segmented and illiquid capital market. The line SS_F represents its decreased marginal cost of capital if it gains access to a more liquid capital market. The line $S'S_U$ shows the effect of moving from a segmented to an integrated capital market. As a result of the combined effects of greater availability of capital and international pricing of the firm's securities, the marginal cost of capital declines from 20% (at K_d) to 13% (at K_u), and the optimal capital budget climbs from LC 400 to LC 600. The marginal cost of capital schedule $S'S_U$ is lower than SS_D at all levels of the capital budget.[1] It should be noted that the menu of potential projects (the line DD1) may also shift to the right if a project needs to be financed abroad due to government regulations, or a foreign acquisition depends on local financing.

Although Exhibit 5.2 is designed to show the impact of sourcing equity

---

1.   Dullum and Stonehill (1983), p. 49.

Exhibit 5.2: *Market Segmentation, Availability of Funds and the Cost of Capital.*

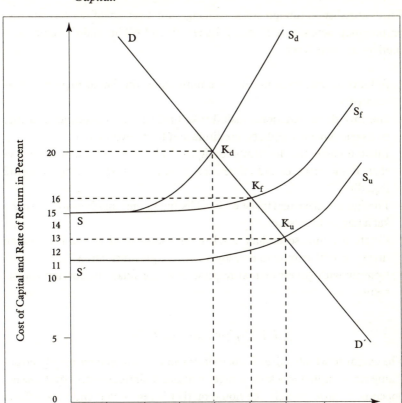

Source: Dullum and Stonehill (1983), page 48.

abroad on a single firm's cost and availability of capital, it can also be used to depict the potential benefit for all Nordic firms of the transition of Nordic equity markets from being segmented to being integrated with global equity markets. Theoretically, the equities of Nordic firms should now be correctly priced with respect to worldwide standards. In practice, however, it is probably only the firms that are large enough and visible internationally that can actually raise funds and list abroad. Therefore, some of the smaller firms must feel that their home Nordic equity market is still partly segmented and illiquid from their own perspective.

5.4. Crosslisting on Foreign Stock Exchanges

Firms crosslist on foreign stock exchanges for a variety of reasons whether or not they actually sell equity issues abroad.[2] The main documented motives are as follows.

- Achieve a world pricing of its equity when the home market is segmented.
- Improve the international visibility of the firm's products and securities to its customers, suppliers, creditors and host governments.
- Make it easier for the firm's foreign stockholders to trade its shares in their home markets and currencies, thus increasing the stock's overall liquidity.
- Foreign underwriters insist on local listing in their markets to help market a new equity issue.
- Create a liquid secondary market for shares used to acquire foreign firms, or to distribute to employees of foreign subsidiaries.
- Comply with governmental requirements for financing foreign investments.

5.4.1. Effects on Stock Price

The extent to which a firm's stock price can be increased by merely crosslisting on a foreign stock exchange, without a simultaneous equity issue, depends on how severely the home market is segmented and what efforts the firm has made to attract international investors.[3] For example, Novo Industri's stock price had already achieved world pricing before its 1981 equity issue and New York Stock Exchange listing (See the Novo Industri case in Part IV). However, as shown by Modén and Oxelheim (1997), in most Swedish cases only a combined equity issue and crosslisting offered full stock price advantages.

---

2. For further analysis see Shahrokh M. Saudagaran (1988) pp. 101-28.
3. Sundaram and Logue (1996) found a favourable effect on stock prices for foreign firms that crosslisted on the New York and American Stock Exchanges during 1982-92.

5.4.2. Improving the International Visibility of a Firm's Products and Securities

Even without selling a new equity issue large multinational firms often crosslist on multiple foreign stock exchanges. Their motivation is to improve their corporate image, advertise their products, obtain good press coverage, and support efforts to raise working capital from host country financial institutions.

5.4.3. Improving Overall Liquidity

Foreign investors can acquire a firm's stock through transactions on foreign stock exchanges. By crosslisting on their investors' home stock markets, a firm can help those investors to trade shares and receive dividends in their home currency. The hope is to increase overall liquidity for trading the firm's shares and to encourage the foreign investors to hold the firm's shares rather than selling them back to the firm's home market.

Crosslisting usually entails creating a *depositary receipts* system. These are negotiable instruments issued by a bank. Depositary receipts are collateralized by original shares of stock held in custody by the bank. For example, in April, 1981, Novo Industri established an *American Depositary Receipts (ADR)* program, with Morgan Guaranty Bank in the United States as custodian. This occurred prior to Novo's new equity issue and NYSE listing in July 1981. In this case five *American Depositary shares (ADS)* were issued for every share of Novo's B-shares held in custody by Morgan Guaranty. This enabled U.S. investors to trade Novo's shares in dollars at a price appropriate for the U.S. market.

5.4.4. Other Motivations to Crosslist on Foreign Stock Exchanges

As will be shown in the next section, listing on a host country's stock market is usually required by underwriters of a firm's new equity issue sold in that market. For example, Goldman, Sachs and Company, Novo's lead underwriter in its U.S. stock issue of 1981 insisted that Novo should be listed on the New York Stock Exchange.

It is often desirable to create a liquid secondary market for shares used to acquire foreign firms. For example, Hafslund Nycomed (See Part VI) crosslisted on the New York Stock Exchange in order to acquire U.S. firms with related technology. It crosslisted in London for the same reason. In both cases the crosslistings were also motivated by the need to support new equity issues in the United States and United Kingdom, respectively.

In Chapter 2, it was stated that it was typical for Nordic regulators to require foreign financing of foreign acquisitions or greenfield investments during the pre-deregulation period. This is no longer true for firms resident in Nordic markets but is relevant for firms resident in many of the emerging markets.

5.5. Motivations to Sell Equities Abroad

It should be emphasised here that a crosslisting abroad may be done without doing a new equity issue at the same time. What benefits can then be reaped by having an issue in addition to the crosslisting? In principle most benefits accrue already through the crosslisting. However, an issue signals a stronger commitment by the company (See Modén and Oxelheim, 1997).

5.5.1. Sweden

In Exhibit 5.3 some arguments are presented for making an issue abroad as they appear in annual reports of Swedish companies involved in such issues. The ranking of the arguments is, in addition to what has been found in the annual reports, based on interviews with relevant decision-makers in these companies. As was found in the Appendix to Chapter 2, some of the companies were listed prior to the time of the international equity offer; others were not. It is apparent that the marketing reason is regarded as important in many cases. In case a company is already listed, the marketing effect is probably enhanced if the company's shares are regularly traded on the foreign stock market. Consequently, an issue directed to foreign investors (to the general market or to a limited set of large investors) may contribute to the marketing effect by fuelling the liquidity of the shares (financial marketing) or by highlighting the company name in local and international media (commercial marketing).[4]

4.   Modén and Oxelheim (1997).

Exhibit 5.3: Ranking of Arguments for Undertaking a Foreign Equity Issue.

Motive	Marketing	Limited domestic supply	Preferential Price Difference	Legal Restrictions	Diversification	To satisfy foreign demand for shares	The issue caused by an imminent funding need
Pharmacia, 1981	1		3		2		No
Cardo, 1982	2	1					No
Perstorp, 1982				1			Yes
Alfa Laval, 1983			1	2			No
Ericsson, 1983	2				1		No
Gambro, 1983	2	1					No
Volvo, 1983		1		3	2		Yes
Sonesson, 1983	2	1					Yes
AGA, 1983	1				2		Yes
PLM, 1983	1					2	Yes
Pharmacia, 1983	1						No
PLM, 1984	1						Yes
Bilspedition,1985	1			3	2		Yes
Bilspedition,1985	1			3	2		Yes
Electrolux, 1986				1			Yes
Skåne-Gripen, 1986	1		2		1		No
Ellos, 1987	1						Yes
Perstorp, 1988	1						Yes
Atlas Copco, 1990		1					Yes
Gambro, 1990		1			2		Yes
Securitas, 1991						1	Yes
Frontline, 1993						1	Yes
Svedala, 1993	3	1				2	No
Arjo, 1993	2		1				Yes

Source: Modén & Oxelheim,1995.
*Note:*Based on annual reports and interviews. (1) is the most important argument for a foreign equity issue, (2) the second most important and (3) the third most important.

5.5.2. Denmark

Novo Industri A/S was motivated by the need to escape a segmented and illiquid Danish home market when it issued a convertible Eurobond (1978) and listed on the London Stock Exchange. Its U.S. equity issue (1981) was motivated by a desire to increase the liquidity of its shares. The underwriting syndicate led by Goldman, Sachs and Company, required Novo to list on NASDAQ and subsequently on the New York Stock

Exchange (NYSE) to help market the issue and meet the dispersion of ownership requirement of the NYSE.

Tele Danmark needed to use the Euroequity market to distribute its mammoth privatisation issue in 1994. It listed on the NYSE and other stock exchanges to provide liquid secondary markets for its new foreign and domestic investors.

5.5.3. Finland

Two of the Finnish case study firms, Amer and Nokia (Part V), raised equity in the United States and United Kingdom in order to gain liquidity for their shares, to help finance foreign acquisitions, and to improve the visibility of their products. To help market their issues the firms listed in London and New York.

5.5.4. Norway

Norsk Data sold equity issues abroad and listed in London and New York (NASDAQ) in order to escape Norway's segmented market and to raise funds for capital investments beyond what could be supplied in Norway. As was mentioned earlier, Hafslund Nycomed used equity shares to purchase acquisitions in the United States and United Kingdom. It also listed on the London and New York Stock Exchange in order to provide a liquid secondary market for its resulting foreign investors and to improve its credibility with its customers in the foreign medical communities.

5.6. Instruments Used to Sell Equity Abroad

Foreign equity markets are normally tapped using one of three instruments.

- A directed issue of stocks, convertible bonds, or a hybrid instrument, sold in a specific foreign equity market. A directed private placement is also feasible.
- An Euroequity issue sold in several equity markets simultaneously. This usually includes the home market in addition to foreign markets.
- Receiving an equity injection from a foreign partner as part of a strategic alliance.

5.6.1. Directed Stock Issue

A directed stock issue is defined as one targeted at investors in a single country and underwritten in whole or in part by investment institutions from that country. The issue might or might not be listed on a stock exchange in the target market.

Directed stock issues were the investment of choice for Nordic firms during the early 1980s. Segmentation of the home equity markets would have made it difficult to attract international investors with a "shotgun" approach. Indeed, the early Nordic equity issues abroad were focused and heavily promoted by Goldman, Sachs and Company (Novo Industri A/ S), and Morgan Stanley (L.M. Ericsson AB, Fortia AB/Pharmacia, and Gambro). The Ericsson and Fortia cases are presented in Part VII.

Directed stock issues have been particularly useful to Nordic firms desiring to improve the liquidity of their shares, to achieve international pricing of their shares, and to become more visible to customers and suppliers. This was certainly the case for the aforementioned four firms in the early 1980s.

Even after the Nordic equity markets became less segmented, directed stock issues have been useful to fund acquisitions or new capital investments in the targeted foreign market. As was mentioned above, this was the motivation for Norwegian-based Hafslund Nycomed's directed share issues in London (1989) and the United States (1992), as well as its listing on the New York Stock Exchange (1992). The Hafslund Nycomed case is presented in Part VI.

5.6.2. Euroequity Issues

Not only have Nordic equity markets become less segmented but this trend is happening worldwide. It is occurring simultaneously with a rapid increase in international portfolio investment. As a result, a robust Euroequity market has evolved starting in the mid-1980s.

Firms are able to issue equity, which is underwritten and distributed in more than one foreign equity market, sometimes simultaneously with distribution in the home market. The same financial institutions that form the backbone of the Eurobond market are the main players in the newer Euroequity market.

The Euroequity market has been the main vehicle for privatising large public utilities from both industrialised and emerging markets. Nordic privatisation's have in the recent past made use of the Euroequity market and are expected to do more of the same in the future. Notable recent examples are the privatisation of Tele Danmark (See case in Part IV), Girobank A/S (Denmark) and Copenhagen Airports A/S (Denmark). A Euroequity issue by Electrolux in 1986 is presented in Part VII. It should be noted that the market only developed during the past decade, so earlier Nordic equity issues did not really have a choice to use it.

Simultaneous distribution in several equity markets implies a single worldwide price. This price is often somewhat different than the previous home market price but results from a compromise among the various national underwriters.

5.6.3. Strategic Alliances

Strategic alliances are usually created to take advantage of some perceived synergies in joint marketing, product development, or other commercial activities. However, financial synergy may also arise if a financially strong firm helps a financially weak partner by injecting favourably-priced equity or debt into it. Such was the case with the Philips NV alliance with Danish Bang & Olufsen A/S in 1990. This case is presented in Part IV. Other cases of strategic alliances which are presented in Parts V and VI are Huhtamaki and Procordia, Elektrisk Bureau A/S and Asea AB.

The key to financial synergy with respect to equity pricing is that portfolio investors price shares according to their expected risk-adjusted rate of return and their Beta. This is necessarily somewhat biased by past performance, but in any case cannot usually anticipate the synergistic effects of a strategic alliance that does not yet exist. Thus, the value of equity in Bang & Olufsen was higher from the perspective of Philips NV, which anticipated the operating and financial synergies, than Bang & Olufsen's value to the existing market of portfolio investors. As of October 1996, many of the anticipated synergies were realised by Bang & Olufsen. Its operating performance has improved dramatically. It has also enjoyed a hefty share price increase compared to the Danish market as a whole.

Contrary to the Bang & Olufsen experience, strategic alliances have been notoriously unstable. They have often been "trial marriages" leading to either a consummated merger or to a divestment. For example in the Norwegian case studies, Elektrisk Bureau was eventually acquired by ASEA AB even though it started out as a strategic alliance.

5.7. Barriers and Costs

The Nordic companies which have listed and sold equity abroad have discovered several uncomfortable burdens. The foreign investors expect them to provide initial and continuing full disclosure of operating results, usually quarterly rather than semi-annually. They also expect to have a professional investor relations program presented to them locally. This puts a strain on a company's financial staff and top management, who are expected to participate on a regular basis.

5.7.1. Disclosure

For those firms choosing to list or sell equity in the U.S. equity market, the Securities and Exchange Commission (SEC) imposes rather stringent and costly disclosure rules. These are reflected in the cost of preparing a "prospectus", which is distributed to potential stockholders. The prospectus and other communications with stockholders must reconcile foreign and U.S. accounting systems (U.S. G.A.A.P). Raising funds and listing on the London Stock Exchange requires less of a commitment to disclosure but an equally time consuming investor relations program. Other stock markets are less stringent but also less liquid. Relative disclosure costs are one of the main reasons that about twice as many foreign firms list in London and are traded on SEAQ International as list on the New York Stock Exchange (NYSE). However, those that list on the NYSE are usually rewarded with greater trading liquidity for their stocks.

Even though it is costly, full disclosure may actually lower a firm's cost of capital because it removes many of the uncertainties about past activities, and provides a more solid basis for assessing future cash flows and opportunities.[5]

5.7.2. Investor Relations

In addition to the costs of disclosure, firms desiring to crosslist or raise equity on foreign equity markets need to invest both money and time in the effort. The transaction costs of preparing a prospectus include

---

5. This defence of disclosure was first proposed by Choi (1973). The relationship between level of disclosure and the decision to crosslist is analysed by Saudagaran and Biddle (1992).

accounting, legal and printing components. Distribution via an underwriting syndicate can also be costly but necessary. For small size issues these combined out-of-pocket costs can easily reach 10% of the issue's gross proceeds. The larger the issue, the smaller the percent since the costs are spread over more proceeds. In the first part of the 1980s, Rutherford (1985) and Hansen (1986) estimated that transaction costs, including preparing the prospectus and distribution, ranged from 3% to 10% of the total amount issued. Oxelheim (1996) estimated that these transaction costs had been reduced, at least for Swedish firms, for equity issues in the 1990s due to greater competition.

In addition to considerable time spent on preparing the prospectus, top management needs to be involved in "road shows" designed to inform investors, security analysts, portfolio managers, and the business press about the forthcoming equity issue or crosslisting. The reason for top management's deep time involvement is that the investment community needs to make a judgement about the quality of top management, as well as the firm's strategic plan for the future. The commitment by top management continues forever since investors expect continuing access to information and an ability to monitor the firm's management and strategy continuously. These are the "agency" costs of gaining continuous access to foreign investors.

5.8. The Future

It appears that Euroequity issues will increasingly dominate corporate efforts to raise equity globally. Euroequity issues have the advantage of being able to raise huge amounts of money at a relatively low cost compared to directed issues.

Crosslisting on foreign stock exchanges will probably continue because of the motives previously described, but as more markets become unsegmented, some of the benefits of directed issues will disappear.

Despite the increased correlation of returns between national stock markets, the benefits of international diversification should continue to motivate crossborder portfolio investment. Indeed, as the benefits become better known and demonstrated, one could expect a much larger proportion of equity portfolios to contain foreign stocks. At the moment, most portfolios are less than optimally diversified internationally due to such variables as "home country bias", foreign exchange risk, differences in taxation, differences in accounting and disclosure, and perceived political risk. The outcome depends a great deal on maintaining political stability in the world, as well as continuation of the trend towards more standardisation of accounting, disclosure, and taxation rules.

References

Choi, F.D.D., Autumn 1973. "Financial Disclosure in Relation to a Firm's Capital Costs". *Accounting and Business Research*, pp. 106-48.

Dullum, K. B. and Stonehill, A., 1983. "Towards an International Cost of Capital". *Nationaløkonomisk Tidsskrift, No. 1*, pp. 43-60.

Eiteman D., A. Stonehill, and M. Moffett, 1995. *"Multinational Business Finance"*. 7th Edition, Reading, MA.: Addison-Wesley Publishing Company.

Hansen, R., 1986, "Evaluating the Costs of a New Equity Issue". *Midland Corporate Finance Journal 4*, pp. 42-55.

Modén, K-M and L. Oxelheim, 1995. "Why issue equity abroad – the experience of small country companies". *Working Paper, No.13*. Institute of Economic Research, Lund University.

Modén, K-M and L. Oxelheim, 1997. "Why issue equity abroad – corporate efforts and stock market responses". *Management International Review*, Vol. 37, No 3, pp. 223-241.

Oxelheim, L., 1996. *"Financial Markets in Transition – Globalization, Investment and Economic Growth"*. London and New York: Routledge.

Oxelheim, L., 1997. "The routes to equity market integration – the interplay among regulators, investors and managers". *Working Paper*. Institute of Economic Research, Lund University.

Rutherford, J., 1985. "An International Perspective on the Capital Structure Puzzle". *Midland Finance Journal, 3*, pp. 60-72.

Saudagaran, M.S., 1988. "An Empirical Study of Selected Factors Influencing the Decision to List on Foreign Stock Exchanges". *Journal of International Busines Studies, Spring*, pp. 101-28.

Saudagaran, M.S., and Gary C. Biddle, 1992, "Financial Disclosure Levels and Foreign Stock Exchange Listing Decisions". *Journal of International Financial Management and Accounting, Summer*, pp. 106-48.

Sundaram, A.K. and D. Logue, 1996. "Valuation Effects of Foreign Company Listings on U.S. Exchanges". *Journal of International Business Studies, First Quarter*, pp. 67-88.

Part IV

Strategies of
Danish Corporations

The trilogy of Danish cases illustrates three different scenarios for raising equity capital internationally. Novo Industri A/S (NOVO) illustrates a directed share issue. Tele Danmark A/S is an example of a modern Euroequity issue motivated by a desire to privatise. Bang & Olufsen A/S shows how a firm can raise equity capital on favourable terms through a strategic alliance when a public issue would not generate an acceptable revenue.

The Novo case was very significant for Nordic companies because it was the first Nordic company to float a convertible bond issue in the Eurobond market (1978) accompanied by a listing on the London Stock Exchange. It was also the first Nordic firm since World War II to float a successful public stock issue in the United States and to list on NASDAQ and subsequently on the New York Stock Exchange (1981). As was pointed out in earlier chapters, the Novo bond and stock issues were floated during the period when all four Nordic stock markets were still very much segmented from world equity markets. However, it should be noted that Novo had escaped the segmented Danish market during the one year period preceding its US share issue and listing. In fact, discovery by US, UK, and other foreign investors had driven Novo's share price up over sixfold between May, 1980 and May, 1981. Indeed, it was this historical high share price which motivated at least the timing of Novo's US offering. The Novo case describes the path taken by Novo to internationalise its cost of capital and the obstacles it faced along the way.

The Tele Danmark case unfolds in April 1994, long after the Danish and other Nordic equity markets had become deregulated. The path to its Euroequity issue was also made much easier by the many successful privatisations issues by other (non-Danish) companies during the 1980s and the early 1990s. In fact, its USD 2.9 billion issue was not at all unusual for the modern Euroequity market, but it was by far the largest Danish equity issue ever floated.

The Bang & Olufsen strategic alliance with Philips NV shows that a company need not have a sparkling stock market track record in order to attract foreign investors. International portfolio investors are not the only fish in the pond. Both Bang & Olufsen and Philips NV recognised the synergies that might be obtained through a strategic alliance, with an equity infusion by Philips into Bang & Olufsen. Philips was even willing to pay a 30% premium over Bang & Olufsen's stock market price to capture anticipated operating as well as other synergies. Portfolio investors, both Danish and foreign, could neither measure nor benefit directly from those synergies. They were more interested in how Bang & Olufsen would influence the rate of return and risk of their portfolios. Thus, they believed Bang & Olufsen's shares had been correctly priced by an efficient market. Furthermore, their portfolios already contained enough Bang & Olufsen shares.

6. NOVO Industri A/S (NOVO): A Directed Issue[1]

Arthur Stonehill and Kåre B. Dullum

6.1. Background

Novo Industri (Novo Nordisk today) is a Danish multinational firm which produces industrial enzymes and pharmaceuticals (mostly insulin). In 1977, Novo's management decided to "internationalise" its capital structure and sources of funds. This decision was based on the observation that the Danish securities market was both illiquid and segmented from other capital markets. In particular, the lack of availability and high cost of equity capital in Denmark resulted in Novo having a higher cost of capital than its main multinational competitors, such as Eli Lilly (U.S.), Miles Laboratories (U.S. – a subsidiary of Bayer, Germany), and Gist Brocades (The Netherlands).

Apart from the cost of capital, Novo's projected growth opportunities signalled the eventual need to raise new long-term capital beyond what could be raised in the illiquid Danish market. Since Novo was and is a technology leader in its specialties, planned capital investments in plant, equipment and research could not be postponed until internal financing from cash flow became available. Novo's competitors would preempt any markets not served by Novo.

Even if an equity issue of the size required could have been raised in Denmark, the required rate of return would have been unacceptably high. For example, Novo's price/earnings ratio was typically around five, while that of its foreign competitors was well over ten. Yet, Novo's business and financial risk appeared to be about equal to that of its competitors. A price/earnings ratio of five was considered appropriate for Novo in a Danish context, when Novo was being compared with other domestic firms.

If Denmark's securities markets were integrated with other capital mar-

1. This case is adapted from Kåre B. Dullum and Arthur Stonehill, «Towards an International Cost of Capital», *Nationaløkonomisk Tidsskrift*, No. 1, 1983, pp. 49-58.

kets, one would expect foreign investors to rush in and buy "undervalued" Danish securities. In that case, firms like Novo would enjoy an international cost of capital comparable to their foreign competitors. Strangely enough, no Danish governmental restrictions existed which would prevent foreign investors from holding Danish securities. Therefore, one must look for investor perception as the main cause of market segmentation in Denmark.

6.2. Market Segmentation in Denmark

At least some of the characteristics for market segmentation, as mentioned in Chapter 5, were valid for the Danish equity market in 1981.

Disparity in the information base of Danish and foreign investors existed. Danish taxation was unfavourable for equity investors. Danish investors could not optimise their portfolios because they were not allowed to buy foreign equities. Financial risks of Danish firms were somewhat higher than in the Anglo-American markets. Foreign exchange and political risks were present but not as severe as in many other countries.

6.2.1. Disparity in the Information Base

Certain institutional characteristics of Denmark caused Danish and foreign investors to be uninformed about each other's equity securities. The most important information barrier was the Danish regulation which prohibited Danish investors from holding foreign private sector securities. As a result of this rule, Danish investors had no incentive to follow developments in foreign securities markets, nor to factor such information into their evaluation of Danish securities. Another detrimental effect of this regulation was that foreign securities firms did not locate offices or personnel in Denmark since they had no product to sell. Lack of physical presence in Denmark reduced the ability of foreign security analysts to follow Danish securities. Therefore, Danish securities might have been priced correctly in the efficient market sense, relative to each other considering the Danish information base, but priced incorrectly considering the combined foreign and Danish information base.

A second information barrier was lack of enough Danish security analysts following Danish securities. Only one professional security analysts service was published (Børsinformation), and that was in Danish. A few Danish institutional investors employed in-house analysts, but their findings were not available to the public. Thus both domestic and foreign investors were deprived of the broad analytical coverage of securities available in many other markets.

Other information barriers included language and accounting principles. Naturally, financial information was and still is normally published in Danish using Danish accounting principles. Most major firms, such as Novo, published English versions, but almost none used U.S. or British accounting principles or attempted to show any reconciliation with such principles. Lack of comparability might have discouraged some foreign investors who did not find it worthwhile to invest the time and money to derive comparable data.

6.2.2. Taxation

Until deregulation, Danish taxation policy had all but eliminated investment in common stock by individuals. Until a tax law change in July 1981, capital gains on shares held for over two years were taxed at a 50% rate. Shares held for less than two years, or for "speculative" purposes, were taxed at personal income tax rates, with the top marginal rate being 75%. In contrast, capital gains on bonds were tax free. This resulted in bonds being issued at deep discounts because the redemption at par at maturity was considered a capital gain. As a result, most individual investors held bonds rather than stocks. This reduced the liquidity of the stock market and increased the required rate of return on stocks if they were to compete with bonds.

6.2.3. The Feasible Set of Portfolios

Because of the prohibition on foreign securities ownership, Danish investors had a very limited set of securities from which to choose a portfolio. In practice, Danish institutional portfolios were composed of Danish stocks, government bonds, and mortgage bonds. Since Danish stock price movements are closely correlated with each other, Danish portfolios possessed a rather high level of systematic risk. In addition, government policy had been to provide a relatively high real rate of return on government bonds after adjusting for inflation. The net result of taxation policies on individuals, and attractive real yields on government bonds, was that *ex ante* required rates of return on stocks needed to be relatively high by international standards, although *ex post* realised rates of return were unexpectedly low during the relevant 1975-81 period.

From a portfolio perspective, Danish stocks were an opportunity for foreign investors to diversify internationally. If Danish stock price movements were not closely correlated with world stock price movements, inclusion of Danish stocks in foreign portfolios should have reduced these portfolio's systematic risk. Furthermore, foreign investors were not subjected to the high Danish income tax rates since they were normally protected by tax treaties, which typically limit their tax to 15% on dividends and capital gains. As a result of the international diversification potential, foreign investors might have required a lower rate of return on Danish stocks than Danish investors, other things being equal. However, other things may not have been equal, because foreign investors might have perceived Danish stocks to carry more financial, foreign exchange and political risk than their own domestic securities.

6.2.4. Financial, Foreign Exchange and Political Risks

Financial leverage utilised by Danish firms was relatively high by U.S. and U.K. standards but not abnormal for Scandinavia, Germany, Italy, or Japan. In addition, most of the debt was short term with variable interest rates. Just how foreign investors would have viewed financial risk in Danish firms depended on what norms they followed in their home countries. We know from Novo's experience in tapping the Eurobond market in 1978 that Morgan Grenfell, its British investment banker, advised Novo to maintain a debt ratio (debt/total capitalisation) closer to 50% rather than the traditional Danish 60%.

Foreign investors in Danish securities are subject to foreign exchange risk. Whether this is a plus or minus factor depends on the investor's home currency, perception about the future strength of the krone, and its impact on a firm's economic exposure. Through personal contacts with Novo's foreign investors and bankers, the authors do not believe foreign exchange risk was a factor in Novo's stock price, because Novo's operations were perceived as being well-diversified internationally. In fact, 97% of sales were outside of Denmark. Based on the same interviews, with respect to political risk, Denmark was perceived as a stable western democracy but with the potential to cause periodic problems for foreign investors. In particular, Denmark's national debt was at this time regarded as too high for comfort, although this had only begun to show up in the form of risk premiums on Denmark's Eurocurrency syndicated loans. The other threat perceived by foreign investors was that Denmark would move toward implementing "economic democracy" in a more substantial manner. Economic democracy implied that mandatory profit sharing plans would be implemented in industry. Employees' share of the profit would be exchanged for stock in the firms. This stock would be held and voted by centralised, labour union-controlled funds. This differs from present practice whereby pension funds are encouraged to purchase equity in private sector firms. Ultimately, of course, this could lead to employee control of these firms and a weak bargaining position for foreign portfolio investors. Despite these general concerns about Denmark's political situation, investors in Novo, in particular, indicated that their evaluation of Novo's prospects were not influenced by political risk.

6.3. Preparations for Internationalising the Cost of Capital

Although Novo's management in 1977 wished to escape from the shackles of Denmark's segmented and illiquid capital market, many barriers needed to be overcome. It is worthwhile to describe some of these, since they would also be typical of the barriers faced by other firms from segmented markets.

6.3.1. Overcoming the Information Gap

Novo had been a family-owned firm from its founding in the 1920's by the two Pederson brothers until 1974, when it went public and listed on the Copenhagen Exchange. However, prior to the decision to internationalise its financial sources of funds, Novo was essentially unknown in investment circles outside of Denmark. In order to overcome this disparity in the information base, Novo adopted a policy of increasing the breadth and depth of its financial and technical disclosure in both Danish and English versions. This was aided in late 1977 by Grieveson, Grant and Company, a British stock brokerage firm, which had started to follow Novo's stock. They issued the first professional security analysis report about Novo in English.

6.3.2. The Convertible Eurobond Issue

The information gap was further closed when Morgan Guaranty Trust Company of New York, Novo's main foreign commercial banker, was consulted about alternative strategies to tap international capital markets. Its advice was to try a Eurobond issue. It then introduced Novo to Morgan Grenfell & Co., a leading U.K. investment bank, which confirmed the recommended strategy. In 1978, Morgan Grenfell successfully organised a syndicate to underwrite and sell a $20 million convertible Eurobond issue for Novo. In connection with this offering, Novo listed its shares on the Stock Exchange in London to facilitate conversion and to gain visibility. These twin actions were the key to dissolving the information barrier as far as foreign investors were concerned and, of course, also raised a large amount of long-term capital on favourable terms, which would have been unavailable in Denmark.

Despite the favourable impact of the Eurobond issue on availability of capital, Novo's cost of capital actually increased when Danish investors reacted negatively to the potential dilution effect of the conversion right. During 1979, Novo's stock price declined from around DKK 300 per share to around DKK 200-225 per share.

6.3.3. Positioning Novo with Respect to Biotechnology

During 1979, a fortuitous event occurred. Biotechnology began to attract the interest of the U.S. investment community, with several sensationally oversubscribed stock issues by such start-up firms as Genentech and Cetus. Thanks to the aforementioned domestic information gap, Danish investors were unaware of these events and continued to value Novo at a low price/earnings ratio of 5, compared to over 10 for its established competitors and 30 or more for these new potential competitors.

At this point Novo felt it had to position itself with its customers in the U.S. market as a firm which had a proven track record in biotechnology, compared to the "blue sky" promises of the recent start-up firms. A failure to do so could lead to the faulty conclusion that Novo was not at the forefront in technology. Therefore, in order to protect its customer base, Novo organised a seminar in New York City on April 30, 1980. About 40 journalists and financial analysts attended the seminar. Soon after the seminar a few sophisticated individual U.S. investors began buying Novo's stock and convertibles through the Stock Exchange in London. Danish investors were only too happy to supply this foreign demand. Therefore, despite relatively strong demand from U.S. and British investors, Novo's share price increased only gradually, climbing back to the DKK 300 level by mid-summer. However, during the following months foreign interest began to snowball. By the end of 1980 Novo's stock price had reached the DKK 600 level. Moreover, foreign investors had increased their proportion of B share ownership from virtually nothing to around 50%. Novo's price/earnings ratio had risen to around 16, which was now in line with that of its international competitors but not with the Danish market. At this point one must conclude that Novo had succeeded in internationalising its cost of capital and that U.S. investors were driving its stock price.

Other Danish securities remained locked in a segmented market. Indeed, movement in the Danish stock market in general was not correlated with the rise in Novo's stock price in 1980, nor could Novo's stock price be explained by movement in the U.S. or U.K. stock markets as a whole. Exhibit 6.1 compares an index of Novo's stock price to Stock Exchange Indices in Copenhagen, London, and New York during the period 1977-1982. Note the extreme divergence after the seminar in New York in April 1980.

6.3.4. The ADR System

In order to improve the liquidity of its shares held by U.S. investors and to increase the availability of capital by tapping the U.S. new issue market, Novo's management in the Fall of 1980 decided to sponsor an "American Depositary Receipts" (ADR) system in the U.S., list its shares on the over-the-counter market (NASDAQ), and retain a U.S. investment banker to advise it about a U.S. stock issue. Goldman, Sachs and Company was selected for this purpose. Morgan Guaranty established the ADR system for Novo in April 1981.

6.3.5. Approaching the Target Market with a U.S. Stock Issue

During the first half of 1981, under the guidance of Goldman, Sachs and Company and the assistance of Morgan Grenfell, Deutsche Bank, Swiss Bank Corporation, and Copenhagen Handelsbank, a prospectus was prepared for S.E.C. registration of a U.S. stock offering and eventual listing on the New York Stock Exchange. The main barriers encountered in this effort, which would have general applicability, were connected with preparing financial statements which could be reconciled with U.S. accounting principles, and the higher level of disclosure required by the S.E.C. In particular, industry segment reporting was a problem both from a disclosure perspective and because the accounting data was not available inter-

Exhibit 6.1: Novo's B Share Prices Compared to Stock Market Indices 1977-1982.

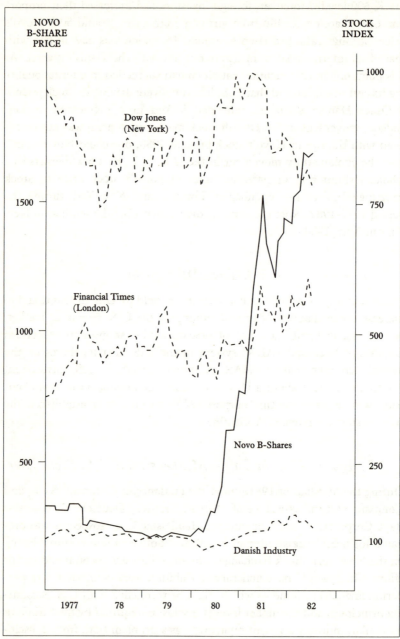

Source: Kåre B. Dullum and Arthur Stonehill (1983), page 55.

nally in that format. As it turned out, the investment barriers in the U.S. were relatively tractable although expensive and time consuming to overcome.

The more serious barriers were caused by a variety of institutional and governmental regulations in Denmark. They were never designed for firms to issue stock at market value, since Danish firms typically issued stock at par value with pre-emptive rights. Even Novo's own stockholders had to be educated as to the value of giving up their pre-emptive rights, but, by this time, Novo's stock price – driven by continued foreign buying – was so high that virtually nobody in Denmark thought it was worth the price which foreigners were willing to pay. In fact, by May 1981 Novo's stock price had risen to over DKK 1500, before settling down to a level around DKK 1400. As of July 1981 foreign ownership had increased to over 75% of Novo's B shares outstanding.

It should be noted that despite the shift to foreign ownership of the majority of B shares, voting control remained in Denmark. Prior to going public in 1974 Novo's owners had established two classes of stock. The A shares were entirely assigned to the Novo Foundation and made non-transferrable. The B shares were eventually mostly sold to the public by the heirs of the founders. Each A share had 10 votes but each B share had only 1 vote. The Novo Foundation was and still is run by an independent Board of Directors composed mainly of scientists, businessmen, and academicians. Its income is distributed primarily for scientific, humanitarian, and cultural purposes.

Market segmentation was very apparent during the first half of 1981. Published and unpublished reports by Danish security analysts, bankers, and the popular press consistently claimed that Novo was seriously overvalued, while their foreign counterparts were consistently touting Novo as being undervalued. The difference in views was based partly on investor perceptions of the importance of biotechnology and Novo's role in this field.

One final piece of evidence on market segmentation can be gleaned from the way Danish and foreign investors reacted to the announcement of the proposed new U.S. share issue on May 29, 1981. Novo's stock price dropped 156 points the next trading day in Copenhagen, equal to about 10% of its market value. As soon as trading started in New York, the stock price immediately recovered all of its loss. The Copenhagen reaction was typical for an illiquid market. Investors worried about the dilution effect of the new share issue, since it would increase the number of shares outstanding by about 8%. They did not believe that Novo could invest the new funds at a rate of return which would not dilute future earnings per share. They also feared that the U.S. shares would eventually flow back to Copenhagen if biotechnology lost its glitter.

The U.S. reaction to the announcement of the new share issue was consistent with what one would expect in a liquid and integrated market. U.S. investors viewed the new issue as creating additional demand for the stock as Novo became more visible due to the selling efforts of a large aggressive syndicate. Furthermore, the marketing effort was directed at institutional investors who were previously underrepresented among Novo's investors. This is because U.S. institutional investors want to be assured of a liquid market in a stock in order to be able to get out, if they desire, without depressing the stock price. The wide distribution effected by the new issue, plus Securities and Exchange Commission (S.E.C.) registration and a New York Stock Exchange listing, all added up to more liquidity.

On July 8, 1981, Novo became the first Nordic firm since World War II to sell equity through a public issue in the United States, as well as the first to list on the New York Stock Exchange. The issue price was equivalent to DKK 1399 per share ($36 per ADS). Immediately after July 1981, Novo's stock price performed better than the U.S. market as a whole. As of January 1982 the price was around $50 per ADS. Thus the dilution effect feared by Danish investors was not realised. In addition to the predicted lowering of the cost of capital due to access to an integrated capital market, the predicted liquidity improvement also occurred. The U.S. equity issue was partial evidence of this, but also the trading volume shortly after listing on the New York Stock Exchange averaged about $2 million per day. This was approximately the same as average daily trading volume of the combined stocks on the Copenhagen Stock Exchange at that time.

6.4. Novo PostScript

Exhibit 6.2 tracks Novo's stock price compared to the Copenhagen Stock Exchange Index and the Standard & Poor 500 Index from 1974 (first listing in Copenhagen) through 1995. Novo has outperformed both of these indices but has experienced considerable volatility in its stock price. The big rise between 1980 and 1981 reflected the events just described. Novo's stock price continued to rise through 1983. It was driven up by excellent operating results and the strength of the U.S dollar, the currency in which a significant share of Novo's sales are billed. In 1983 Novo was able to sell

Exhibit 6.2: Novo Nordisk versus Copenhagen Stock Exchange Index and Standard & Poor 500 index.

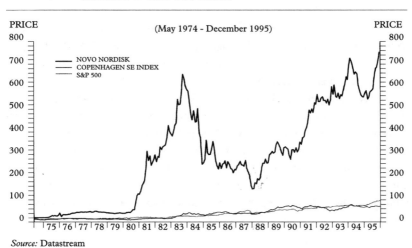

PRICE   (May 1974 - December 1995)   PRICE

NOVO NORDISK
COPENHAGEN SE INDEX
S&P 500

Source: Datastream

a $100 million equity issue in the United States at a higher price than the original 1981 issue. ($53.00 per ADS compared to $36.00 per ADS in 1981).

Novo's stock price declined rapidly between the midle of 1984 and the middle of 1987. Initially this was caused by management missing two forecasts in 1984/85. Management failed to meet their own forecast for two quarters in 1984/85. Novo's management learned the unpleasant way that one missed forecast with international investors spells problems, and two missed forecasts spell disaster. On top of this, competitive pressures in the insulin industry after Eli Lilly introduced its human insulin and Novo was a little late in receiving FDA approval of its own version of human insulin magnified the problems with investors.

From 1985 to 1986 the U.S dollar declined rapidly in value. This had an unfavourable effect on Novo due to its operating exposure. Most of its production of both insulin and industrial enzymes was located in Denmark, whereas 97% of its sales were abroad.

Novo's operating results and foreign exchange exposure began to improve in 1987 and 1988 but one of the main reasons for its stock price recovery was Novo's merger with Nordisk Gentofte in 1989. Nordisk Gentofte was its main Danish (and European) competitor in the insulin industry. Both firms were strong in research and development. Novo had a more complete worldwide distribution system. The attraction for Nordisk Gentofte was Novo's already internationalised cost of capital and its access to global capital markets.

Since 1989 Novo Nordisk has enjoyed impressive operating results as the synergies anticipated in the merger became realised. The brief dip in stock price in 1994 resulted partly from a delayed FDA approval for operating its new plant in Denmark.

The Novo experience has been described in hopes that it can be a model for other firms wishing to escape from segmented and illiquid home equity markets. However, a word of caution is advised. Novo had an excellent operating track record and a very strong worldwide market niche in two important industry sectors (insuline and industrial enzymes). This record continues to attract investors in Denmark and abroad. Other companies would also need to have such a favourable track record to attract foreign investors.

7. Tele Danmark A/S: Privatisation Via an Euroequity Issue

Arthur Stonehill and Kåre B. Dullum

7.1. Introduction

During April 1994, Tele Danmark, Denmark's national telecommunications company, was partially privatised by means of a DKK 19.5 billion (USD 2.96 billion) stock issue, floated on a number of national equity markets, including the Danish market.

This was the third step by the Danish government to privatise national companies. The first step was to sell to the public and employees 51% of the stock in Girobank A/S in November 1993. Girobank A/S had previously taken over the Danish postgiro system, which handled most cash transfer payments through the nation's post office locations.

The second step was to sell 25% of the stock of Copenhagen Airports A/S to private investors in Denmark and abroad. This was completed in March 1994. As the name implies, the company operates the airports in Denmark as well as their duty-free shops.

Tele Danmark was founded by the Danish government in 1990 as a holding company for consolidating the four existing regional telecommunications companies and Telecom A/S, which provided international services. The "Kingdom of Denmark" owned 89.9% of the controlling A-shares. A "Political Agreement", passed in 1990, required reduction of government ownership to 51% of Tele Danmark's nominal share capital and voting power. The government had also agreed to give Tele Danmark the operating independence to compete with anticipated increased competition coming from deregulation in Denmark and in the European Union.

At the time of privatisation Tele Danmark was the main source in Denmark of domestic and international telephone services, as well as leased lines. It was also one of two public mobile phone services. It supplied and serviced most other telecommunication services and cable television in Denmark.

7.2. Preparations for Privatisation

Preparation for privatisation typically involves at least three elements. First, there needs to be political agreement that the government should sell all or part of its shares. Second, the company needs to transform itself into a profit-making entity rather than a government-subsidised burden. Third, agreement needs to be reached with the underwriters with respect to the appropriate initial stock price, and the strategy for distribution and marketing of the shares domestically and internationally.

7.2.1. Gaining Political Agreement

In 1990, political agreement was reached among the major political parties to privatise certain Danish government-owned companies. The Danish government also recognised officially the need to operate the selected companies as private, profit-making units, with minimal government interference. They should operate in the same manner as any other private company.

7.2.2. Transformation into a Profit-making Entity

Once political agreement had been reached, management of Tele Danmark made some hard operating decisions. They reduced the size of the work force, and focused the company on future growth areas. They also reduced the price of telephone services in anticipation of future competition once Tele Danmark's monopoly position was relinquished. These efforts were rewarded by a dramatic increase in earnings per share (EPS), profit after tax, equity size, equity ratio, and operating margin. The improvement in operations can be seen in Exhibit 7.1, which covers the key figures for the period 1991-1993. Of course, no stock price existed since the company was still nearly 90% government-owned.

7.2.3. Setting the Initial Stock Price and Strategy for Distribution and Marketing

Since Tele Danmark's privatisation was one of the first in telecommunications in Europe, few precedents existed to help determine its initial stock price and strategy for distribution. The underwriters and government officials needed to use stock price comparisons with other telecommunica-

Exhibit 7.1: Income Statement, Balance Sheet & Key Figures for Tele Danmark.

Income statement Mill. DKK	1991	1992	1993
Turnover	15,288	15,653	16,293
Employee costs	4,925	5,424	4,397
Depreciations	3,503	3,547	3,504
Operating profit	1,939	2,072	3,110
Net finance	-815	-780	-348
Currency adjustments	34	88	-92
Profit before tax	1,158	1,380	2,670
Tax	510	446	848
Profit after tax	648	934	1,822
Extraordinary items	0	-18	-261
Cash earnings	4,151	4,481	5,326
Net investment	2,921	2,508	2,383
Balance sheet Mill. DKK			
Fixed assets	19,847	18,800	17,719
Current assets	7,404	7,870	8,389
Short debt	6,968	7,549	6,051
Long debt	12,720	10,288	9,776
Equity	6,502	7,322	8,752
Balance	27,651	26,670	26,108
Key figures			
EPS	4.9	7.1	13.9
CEPS	31.7	34.2	40.7
BV	49.6	55.9	66.8
Dividend/A-share DKK	10.0	10.0	10.0
Dividend/A-share total	131.0	131.0	131.0
Yield A-share	3.3	3.3	3.3
ROE %	N/A	14.4	24.9
Equity ratio %	23.5	27.5	33.5
Operating margin %	12.7	13.2	19.1
Asset turnover	1.8	1.7	1.6
Interest cover	2.4	2.7	8.9
Depreciations/net investments	1.2	1.4	1.5
Current ratio	1.1	1.0	1.4

Source: Rammer (1994), page 9.

tions companies that had publicly-traded shares. Exhibit 7.2 presents such a comparison. Based on these comparisons and estimates of future growth potential, the initial stock price was set at DKK 310 per B-share.

Distribution and marketing strategy was jointly determined by government representatives, management of Tele Danmark A/S, and the lead underwriters, Goldman Sachs International and Den Danske Bank. They needed to estimate how many shares could be absorbed by the Danish equity market and employee purchases before allocating the rest of the shares to international investors. In the end about 18% of the shares were placed in Denmark, 41% in the United States (ADS) and 41% in the rest of the world.

Exhibit 7.2:   Price-related Key Figures for European and American Telecommunications Companies.

	Price 24.3.1994	Currency	Market Cap. DKK mill	P/E 1992	P/E 1993	P/E 1994	Yield 1993
Denmark							
GN Great Nordic	615.0	DKK	3,146	30.8	22.9	27.7	1.95
Sweden							
Kinnevik	177.0	SEK	4,800	-25.1	16.1	29.2	2.82
Ericsson	362.5	SEK	65,733	129.0	38.7	25.3	1.14
Germay							
Mannesman	424.0	DEM	60,634	52.9	-41.9	79.1	1.08
France							
Alcatel Alsthom	680.0	FFR	105,588	12.8	12.9	13.3	2.26
United Kingdom							
British Telecom	396.0	GBP	239,992	17.9	13.6	12.3	4.35
Cable & Wireless	434.0	GBP	94,606	20.3	19.0	16.9	1.95
Vodafone	540.5	GBP	53,262	24.8	22.7	20.2	1.57
Security Services	768.0	GBP	8,325	37.1	29.1	22.9	0.73
Total telecommunications	EU		636,085	18.9	19.5	21.0	1.98
USA							
AT & T	53.0	USD	479,554	18.5	16.8	15.8	2.49
GTE Corp.	31.6	USD	199,784	16.2	14.4	13.5	5.75
Motorola	105.1	USD	195,772	48.7	29.6	24.2	0.42
Bellsouth	54.6	USD	179,730	16.2	15.6	14.6	5.05
Bell Atlantic	53.6	USD	153,855	16.6	15.5	14.7	5.00
Pacific Telesis	53.0	USD	147,982	18.7	18.9	18.3	4.11
Ameritech	40.5	USD	146,474	16.1	15.6	14.5	4.94
McCaw Cellular	50.5	USD	74,771	24.9	126.3	252.5	0.00
Alltel Corp	26.8	USD	34,000	21.9	19.1	16.7	3.29
US Cellular	26.9	USD	13,724	62.5	59.7	26,875.0	0.00
Total telecommunications	USA		1,625,646	18.6	18.2	16.5	3.11

P/E averages are excl. observations > 30
Sources: Gudme Raaschou, Value Line, Euro Equities, and Rammer (1994), page 3.

The marketing plan involved the traditional "road shows." Top management was asked to describe the company's future strategy, the role of the government, and answer questions from investors, security analysts, portfolio managers, and the Press in a variety of geographic locations.

7.3. The Share Offering

The offering consisted of an international issue and a United States issue of new B shares and American Depositary Shares (ADS). Danish citizens and Tele Danmark employees were included in the international issue. The subscription price was, as mentioned, DKK 310 per share during the subscription period of April 11-22, 1994. Simultaneously, Tele Danmark's

Exhibit 7.3: Prospectus Cover.

 DANMARK

Tele Danmark A/S

37,310,000 B Shares
in the form of American Depositary Shares or B Shares

Tele Danmark A/S is offering hereby, through the several International Underwriters, (i) American Depositary Shares, each representing one-half of one Class B Share, nominal value DKK 10, of the Company, and (ii) B Shares, as part of a worldwide offering described herein. The ADSs are evidenced by American Depositary Receipts. In addition to the ADSs and B Shares offered hereby, the Combined Offering includes an offering of 25,919,770 B Shares, in the form of B Shares and ADSs, in the United States. The International Offering includes an offering of B Shares in the Kingdom of Denmark.

After the Combined Offering, the share capital of the Company will consist of 6,777,023 Class A Shares, nominal value DKK 100 each, and 63,229,770 newly-issued B Shares, representing approximately 51.7% and 48.3%, respectively, of Tele Danmark's nominal share capital. Dividends on each A Share will be limited to an annual maximum of DKK 10, but there will be no such restriction on the amount of dividends that may be paid on the B Shares. See "Dividend Policy." Each A Share, nominal value DKK 100, will carry ten votes, while each B Share, nominal value DKK 10, will carry one vote.

After the Combined Offering, the Kingdom will own 6,681,000 A Shares, representing 51% of the nominal share capital and voting power of the Company. Another 96,023 A Shares, representing 0.7% of the nominal share capital and voting power of the Company, will be owned by private shareholders. The government of the Kingdom will purchase on March 1, 1997 all A Shares not then held by it at a price per A Share of DKK 125, plus an amount corresponding to a proportionate amount of A Share dividends, following which all A Shares will be converted into B Shares on a one-for-ten basis. Upon such purchase, the Kingdom will hold A Shares representing 51.7% of the nominal share capital and voting power of the Company, which will then again be reduced to 51%. See "Relationship with the Danish Government — Shareholding."

Prior to the Combined Offering there has been no public market for the ADSs or the B Shares. Application has been made to list the ADSs on the New York Stock Exchange and to list the B Shares on the Copenhagen Stock Exchange. In addition, it is expected that the ADSs and the B Shares will be quoted on the SEAQ International System of The International Stock Exchange of the United Kingdom and the Republic of Ireland Limited.

The initial offering price is DKK 310 per B Share and $23.526 per ADS, based on an exchange rate of DKK 6.5885 per US dollar and adjusted to reflect the ratio of one-half of one B Share to one ADS.

The B Shares and the ADSs are offered severally by the International Underwriters, as specified herein, subject to receipt and acceptance by them and subject to their right to reject any order in whole or in part. It is expected that on or about May 5, 1994, the B Shares will be delivered in book-entry form through the facilities of the Danish Securities Center (*Værdipapircentralen*), Euroclear or Cedel and the ADRs evidencing the ADSs will be ready for delivery in New York, New York.

Joint Global Coordinators

Goldman Sachs International   **Den Danske Bank**

Regional Lead Managers

Europe	*Nordic*
UBS Limited	**Den Danske Bank**

Rest of World	*United Kingdom*
Goldman Sachs International	**Barclays de Zoete Wedd Limited**

The date of this Prospectus is April 27, 1994.

---

shares were listed on the Copenhagen, and New York Stock Exchanges, and quoted on SEAQ International in London. The Danish Government would continue to own and vote 51% of Tele Danmark after the new share issue, including a later conversion of the Government's A shares to B shares.

Exhibit 7.4:   Tele Danmark's Press Release.

To the Copenhagen Stock Exchange   April 27, 1994
and the press outside the United States   OJ.647/6-006/67

The initial public price for Tele Danmark B Shares is fixed at DKK 310

Following consultations with the underwriters, Tele Danmark has decided to fix the offer price at DKK 310 per share and USD 23,53 per American Depositary Share (ADS). The price of the ADSs is based on an exchange rate of 6.5885 per US dollar and adjusted for a ratio of one half of one B share per ADS.

A total of 63,229,770 new B shares of nom. DKK 10 each were on offer. Approximately 18% of the total offer is being placed in Denmark, approximately 41% in the USA and approximately 41% in the rest of the world. A total of around 28,000 Danish individuals and around 10,500 employees of Tele Danmark have purchased new shares.

Following the completion of the offering, the Danish government will hold 51% of the company's share capital in the form of A shares, while private A-shareholders will own 0.7% of the company's share capital and new shareholders will hold the remaining 48.3% in the form of B shares.

The offering has been managed by an international management group, with Goldman Sachs International and Den Danske Bank as the Joint Global Coordinators.

Gross proceeds at DKK 19.5 bn

Tele Danmark's gross proceeds at the prices agreed to amount to approximately DKK 19.5 bn for the total offering. This makes the stock issue the biggest made on the Copenhagen Stock Exchange.

DKK 1.1 bn of the total offering will be used to acquire and write down A shares for the same nominal amount for which B shares have been issued. Tele Danmark's nominal share capital will thus remain unchanged after the offering.

Retail allotment (orders up to and including DKK 2,000,000)

Purchase offers will be accepted in full up to DKK 155,000 of market value (corresponding to 500 shares), but orders for more than DKK 155,000 of market value will be allotted 500 shares and a number of shares corresponding to 65% of the remainder of their market value.

Employee Shares

As an integrated part of the offer, approximately 718,000 shares have been acquired by Tele Danmark employees. The subscription price for employees is DKK 100 per B share. A total of approximately 10,500 employees, or 62% of the group's employees have subscribed for new shares.

Simultaneous listing in New York and Copenhagen

The B share will be listed on the Copenhagen Stock Exchange, whereas the ADSs, which are issued in the form of American Depositary Receipts (ADR), will be listed on the New York Stock Exchange. The B Shares and ADSs will also be quoted on SEAQ International in London.

Trading will commence tomorrow on the Copenhagen and New York Stock Exchanges. The trading on the Copenhagen Stock Exchange will start at 3.30 p.m. because of the time difference between New York and Copenhagen. The Copenhagen Stock Exchange will extend opening hours tomorrow until 7.00 p.m.

Tele Danmark A/S

Knud Heinesen   Hans Würtzen
Chairman of the Board   Chief Executive

Exhibit 7.3 reproduces the "Tombstone" for the issue. Exhibit 7.4 reproduces the press release from Tele Danmark dated April 27, 1994, after the successful completion of the share issue. Trading in the shares commenced on April 28, 1994.

7.4. The Stock Market Reaction

The initial stock market reaction was to confirm the pricing of the shares. Exhibit 7.5 shows both the price and volume of trading during the period between the issue date and December 31, 1995. Visual inspection suggests that Tele Danmark's share price pretty much followed the pattern of the overall Copenhagen Stock Market Index, rather than the S&P 500 Telephone Index. This suggests that it had not yet achieved an international price for its shares.

Proceeds of the sale of equity were targeted to repurchase the A-shares, which were to be converted to B-shares, to reduce the annual pension costs of Tele Danmark, to repay the company's debt to its pension fund, to make some desired capital expenditures, to repay other non-pension related debts, and to increase its working capital.

Exhibit 7.5: Tele Danmark v.s. Copenhagen Stock Index and S&P 500
Telephone Index

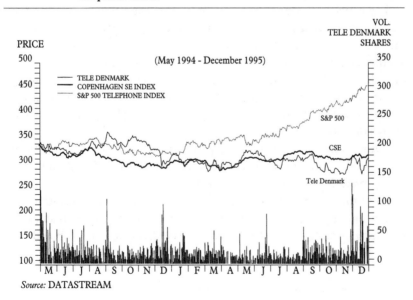

Source: DATASTREAM

7.5. Key Issues after Privatisation

As was the case with other privatisations in Denmark and elsewhere, Tele Danmark's future hinged on the resolution of a number of key operating and financial issues:

- Could Tele Danmark compete in an increasingly deregulated market, including expected increased competition from non-Danish companies?
- Would it be too small to keep up with rapid technological changes?
- With the Danish Government still owning 51% of the shares, would this lead to being saddled with non-profit oriented requirements because of political or social needs?
- Given an increased expectation for dividends, would it be able to raise enough new funds in the future to invest in growth opportunities?

In the long run, the success or failure of Tele Danmark to live up to its shareholders' and the Government's expectations would depend on its ability to improve its financial and operating performance. According to a recently published benchmark study of privatised firms worldwide, prospects for achieving favourable results were good.[1]

The benchmark study's data base was comprised of 61 companies from 18 countries and 32 industries. All had fully or partially privatised during the period 1961 to 1990, through stock sales to the public rather than to another company. Most were secondary sales by the governments of their own shares rather than newly issued shares, where the proceeds would go to the company, rather than the government. Thus, any change in performance was not merely due to an increased equity base. The benchmark study concluded as follows:

"Our results document strong performance improvements, achieved surprisingly without sacrificing employment security. Specifically, after being privatised, firms increase real sales, become more profitable, increase their capital investment spending, improve their operating efficiency, and increase their work forces. Furthermore, these companies significantly lower their debt levels and increase dividend payout. Finally, we

---

1. Megginson, Nash, and Randenbough (1994).

document significant changes in the size and composition of corporate boards of directors after privatisations."[2]

2. Ibid, Page 403.

References

Meggenson, W.L, R.C. Nash and M. I. Randenbough (1994), "The Financial and Operating Performance of Newly Privatised Firms: An International Empirical Analysis". *Journal of Finance, June*, pp. 403-452.

Rammer, S. (1994), *"Tele Danmark Issue"*. Copenhagen: Gudme Raaschou Investment Bank, April 5, pp. 1-9.

Tele Danmark (1994), *Prospectus*. Copenhagen, April 27, cover sheet.

Tele Danmark (1994), *Press Release*. Copenhagen, April 27, pp. 1-2.

8. Bang & Olufsen/Philips NV: A Strategic Alliance

Arthur Stonehill and Kåre B. Dullum

8.1. Bang & Olufsen's Situation in June 1990

Although strategic alliances are normally based on anticipated synergies in technology or marketing, the Bang & Olufsen's (B&O) strategic alliance with Philips N.V. (Philips) in June 1990 is a good example of capturing financial synergies in addition to the traditional synergies. It also demonstrates that a stock market price determined by portfolio investors can underestimate the intrinsic value of a firm, in this case B&O, to an industrial partner that can anticipate gaining synergies that are not obvious to portfolio investors. B&O was able to raise equity capital at a 35% premium over its market-based share price while also gaining the potential synergies it needed to implement its capital intensive strategy.

B&O was and still is Denmark's premier audiovisual firm but was a pygmy among giants in global terms. Prior to the strategic alliance in 1990, under the strategic leadership of Vagn Andersen, it had somehow survived the shakeout in the European consumer electronics industry which left only a few large multinational firms as the surviving competitors worldwide.

B&O had serious financial problems both because of its historic lack of consistent profitability and because its high end niche strategy was of necessity very capital intensive. It faced the usual problems of a small firm located in an illiquid home capital market that has more growth opportunities than the financial resources to take advantage of them. Most of its problems were structural and could be traced to B&O's small size relative to its competitors.

By the late 1980s, top management of B&O could identify at least eight problems of major concern. They were:

• Niche Strategy

Because of its small size B&O did not compete across the board in consumer electronics but rather followed a niche strategy. This emphasised outstanding design, systems solutions, and rapid response to changing customer tastes. Despite heavy emphasis on research and development, it was becoming increasingly difficult to get new products to market in a timely enough manner.

• Economies of Scale

Although B&O designed and produced some proprietary components for its own use, it lacked economies of scale relative to its competitors. B&O purchased the rest of its components from others but lacked the buying power to get the best volume discounts.

• Dependence on Competition for Supply

Most of the purchased components were bought from Philips, and to a lesser extent from other potential competitors. This left B&O potentially vulnerable to delivery schedules over which it had no control. If component shipments were delayed for even a few months, it would seriously impair B&O's strategy of timely introduction of a constant stream of new products. On the other hand, B&O's longtime purchasing experience with Philips had always been highly satisfactory.

• Economies of Scope

Following a niche strategy meant that B&O could not offer its sales outlets a complete line of products. Thus the products of competitors were nearly always displayed side-by-side with B&O's products, competing for floor space and the sales forces' attention.

• Price

Since B&O needed to cover heavy investments in research and development with relatively modest sales volume, its products were always high-priced compared to those of its competitors.

• Sensitivity to Business Cycles

B&O's sales were extremely sensitive to business cycles. On the other hand, its cost structure was not flexible enough to adjust quickly to variable sales volume. The result was periodic losses even with modest swings in sales.

* Foreign Exchange Exposure

Since B&O produced nearly all of its products in Denmark but sold 77% outside of Denmark, it was potentially very sensitive to foreign exchange operating and transaction exposures. For example, when foreign currencies strengthened relative to the Danish krone, B&O's exported products could become more price competitive. This would be only partially offset by the higher foreign exchange costs of imported components. The reverse was also true. If foreign currencies weakened, B&O could face a negative foreign exchange effect. With respect to transaction exposure, B&O hedged most exposures with forward contracts.

* Shareholder Strength

Although B&O's B-shares were listed on the Copenhagen Stock Exchange, the controlling A-shares were held by foundations, representing descendants of the founders, and a group of five Danish institutional investors. An investment agreement among the A-shareholders ensured that no unfriendly takeover could occur. However, the family members, in particular, did not have outside funds that could be used to finance additional A- or B-share issues. B&O's modest financial results during the 1980's also precluded significant internal financing for growth and would make it difficult to attract new investors if a public equity issue should be attempted. Additional equity at an international price was called for, but without giving up control.

8.2. The Consumer Electronics Industry

The worldwide consumer electronics industry was and is characterised by rapid technological development and obsolescence, significant economies of scale and scope, a high degree of capital intensity, declining unit prices, and fierce global competition among multinational firms.

The pace of technological development up to 1990 is illustrated in Exhibit 8.1. The main audio/video product lines in the 1990's are derivatives of the old television, videorecorder, phonograph and radio industries. In 1990 about 80% of B&O's sales were of products first introduced in the same or the two preceding fiscal years. This was typical of the industry worldwide. Thus the technological pace placed a heavy emphasis on timely research and development, which necessitated heavy capital investment costs.

Exhibit 8.1:   Technological Developments Within the Consumer Electronics Industry as of 1990.

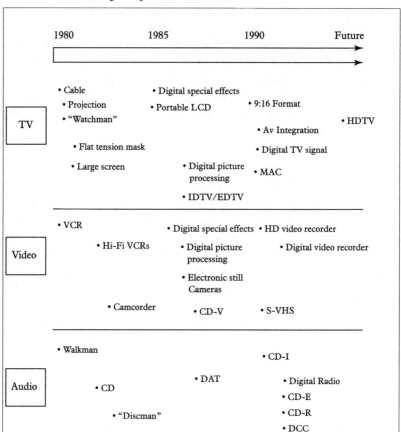

8.3. The Competition

B&O's main competitors in 1990 included six large Japanese and three large European companies. Notably absent were any significant U.S. competitors since they were mostly eliminated by intense Japanese competition during the 1980's. The main Japanese competitors were Sony, Sanyo, Hitachi, Toshiba, Yamaha, and Matsushita.

The three principal European competitors were survivors of an ongoing consolidation process in Europe. Exhibit 8.2 shows that Philips, Thomson

CSF, and Nokia were the survivors of 16 European companies in the television sector of consumer electronics.[1] In addition, the two principal British competitors, GEC and Rank, were taken over by Hitachi and Toshiba, respectively.

The nature of consumer electronics products lends itself to mass production and mass distribution methods. Gaining economies of scale and scope, while denying these to competitors, is a critical determinant of competitive advantage. However, a few niche companies, such as B&O, have managed to survive despite lacking such economies.

Looking ahead from 1990, B&O's management felt that historically-intense competition for the European market could become even fiercer. Protective barriers were being dismantled as a result of the drive to form a single internal market within the EU by 1992, and possibly within an expanded EU. Indeed some of the mergers shown in Exhibit 8.2 were motivated by the need to restructure in anticipation of the single internal market. The type of barriers in consumer electronics most likely to disappear were expected to be: disparate technical standards, government purchasing preferences for national firms, and corporate charter provisions preventing unfriendly takeovers.

On the other hand, EU subsidies and regulatory support were expected by management to continue for European-based electronics firms operating in such critical high technology areas as computers, semiconductors, and telecommunications. Two of the beneficiaries were expected to be Philips and Thomson. As we will see shortly, Philips was both a competitor and an ally of B&O. Evidence of EU support for Philips and Thomson had been demonstrated when the EU rejected Japan's broadcasting standard for high-definition television (HDTV) in favour of a European standard developed with heavy subsidies from the Dutch and French governments.

8.4. Ownership and Control

B&O was founded in 1925 by Peter Bang and Svend Olufsen. It remained a privately-owned company until 1977, when B-shares were sold to the public and B&O listed on the Copenhagen Stock Exchange. In the follow-

---

1. Although Grundig was controlled by Philips, which owned 32% of its shares, it could be considered a fourth European competitor because it competed as if it were an independent company.

Exhibit 8.2:   Mergers in the European TV Industry.

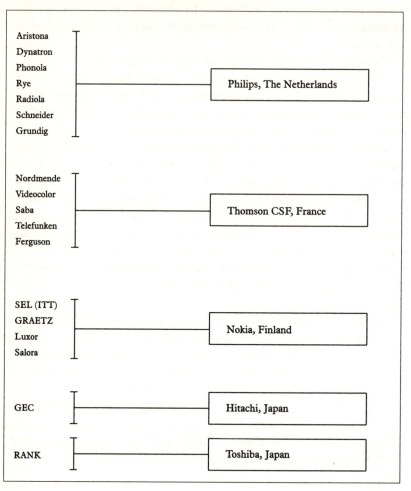

ing years public ownership was gradually increased, with a participating preferred share issue sold to institutional investors in 1981, and a public B-share issue in 1983. In 1988 the family heirs and institutional investors signed an investment agreement which gave the right of first refusal to each other on A-share transfers. An important objective of both the heirs and institutional investors was to maintain control in order to ensure that B&O could continue to pursue its long range strategy while remaining a Danish-owned company.

8.5. Finance

B&O's historical financial results prior to the strategic alliance in 1990 were typified by extreme volatility both in operating results and share price development. The cumulative returns to stockholders were also quite modest. Exhibit 8.3 shows the key financial results for the period 1986-1991. Exhibit 8.4 presents the income statements for fiscal 1990 and 1991. Exhibit 8.5 shows the balance sheets as of May 31, 1990 and 1991. Exhibit 8.6 shows the share price development during the period 1983-1991. Cumulatively, Exhibits 8.3 to 8.6 capture the financial situation both before and after the strategic alliance (June 1990).

Exhibits 8.3: B&O Financial Highlights for the Group.

(million kr.)	86/87	87/88	88/89	89/90	90/91
Turnover					
Turnover	1,902.1	1,955.7	2,098.8	2,279.5	2,180.1
Turnover outside Denmark	1,451.9	1,472.9	1,591.1	1,729.4	1,677.8
Turnover outside Denmark as a percentage of total turnover	76.3	75.3	75.8	75.9	77.0
Earnings					
Operating earnings	137.8	39.5	85.3	91.1	(47.1)
Earnings before extraordinary items	81.1	(19.5)	47.6	28.5	(115.5)
Earnings before tax	81.1	(19.5)	48.8	68.0	(135.5)
Earnings after tax and minority interests	53.1	(8.6)	32.3	55.3	(74.4)
Total Assets					
Total assets	1,332.9	1,337.2	1,459.4	1,715.6	1,685.2
Shareholders' fund at year-end	478.3	477.9	505.3	603.5	656.5
Attributable to minority shareholders	–	–	–	–	183.4
Asset cover, % incl. shares held by minority shareholders	35.9	35.7	34.6	35.2	49.8
Return on investment on June 1. 1990, %	18.4	(4.1)	10.2	13.5	(22.5)
Share Capital					
Share capital	100.0	124.0	124.0	124.0	124.0
Earnings after tax per nominal 100 kr. share (kr)*)	43	(/)	26	45	(60)
Dividend, % of nominal value	10	0	10	10	0
Quoted share price at May 31	432	432	277	402	530
Employment					
Number of employees at year-end	3,177	2,856	3,357	3,200	3,301

* Adjusted for share capital increases under market price

Exhibit 8.4:   B&O Income Statement for the Group.

(DKK million)	1990/91	1989/90
Turnover	2,180	2,280
Production costs	(1,465)	(1,514)
Gross earnings	715	766
Research and development costs	(167)	(165)
Sales and marketing costs	(477)	(416)
Administrative costs	(120)	(98)
Other operating income	2	4
Operating earnings	(47)	91
Net financing costs	(68)	(63)
Extraordinary items	(20)	40
Earnings before tax	(135)	68
Corporate taxes	35	(13)
Net earnings (loss)	(100)	55
Minority interest	26	–
B&O Holding's share of earnings	(74)	55

Exhibit 8.5:   B &O Balance Sheet for the Group (May 31).

(DKK million)	1991	1990
Assets		
Cash in hand	41	24
Inventory	531	638
Accounts receivable	422	425
Total current assets	994	1,087
Tangible fixed assets	600	539
Intangible fixed assets	86	84
Financial investments	5	5
Total fixed assets	691	628
Total assets	1,685	1,715
Liabilities		
Accounts payable	145	123
Short-term debt	489	738
Long-term debt	188	199
Total debt	822	1,060
Provisions (taxes, etc.)	23	52
Retained earnings	321	347
Reserves	–	31
Capital surplus	212	101
Common stock (nominal/value)	124	124
Total net worth	657	603
Minority interest	183	–
Total liabilities and net worth	1685	1,715

Exhibit 8.6: Share Price Development 1983-1991.

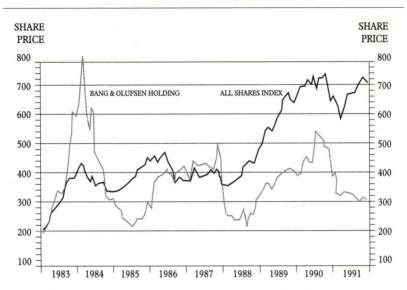

Source: Copenhagen Stock Exchange.

8.6. Marketing

B&O produced a line of audio/video products, such as televisions, videorecorders and stereo systems, which could easily be connected into a coordinated household entertainment system. B&O products had a worldwide reputation for advanced design, ease of use, and systems integration. In addition to excellent technical qualities, B&O products were designed to appear as ultramodern furniture pieces.

B&O marketed its products worldwide through its own sales subsidiaries and independent distributors. In the United States it experimented with franchised outlets selling exclusively B&O products. About 77% of B&O's sales were outside of Denmark. Although it had a respectable share of the Danish audio/video market it had a relatively small share of each of its other geographic markets.

B&O products appealed to those who placed a high value on lifestyle. Its customers were willing to pay a premium price for high quality, user-friendly products featuring a futuristic design. B&O had a rather large share of this narrow product market niche.

8.7. Production

Most of B&O's production was located in Jutland, Denmark, in the towns of Struer, Lemvig, and Skive. As of mid-1990, B&O employed about 3,300 persons, of which about 85% were located in Denmark. The rest were located in numerous sales and service subsidiaries abroad. About 10% of the Danish employees were engaged in product development.

B&O produced a significant share of the components it needed. Some of these were proprietary products based on B&O's own research and development. The rest were standard items but were self-produced in order to guarantee quality and assurance of delivery. The balance of components were sourced outside. Philips was a major European supplier. Some of the Japanese electronic firms were also suppliers.

B&O assembled all of its products at its manufacturing locations in Jutland. Although labour was relatively costly in Denmark, its reliability and productivity were also high, The direct labour content of most of B&O's products was modest, but the research and development overhead was quite significant because of the relatively small production runs of each product.

8.8. Restructuring the Corporate Organization

In anticipation of future cooperative agreements, during 1989 B&O, in cooperation with its financial advisors, Gudme Raaschou Investment Bank, devised a creative reorganisation plan which became effective on June 1, 1990. B&O A/S changed its name to B&O Holding A/S and continued as the listed company. A new company was established by B&O Holding A/S as a 100%-owned subsidiary. It was called B&O A/S and took over the audio/video activities, comprising about 85% of the group's activities. Exhibit 8.7 shows B&O's corporate organization before and after the change.

The new corporate• organization had several advantages over the old one:

• B&O's fundamental image, product concepts, management situation and strategies were preserved.
• B&O Holding remained controlled by the existing shareholders and had the same Board of Directors as B&O A/S. The latter accounted for about 85% of the group's total business.

Exhibit 8.7:   Corporate Reorganisation of June 1, 1990.

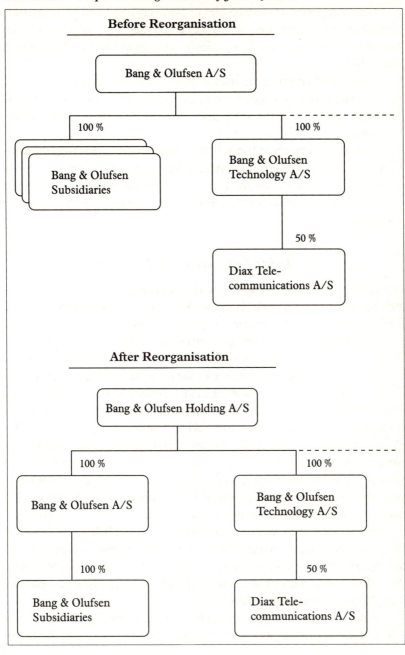

- In the future, new subsidiaries of B&O Holding could be easily established to exploit new technologies or products unrelated to the existing product line. These new subsidiaries could then form alliances or joint ventures with whatever companies were appropriate for their type of activities.
- The terms of equity participation in the new subsidiaries could vary with market conditions and their synergistic value to specific partners without reference to the share price of B&O Holding or its other subsidiaries.
- Potential partners could buy into just those activities that were valuable to them and not be forced to invest in less suitable activities.
- In the future B&O Holding could sell off subsidiaries that it no longer wanted, perhaps to its partner, or to another company acceptable to its partner.

8.9. Joint Venture with Ericsson

During the 1980's, B&O had received numerous feelers from companies attracted by its upscale market niche. Some were interested in acquiring B&O. Some wanted to conduct cooperative activities, while others proposed joint ventures or strategic alliances. Among the most interesting of these possibilities were proposals from Ericsson (Sweden) and Philips.

During 1989, prior to the strategic alliance with Philips, a joint venture to develop and market products in the telecommunications industry was proposed by Ericsson, one of the leading multinational firms in the world in the industry. Ericsson was particularly interested in a small digital telephone concentrator which had been developed by B&O. This product was complementary to the telephone exchanges for which Ericsson was famous. Although the B&O digital telephone concentrator was not fully-developed, it represented potential future competition for Ericsson, particularly if B&O could find another strong partner.

The proposed joint venture was attractive to B&O because it would have had difficulties financing further development and improvement of the digital telephone concentrator. Moreover, this product would be sold through different marketing channels and to a different type of customer than B&O's existing audio/video product line.

The proposal was that B&O provide the technology and product, while Ericsson would provide access to its worldwide marketing network. Ericsson would invest DKK 50 million in return for 50% of a newly-formed corporate joint venture, *Diax*. Agreement was reached and Diax began operations January 1, 1990. B&O's interest was placed under B&O Technology A/S, a subsidiary of B&O Holding, as part of the June 1990 reorganisation. This was such a small investment that there was little stock market reaction. Ericsson is discussed further in Part VII.

8.10. Strategic Alliance with Philips

As a major supplier of components to B&O for nearly 60 years, Philips was very comfortable with B&O and its management. Several times Philips had approached B&O about acquiring an equity interest or cooperating in various activities. Both companies were ripe for something positive to happen when negotiations were opened in 1989.

Philips was eager to join forces with B&O in the upscale consumer electronics market. Philips had a product designed for this market but it did not possess the high quality image of B&O's products. Philips was also worried that if financial pressure continued, B&O might choose a competitor as a partner. A Japanese competitor would be very damaging. Philips had always been supported politically by B&O in their efforts to gain national and EU support to make the remaining European companies more competitive vis-à-vis Japanese competitors. Philips was also interested in cementing relations with B&O as a major customer for Philips' components.

B&O was interested in Philips because a closer relationship could partially solve some of B&O's long run problems. In particular, Philips could give B&O the following advantages:

- More rapid access to new technology,
- assistance in converting Philips' technology into B&O product applications,
- assurance of component supplies at large volume discounts from Philips itself, as well as from its large network of suppliers,
- equity financing from Philips.

During the course of 1989-1990 a strategic alliance between B&O and Philips was agreed upon. It went into effect on June 1, 1990, simultaneously with B&O's corporate reorganisation. The main features of the alliance were:

- Philips would provide B&O with instant access to its new technology, but not vice versa.
- Philips would give B&O access to its supplier network to take advantage of the discounts and delivery terms that Philips enjoyed. However, B&O was not forced to buy from Philips or its suppliers.
- Philips invested DKK 342 million in an equity increase for B&O A/S in return for a 25% ownership of the expanded company.
- Philips agreed not to be represented on the Board of Directors of B&O A/S or B&O Holding but was given the right to veto the choice for President of B&O A/S. However, they could not choose the President.
- Philips was given the right to buy another 25% of the equity in B&O A/S for net book value if the B&O Holding A-shares should in the future be sold to investors outside of the present group. This protected Philips from having a competitor overseeing its activities with B&O A/S.
- B&O was given the right to buy back its shares from Philips at net book value if the alliance did not live up to expectations.

When B&O's strategic alliance with Philips was announced to the public on May 3, 1990, the reaction was instantaneously favourable both in the press and in the stock market. B&O's share price jumped by 35% during the next two days and remained at the new level until the Gulf War crisis depressed the share price once again. Exhibit 8.8 shows B&O's share price development before and after the announcement.

8.11. Synergies: Philips NV Versus Portfolio Investors

Philips anticipated gaining enough operating synergies from its strategic alliance with Bang & Olufsen to justify paying a 35% premium over the existing May 2, 1990 market price for new shares. Investors ratified that decision initially so that all shares, old and new, traded at the price paid by Philips. However, operating synergies do not occur immediately. It takes time to implement fundamental changes in strategy, such as increasing outsourcing, downsizing, reducing scope of product line and geographical areas served, and deepening marketing/ promotional efforts. Furthermore, strategic alliances are historically unstable. They often lead to either a "divorce" or a "marriage," but rarely to retention of the status quo. The marriage usually entails one partner buying out the other.

When the Gulf War started, Bang & Olufsen's sales and earnings

Exhibit 8.8:   Stock Price Development: Bang & Olufsen. From 1/4 1990 to 31/5 1990.

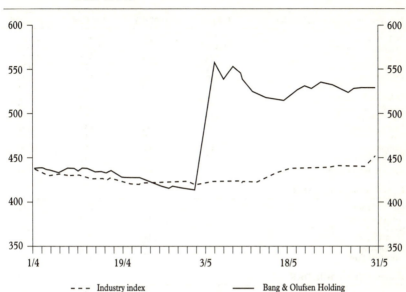

declined due to its structural sensitivity to business cycles. Its high-end products were and still are very dependent on buyers having high disposable income and confidence about the future. The decline in already meager earnings, combined with the gloomy outlook, caused investors to lose patience and dump their Bang & Olufsen shares after the initial euphoria of the Philips alliance wore off. This resulted in a steady share price decline during 1991 and 1992.

8.12. The Aftermath – A Longer Term Perspective

The operating synergies began to be reflected in the financial results in 1993 and continued to impact favourably on earnings in the following years. Bang & Olufsen's share price reflected this recovery and rose rapidly during the next two years (August 1995). Exhibit 8.9 shows the key financial results during the period 1991-1995 (August). Exhibit 8.10 shows the stock price development for the period 1988-1995 (August). Exhibit 8.11 presents a comparison of net profit to stock price during the same period. After 1993 B&O outperformed the Danish Stock Market in both stock

Exhibit 8.9: Bang & Olufsen Holding. Summary of Fiscal 1994/95.
			Financial Statement.

Income Statement Mill DKK	1991/92	1992/93	1993/94	1994/95
Net turnover	2,246	2,126	2,401	2,618
Production costs	1,451	1,422	1,527	1,614
Gross Result	794	704	874	1,004
Prod. devel.	202	177	171	176
Dist&market.	516	459	490	506
Administration costs	69	59	62	73
Other ord. income	13	3	4	-1
Operating profit	19	12	156	248
Net finance	-49	-50	-24	4
Profit before tax	-30	-38	131	252
Tax	15	18	32	75
Minorities	-14	-22	18	38
Profit after tax	-31	-34	81	139
Extraordinary items	0	-4	-6	0
Cashflow data Mill. DKK				
Depreciations	128	144	138	134
Cash earnings	97	110	219	273
Cash flow from operations	97	214	446	245
Investments	171	117	55	92
Dividends	0	0	12	15
Free cashflow	97	97	379	140
Balance Sheet Mill. DKK				
Fixed assets	732	680	600	557
Current assets	998	776	1,081	1,223
Long term debt	167	155	276	248
Net debt	470	357	-35	-184
Equity	623	580	661	776
Minorities	168	144	164	183
Balance	1,730	1,456	1,681	1,780
Key figures				
ROE%	-4.8%	-5.7%	13.1%	19.3%
Equity ratio	45.7%	49.8%	49.1%	53.9%
Operating margin	0.9%	0.6%	6.5%	9.5%
Interest cover	0.39	0.24	6.40	-61.90
Current ratio	2.5	2.35	2.80	2.70
Asset turnover	1.3	1.46	1.43	1.47
EPS	-24.8	-27.7	65.6	109.1
CEPS	177.5	149.2	236.3	285.1
BV	502.4	467.7	533.3	611.0
Dividend DKK/share	0.0	0.0	10	12.0
EBIT/share	15.6	9.8	125.5	199.7
Sales/share	1,811.0	1,714.5	1,936.3	2,111.3
Net cash/share	379.2	287.9	-28.2	-148.4

Source: Søren Gjelstrup, Gudme Raashou Securities A/S, dated 8-21-95.

price and profitability. It attained an international cost of capital by improving its operating performance, with the timely equity injection and some good advice from Philips. That advice was to outsource more of its manufacturing, narrow its geographic scope, and concentrate on design, where it had a competitive advantage. It is to the credit of Managing

Exhibit 8.10: Bang & Olufsen vs. Copenhagen Stock Exchange Index.
(January 1988 - December 1995).

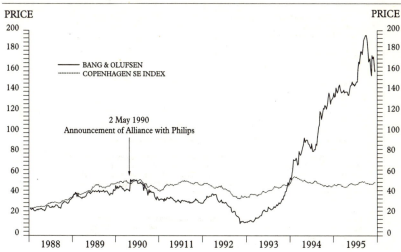

Source: Datastream.

Exhibit 8.11: Bang & Olufsen, Net Profit and Market Value.

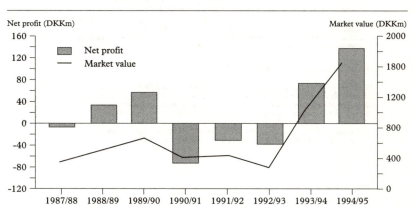

Note: Profit after tax and minorityinterests

Bang & Olufsen

Bang & Olufsen Holding A/S
Peter Bangs Vej 15
DK-7600 Struer

Phone: +45 97 85 11 22
Phone: +45 97 84 00 44 – ext.
Fax: +45 97 85 45 40
Telex: 6 65 19
AS Reg.:   38 303

The Copenhagen Stock Exchange A/S
Nikolaj Plads 6
DK-1067 Copenhagen K

(Translation)

Bang & Olufsen Holding to purchase Philips' equity stake in Bang & Olufsen A/S

Bang & Olufsen Holding is to acquire the 25% shareholding that Philips has owned in
Bang & Olufsen A/S since 1990. The price for the stake will be DKK 540 million.
The two groups' close cooperation will continue. The current cooperation agreement will
be extended five years ensuring both Bang & Olufsen access to Philips' technology and
Philips' status as Bang & Olufsen's preferred supplier.

Bang & Olufsen Holding will return to being the sole shareholder in its audio/video
subsidiary. Today, Philips owns 25% of the share capital, with the remaining 75% held
by Bang & Olufsen Holding.
Philips acquired the 25% shareholding for DKK 342 million in 1990. A substantial
economic recovery during recent years has made it possible for Bang & Olufsen to
re-purchase the shares.

Some key figures showing the development:

* After accumulating losses of DKK 207 million in three consecutive financial
  years from 1990 to 1993, Bang & Olufsen Holding has achieved pre-tax profits
  amounting to DKK 974 million in the years since, including the DKK 325 million
  being the expectations for 1996/97.

* Between 1990/91 and 1996/97, turnover has increased by approx.
  DKK 820 million to DKK 3 billion. The latter figure being the expectation for
  the financial year 1996/97.

* In 1990, Bang & Olufsen had short-term bank debt of more than DKK 500 million.
  Today, there is a positive cash balance of more than DKK 500 million.

The price of the stake will be based on a formula agreed upon in 1990. The transaction is
conditional upon the approval by a General Assembly of Bang & Olufsen Holding, and the
Board of Management of N.V. Philips Electronics. An extraordinary General Assembly will
therefore be called for 24th June 1997.

Future continued close cooperation

There will be no change in the close relationship between Bang & Olufsen and Philips.
When Philips made its investment in 1990, an agreement was signed providing for the
exchange of know-how, joint exploitation of technology, mutual licensing etc., and
Bang & Olufsen has steadily increased its purchases of components from Philips.

This cooperation has functioned to the satisfaction of both parties - a point which
is underlined by the fact that the agreement will be extended for a further
five years.

Struer, 27th May 1997

Peter Skak Olufsen   Anders Knutsen
Chairman of the Supervisory Board   President, CEO

For further information please call Bang & Olufsen, Mr. Anders Knutsen - tel.: +45 96 84 10 00
or Philips, Mr. Ben Geerts, Press Officer - tel: +31 40 275 70 47

Director Anders Knutsen and his staff, who were responsible for designing and implementing B&O's successful post-alliance strategy.

Repurchase of Philips' 25% Equity share in B&O A/S.

On May 27, 1997, B&O Holding announce that it would repurchase Philips' 25% equity share ownership of B&O A/S for a price of DKK 540 million. The buyout price had been set by formula as part of the original strategic alliance agreement in 1990. Based on the original equity injection of DKK 342 million the repurchase price represented a 58 % capital gain for Philips. Exhibit 8.12 presents the Press Release for this proposed transaction.

◀ *Exhibit 8.12: Press Release on B&O Holding's Proposes Buyout of Philips' 25% Equity Stake in B&O A/S.*

Part V

**Strategies of
Finnish Corporations**

In this part of the book three cases are presented which illustrate strategic dimensions of the transition of the Finnish equity market from segmentation to integration with global capital markets. The Amer case (Chapter 9) describes the whole corporate and capital market transition process with different types of equity issues designed to seize opportunities in the prevailing market conditions. The Nokia case (Chapter 10) demonstrates how a fast growing global company from a small domestic capital market can reduce its cost of capital to the level of its large global competitors by globalizing its capital sourcing. Huhtamaki (Chapter 11) represents a strategic alliance with a foreign partner, where the foreign partner supplied capital, but the controlling interest remained with the old Finnish shareholders.

The 1980s and early 1990s was the era of transition for a number of companies listed on the Finnish stock exchange. As deregulation went on and competition became increasingly international, it was necessary fordomestic conglomerates to become leading international actors in specialised fields. The transition process involved disposal of a number of non-core domestic businesses as well as acquisitions of domestic and international companies in core business areas.

As Finnish companies became more international, they established manufacturing plants in a number of foreign countries, first in Europe, later in North-America and Asia. Their capital sourcing followed the same pattern. Finance departments had to supply the funds to finance both internal growth and foreign acquisitions. Capital sourcing spread out from domestic markets through European markets to global markets.

Many of the first international equity issues of Finnish companies in the early 1980s were directed issues in a single foreign market. Foreign investors saw at the outset of deregulation the capital gains opportunity of the Finnish stock market. As was shown in Chapter 2, some Finnish companies also listed their shares in Stockholm, Sweden.

In the mid-1980s, Finnish companies introduced a new type of shares, free shares, which were freely available for foreign investors. Finnish stocks were considered to be cheap in an international comparison. However foreign ownership, and thus free shares, was first limited to 20% of shares. The limit was later raised to 40 % of shares. Free shares were trading at a premium compared to restricted share series. A number of Finnish companies seized the opportunity to lower their capital costs by targeting equity issues of free shares mainly to UK investors, and listed their shares on the London Stock Exchange or on its International SEAQ-system.

Investors considered Finnish stock as Finnish risk, not as exposure to specific industries. The Finnish capital market was semi-segmented. New issues were priced at a discount. Domestic Finnish banks were typically the lead managers of the underwriting syndicate. Foreign ownership in listed companies was around 10-15%. During the boom period of 1986-1988 many foreign investors made considerable profits in Finland. The Amer case illustrates a pioneer company of that time that used both private placement and international equity offerings, as well as listed its shares abroad.

In the early 1990s Finnish capital markets became more efficient and well integrated with the global capital markets. As described in Chapter 2, regulations were abandoned. The 0.5 % stamp duty on stock exchange transactions was lifted in 1992 and all restrictions on foreign ownership abandoned in the beginning of 1993. Capital markets had become transparent already in 1989 when the new Securities Act, with Anglo-American style disclosure and insider dealing norms, was enforced.

However, international investors, particularly U.S. investors, had lost apetite for country exposures. They were stock pickers, looking for the best global investment alternatives in different industries. Global companies with a dominant market position in a well-defined field rather than conglomerates attracted investors' attention. Investment analysts were moving from country analysts to sector analysts. Pressure to restructure and streamline conglomerates was on.

The first Finnish companies to exploit the U.S. capital market and to crosslist their shares on the New York Stock Exchange were Nokia, Rauma and Valmet. Subsequently Nokia's stock was completely priced in dollars in the United States. The price formation of the other two companies was more ambiguous. The international equity offerings of Finnish companies in the 1990s were lead-managed by the major U.S. and U.K. investment banks. Domestic banks and stock broker companies only took care of the domestic or Nordic placement.

Strategic alliances with foreign companies were mainly used as means to exit from non-core businesses, or to obtain a lacking marketing channel, or resources to develop a product innovation into a world class business. The alliance served as a step-wise divestment suitable to find a proper new home for a former subsidiary. Typically the foreign buyer first bought a minority interest and after a few years the remaining shares of the Finnish subsidiary. Huhtamaki's strategic alliance with Procordia from Sweden incorporated both an acquisition and the potential for a later divestment.

In the 1990s a number of state-owned companies were privatised and listed on the Helsinki Stock Exchange. The majority of their initial public offerings were placed with international investors.

It seems that Finnish companies have been able to exploit the international capital markets to reduce their cost of capital. During the transition period in the 1980s stock market reactions to international equity issues were mainly positive. Companies were able to issue new equity at favorable prices while the stock market was going up. In the 1990s, stock market reactions to new issue announcements were mainly negative, with the exception of high-tech companies that were enjoying the investor rally. The stock market reactions to the equity issues in Part V can be summarised as follows.

Company	Event date	Pre-issue price development	Immediate reaction	3 months reaction	>1 year price development	Final outcome
Amer						
Amer	May 25, 1984	+/–	+/–	+/–	–	Continues in
Amer	Feb. 25, 1986	++	+	–	+	operation
Amer	May 22, 1989	+/–	+	–	–	
Nokia						
Nokia	Feb. 14, 1983	++	++	+	–	Continues in
Nokia	March 3,1986	+	++	++	+	operation
Nokia	May 13, 1993	+	–	++	++	
Nokia	May 25, 1994	+	++	++	++	
Huhtamaki						
Huhtamaki	June 29, 1993	–	+	–	+	Divestment

9. Amer Group:
A Directed Public Issue,
A Private Placement and
An Euroequity Issue

Kaisa Vikkula

9.1. Introduction

This case actually covers three international equity issues by Amer: A
directed issue in 1984, a private placement in 1986, and an Euroequity
issue in 1989.

Amer was mainly a domestic company until the latter part of the 1980's.
In 1984 Amer acquired the largest Finnish car importer and distributor,
Korpivaara, that exposed it to large scale imports from Japan. The net sales
of Korpivaara were about the size of Amer. The acquisitions of MacGregor
and Wilson changed Amer to become a true multinational corporation with
foreign manufacturing and export operations. The major foreign acquisitions by Amer are presented in Exhibit 9.1. In all acquisitions Amer seeked
to exploit its marketing skills in internationally branded products, market
knowledge, management experience, and financial resources.

In the early 1990's, after these investments Amer was a diversified
Finnish multinational company that concentrated on marketing, manufacturing and importing of internationally known branded products. The
group operated in business areas where it was close to the consumer, that

Exhibit 9.1: *Major International Acquisitions of Amer.*

Year	Company	Line of business	Country	Consideration
1979	Canadian Hockey	Ice-hockey equipment	Canada	
1986	divested			
1987	MacGregor Golf	Golf equipment	USA	
1987	Hobart/McIntosh	Paper wholesaler	USA	
1987	Rias	Plastics wholesaler	Denmark	
1989	Rias divested			
1989	Wilson Sporting Goods Co.	Sporting equipment	USA	$ 197 million
1989	Van Stolk & Reese	Paper wholesaler	Holland	$ 12 million

Exhibit 9.2:   Amer Group's Net Sales (12 months).

By product FIM million.

	1991[1]	%	1990[1]	%
Korpivaara (motor vehicles)	2,503	33	2,903	35
Sporting Goods	2,266	30	2,371	29
Paper	1,662	22	1,622	20
Tobacco	571	7	529	7
Publishing and Printing	403	5	336	4
Marimekko	117	2	110	1
Portfolio Investments	78	1	112	1
Divested operations			226	3
– internal sales	– 16		– 28	
Net sales	7,584	100	8,181	100

By Geographic Area.

	28 Feb. 1991	%	28 Feb. 1990	%
Finland	3,790	50	4,215	52
Europe	785	10	733	9
North America	2,672	35	2,894	35
Others	337	5	339	4
Net Sales	7,584	100	8,181	100

[1] The financial year ending 28 of February.

were not sensitive to economic fluctuations and that did not require heavy expenditure on industrial fixed assets.

In Finland as of 1992, Amer was the leading manufacturer and distributor of cigarettes under a license from Philip Morris. Furthermore, the company was the largest importer of motor vehicles (Toyota, Citroën, Suzuki), one of the largest paper wholesalers, and it had a strong market position in publishing and printing (Time/design, Time/system, non-fiction and textbooks). Overseas operations that consisted of sporting goods, represented 50 % of FIM 7.6 billion (USD 1.8 billion) corporate net sales. Following the acquisition of MacGregor Golf Company and Wilson Sporting Goods Co. in the late 1980's Amer was one of the leading golf and tennis equipment manufacturers in the world. The distribution of net sales is shown in Exhibit 9.2.

9.2. Internationalisation of Capital Structure

Amer was established in 1950 by four foundations; the Student Union of the Helsinki School of Economics, The National Graduates Associations of Engineers, and of BAs' and MBA's, as well as the Land and Water Technology Foundation. The goal was to generate profits for the funding of business and technical education and research in Finland. Amer started out by manufacturing and marketing American blend cigarettes. The 1970's was a decade of growth and diversification for Amer. New business sectors were added to the portfolio.

By 1976 it became clear that the initial founders did not have enough financial resources to finance the growth of Amer. A plan of stock exchange introduction and share issue in 1977 was made. In order to achieve wide enough ownership structure for the listing, Amer targeted a share issue of preference shares to the individual members of the founding foundations at a subscription price of FIM 18 in 1976. The listing issue in 1977, doubling the share capital to FIM 32 million (USD 7.6), was also priced at FIM 18.

The ordinary K shares, all held by the four founders, carried 10 votes each, whereas each 10 shares of Series A or a fraction thereof carried one vote. Thus the difference in voting power between the two series was 100 times. As of 1992, the four founders held 95.5 % of the votes, but 30.9 % of shares. The preference A shares take precedence over ordinary K shares in receiving from the profits available for distribution a dividend amounting to 10 % of the nominal share value. A shares are always entitled to a dividend at least equal to that of K shares. The nominal value of the share was first FIM 10, but was raised to FIM 20 in 1982.

In the early 1980's, Amer was ready for a major new acquisition. The company realised that it was about to outgrow the Finnish market and should start to look for new growth opportunities abroad. Due mainly to its Finnish based operations Amer was totally unknown to foreign investors. In May 1984 Amer was listed on the London Stock Exchange together with a targeted new equity issue to British and US institutional investors. Amer introduced a new Series of shares, free preference shares, that were freely transferable to foreign investors. A total of 600,000 Series A preference free shares were placed, amounting to FIM 78 million (USD 19 million) in total proceeds and representing a 10.7 % increase in share capital. The shares were sold at FIM 130, an 8 % premium over restricted preference shares. The price premium of Amer free shares relative to restricted shares was normally around 20 % in the market.

The lead manager of the issue was Morgan Grenfell. Cazenove, a UK stock broker, selected the long-term investors that were invited to subscribe. Investor presentations were organised in London, Edinburgh and New York. Since the introductory foreign issue, Amer has given an investor presentation twice a year in London and once in Edinburgh and New York.

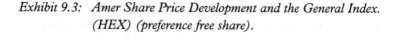

Exhibit 9.3: Amer Share Price Development and the General Index.
         (HEX) (preference free share).

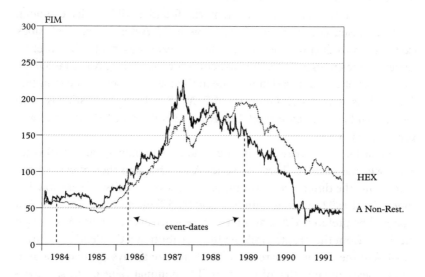

The purpose of the London listing was not to raise capital, but to establish Amer's name internationally and to enhance company reliability for future international acquisitions. Amer was among the first Finnish companies to issue free shares. When foreign investors became aware of the strong economic growth and domestic consumer demand in Finland in the mid-1980's, Amer became their favourite stock. International investors who wanted to have Finnish exposure in their portfolio bought Amer shares. The share price of free shares soared from FIM 50 in the summer of 1985 to an all time high, FIM 266, in the fall of 1987 (Exhibit 9.3).

In April 1986 Amer raised FIM 23.7 million (USD 5.6 million) of new share capital, FIM 162.7 million (USD 38.7 million) in total proceeds, through a private placement to one US institutional investor alone. The arranger of the issue was First Boston. The issue represented an increase of 11.6 % in the share capital. It was priced at FIM 137.34, a small discount to market price. However, shortly after the issue the price climbed to over FIM 170.

After the issue Unitas, a Finnish stock broker, wrote an investment analysis of Amer with a buy recommendation. The recommendation was based on Amer's strong cash position, favourable profit trend (P/E equal to 12), low risk business, and a shareholder friendly policy. Amer had been issuing shares on advantageous terms to shareholders and had increased the adjusted dividend income of its shareholders at an annual rate of 22 % in the period of 1977-1985.

In 1987 Amer established a sponsored American Depositary Receipt (ADR) facility with Citibank N.A. in New York, but the facility has remained passive. US institutional investors developed a knowledge about European equities and preferred trading in Europe where the liquidity and the knowledge of the local stock market was better. In the meanwhile, Continental investment researchers became interested in Amer and wrote investment recommendations. Demand from private investors in Germany, France, and Switzerland arose. Amer arranged institutional investor presentations in Frankfurt, Paris, Zurich and Geneva with Deutsche Bank, Credit Suisse, and Swiss Bank Corporation.

The third major international equity issue was launched in May 1989, just around the time of the deregulation of the Helsinki Stock Exchange. During the two following years the trading volume and the market capitalisation of The Helsinki Stock Exchange shrank to half. The issue, 750,000 free shares priced at FIM 161, a 6 % discount to market price, was targeted mainly to Japanese investors, but also to European institutional investors. The total proceeds of the share issue were about FIM 121 million (USD 29 million), and the increase in equity capital FIM 15 million (USD 4 million). The lead manager of the issue was Japanese Nomura and the co-lead Kansallis-Osake-Pankki, a Finnish stock broker (see Exhibit 9.4). The initial market reaction was positive.

After the issue was launched, Nomura gave an investment recommendation of attractive buy with a P/E estimate of 11 for 1990, and of 10 for 1991. The recommendation was motivated by considerable longer term synergies of Wilson and MacGregor and excellent prospects for leisure business. James Capel, a British stockbrokerage, was more cautious with a long term buy recommendation. Amer's earnings were stagnant but the shares, according to James Capel, were selling at a 10 % discount to the Finnish market as a whole. They also saw an above average long term growth in the leisure and sport business, but considered the price paid for Wilson too high. Their estimate of Amer's P/E for 1990 was 10 and for 1991 it was 9.

Japanese investors had participated in the London presentations already in 1986-1988 and special presentations were organised in Tokyo in 1988 and 1989. Three factors awoke the interest of Japanese investors: Amer was importing Toyota cars to Finland. Finland had the largest market share of Japanese cars of all the European countries. The Japanese consumers found the Marimekko design products (a subsidiary of Amer) attractive.

Exhibit 9.4   The Amer Group 1988-Tombstone

OFFERING CIRCULAR

AMER GROUP LTD

(incorporated with limited liability in the Republic of Finland)

International Offering of
750,000 New Free A-Shares
of nominal value FIM 20 each

Issue Price FIM 161.00 per Share

Pursuant to the authorisation by the shareholders of Amer Group Ltd at the Annual General Meeting held on 22nd June, 1988 Amer Group Ltd (the "Company" or "Amer") proposes to issue 750,000 new free A-Shares (the "New A-Shares"), having a nominal value of FIM 20 each. The New A-Shares are being offered by means of an international offering outside the Republic of Finland.

Application has been made to the Council of The International Stock Exchange of the United Kingdom and the Republic of Ireland Limited for the New A-Shares to be admitted to the Official List. Copies of this document have been delivered to the Registrar of Companies in England and Wales as required by Section 149 of the Financial Services Act 1986. The New A-Shares will also be listed on the Helsinki Stock Exchange.

The New A-Shares will rank *pari passu* with the free A-Shares of the Company which are currently in issue and will be entitled to the full amount of any dividend declared on the free A-Shares of the Company for the financial period ending 28th February, 1990. Dividends paid by the Company to shareholders who are not residents of the Republic of Finland are subject to deduction of Finnish withholding tax, as described under "Taxation".

The New A-Shares, in the form of interim share certificates, are expected to be available on 8th June, 1989. As soon as possible, the Company will issue definitive share certificates in exchange for interim certificates.

Nomura International
Kansallis Banking Group

Banque Indosuez	**James Capel & Co.**
Cazenove & Co.	**Deutsche Bank Capital Markets Limited**
Enskilda Securities Skandinaviska Enskilda Limited	**Goldman Sachs International Limited**
Morgan Stanley International	**Swiss Bank Corporation** Investment Banking

---

The timing of the issue was very successful from Amer's point of view. First, shortly after the issue the share price of Amer started to decline along with the bear market of the Helsinki Stock Exchange and did not recover until 1994. Secondly, during the preparation of the issue Amer engaged itself in the negotiations of the Wilson acquisition. The acquisition was completed in March and the share issue proceeds were needed to finance the acquisition and to reduce leverage.

In summary, Amer has been one of the most active Finnish companies in issuing new share capital. Altogether in the 1980's Amer made five rights issue to existing shareholders, three bonus (capitalisation) issues, three issues targeted to international investors, one bond issue with warrants, and two issues targeted to the shareholders of the acquired company to finance the acquisition. Through these issues the equity capital of the company was raised from FIM 32 million (USD 6.6 million) in 1980 to FIM 379 million (USD 90.2 million) in 1989. Of the total FIM 1.1 billion (USD 260 million) half of the issue proceeds was collected through targeted share issues to new institutional investors. A total of FIM 361 million (USD 86 million) was targeted to international investors. The proportion of free shares relative to all shares outstanding rose from 8.7 % in 1984 to 21.4 % in 1989. The majority of free shares were held by foreign investors.

9.3. Reasons for the Internationalisation of Amer's Capital Structure

The action of Amer to go for international equity markets and raise new capital was motivated by international pull and domestic push factors. The international pull factors were dominating in the company's first international operations. Only in the late 1980's did the domestic push factors play an active role in the internationalisation process of capital costs. The major international pull factors were strong foreign demand and international deregulation of capital markets.

9.3.1. International Pull Factors

In the 1980's the Finnish economy outperformed OECD countries. The GNP growth in Finland in the 1980's averaged 3.7 % p.a. compared with 2.2 % p.a. for the OECD Europe. The growth of real total domestic demand averaged 3.9 % p.a. compared with 2.2 % p.a. for the OECD

Europe. The domestic real consumption growth accelerated to 6-7 % p.a. in 1987-1989. Inflation was in line with the OECD average. The political, foreign exchange and financial risk associated with portfolio investments in Finland was low. The Bank of Finland pursued a monetary policy of strong and stable currency. In fact, the Finnish markka was revaluated upward against other currencies by 4 % in early 1989.

Foreign institutional investors saw investment opportunities in Finland in the mid-1980's. The market forecast was good and stocks were internationally undervalued. For most foreign investors Finland was a totally unknown market. There were only very few Finnish multinationals. As was discussed in Chapter 2, Finnish companies were not listed abroad. Kone was the first one to list its shares in Stockholm in June 1982. Nokia and Wärtsilä followed in 1983. Instrumentarium was listed on NASDAQ in the United States (ADR) in 1983. Amer was the first Finnish company to list in London in 1984. Others followed in the late 1980's.

Foreign net equity investment flow (portfolio investments) to Finland increased by FIM 1.0 billion in 1986 and by FIM 1.3 billion in 1989. Since then foreign portfolio investments in Finnish bonds grew at the expense of equity investments. The increased foreign demand boosted the turnover on the stock exchange. The relative share of turnover in free shares to the total equity turnover on the Helsinki Stock Exchange rose from 13.9 % in 1985 to 30 % in 1988-1989.

The market capitalisation of the listed companies on the Helsinki Stock Exchange rose from FIM 10 billion (USD 2.4 billion) in 1981, to FIM 54 billion in 1986, and FIM 129 billion (USD 31 billion) in 1989. The proportion of free shares grew from FIM 9 billion (USD 2.1 billion) to FIM 20 billion (USD 5 billion) in 1989 representing 16 % of the total market capitalisation.

Amer was one of the favourite stocks of the international investors, because all its business sectors were benefiting from strong domestic consumer demand. The annual average value increase of Amer A restricted shares in 1984-1988 was 35.6 % compared to 21.4 % for the general index. Due to weak performance of Amer in 1989 the annual average value increase in 1985-1989 for Amer A free shares was 26.2 % and for the restricted shares 27.6 % compared with 38.5 % of the index. In 1985-87 Amer outperformed the index by some 25 %. The relative turnover in Amer free shares in Helsinki as a proportion of the amount of free shares outstanding rose to 79 % in 1986 and 88 % in 1988. The corresponding figures for the restricted share were 27-28 % (Exhibit 9.5)

Exhibit 9.5: Amer Share Data 1984-1990.

	1984	1985	1986	1987	1988	1989	1990
Number of shareholders	12,995	16,330	22,653	22,491	27,914	27,315	27,104
Market Capitalisation (FIM mill.)	710	1,798	3,432	2,850	2,983	2,441	933
Number of Shares (mill.)							
A restricted	5.2	7.7	10.2	10.2	12.9	12.9	12.9
A free	0.6	2.1	2.7	2.7	3.3	4.1	4.1
P/E A restr.	5.2	8.9	14.9	10.9	11.0	23.5	neg.
P/E A free	5.2	11.5	16.6	11.4	10.7	30.6	neg.
Relative turnover (%) [a]							
A restricted	8	24	28	20	27	14	4
A free	26	37	79	38	88	$49	89[b]
Proportion of free shares (%)	8.7	18.4	18.3	18.3	18.2	21.4	21.4

a. Annual turnover of Series A restricted (A free) shares on the Helsinki Stock Exchange in proportion to the amount of Series A restricted (A free) shares outstanding.
b. Including SEAQ turnover in London. The relative turnover in London was 62 % of the free share turnover.

Exhibit 9.6: Amer's Financial Performance 1986-1992.

FIM Million	1986	1987	1988	1989	1990	1991	1992
Net sales	2,973	4,516	5,831	8,181	7,584	6,957	7,000
Profit after financial items	184	273	294	185	– 9	– 35	91
Profit before extraordinary items	169	250	251	101	– 38	– 34	74
Shareholders' equity	619	743	1,379	1,438	1,405	1,535	2,160
Total capital employed	2,413	3,395	4,494	7,310	6,657	6,263	6,456
ROI, %	14.5	13.3	11.3	9.2	5.6	6.2	8.1
ROE, %	14.7	15.5	11.3	3.7	– 2.0	– 2.0	2.1
Equity/Assets,%	44	43	47	30	32	30	29

In 1990, this fortunate era came to an end. Finland entered the most severe recession since the 1930s and domestic consumption fell drasticaly. GDP fell by 6.5% in 1991 and another 3.5% in 1992. Unemployment exceeded 17% in 1993, and peaked at 20% in 1994. Amer's domestic sales suffered badly. As shown in Exhibit 9.6 Amer reported losses after financial items in 1990 and 1991. The share price dropped from FIM 120 in early 1990 to FIM 40 in 1991.

9.3.2. Domestic Push Factors

The domestic causes for Amer to launch international equity issues were mainly the illiquidity and segmentation of the domestic equity market, and the non-availability of capital from the existing shareholders. These reasons became more evident in the late 1980's and early 1990's when the Helsinki Stock Exchange was suffering from a deep recession.

Illiquid Finnish Equity Markets

The Helsinki Stock Exchange was relatively liquid in 1988-1989 with an annual share turnover over FIM 30 (USD 7 billion), of which FIM 9 (USD 2.2 billion) in free shares. In 1990 and 1991 the turnover in Helsinki dropped by half from the previous year. However, the liquidity in the SEAQ system in London remained much better. A number of banks and brokers quoted two-way dealing prices for the most liquid Finnish stocks. In Finland, until late 1992, such market making was impossible due to a 1 % turnover tax. The turnover figures in the SEAQ system and in Helsinki are not comparable, since the SEAQ figures include deals between brokers and each trade is recorded twice, whereas the Helsinki turnover represents more or less pure investors' demand.

Nevertheless, in 1990 the turnover of Amer free shares in SEAQ was two and half times that of Helsinki (2 million vs. 0.8 million shares). In 1991 the trading in Amer shares picked up, amounting to 1.4 million in Helsinki and 3.8 million shares in the SEAQ system. With reawakened foreign demand, the Helsinki Stock Exchange turned around in 1993. The annual turnover in shares rose to FIM 46 billion, and in 1994 to FIM 69 billion. The trading volumes of Amer's shares in Helsinki totalled 8.2 million in 1993 and 12 million in 1994. The role of SEAQ was diminishing.

By tradition, all new equity issues were priced at a discount of 2-5 % in Finland. Amer was able to price its first international offering of free shares at an 8 % premium over restricted shares. Since then the premium has increased, in June 1991 up to 54 %. Thus, the high premium reflects the higher value of the stock to internationally diversified portfolios. The latter two international share issues were priced at a small discount to market price.

Segmented Domestic Equity Markets

In the 1980s the Finnish equity market seemed to be somewhat segmented in pricing the shares. Escaping segmentation should reduce the cost of capital for Finnish companies when launching international equity issues or listing the stock abroad. During 1987-1989 the Amer free preference share was valued higher than the conglomerate companies on average in Helsinki. Internationally a P/E ratio of 10-11 was still relatively low. The P/E ratio for the restricted share was below the ratio of the Amer free share, and in 1987-88, under the average of conglomerate companies. International comparisons of individual companies are difficult to make, since Amer's portfolio of businesses is quite unique.

The pricing of Amer shares in Helsinki and on the SEAQ system in London in 1990-1992 did not offer arbitrage opportunities after adjusting for the Finnish turnover tax. Amer's listing in London and quotations on SEAQ have effectively reduced the disadvantages of segmentation. Amer's financial losses, and subsequently high P/E ratio, did not allowed further international equity issues in the early 1990's.

Non-availability of Capital from the Existing Shareholders

To finance the acquisition of Wilson in 1989 Amer needed new equity. The Helsinki Stock Exchange was about to dry up, not the least because of excessive capital issues in 1987-1989. The amount of new capital raised represented 8-9 % of the total market capitalisation in each of those consecutive years. Amer took advantage of foreign investor's demand. The relative ownership and control of the existing holders of Amer ordinary shares were protected by the dual-class share structure.

In the early 1980's the Bank of Finland denied Amer permission to borrow from abroad since its major business sectors, tobacco, and publishing and printing divisions, were purely domestic and the company did not have any exports. However, equity issues to foreign investors were allowed, and Amer raised the capital it needed through an equity issue to international investors in 1984. In 1986 Amer was able to launch its first international syndicated loan. In 1988 Amer entered the Euro commercial paper market.

9.4. Barriers to Internationalising the Capital Structure

In 1992, there were still institutional barriers remaining that prevented a complete internationalisation of the cost of capital. Most serious ones were the restrictions imposed by the Finnish government. Foreign investor perception of Amer and Finland, as well as existing stockholders' dislike of targeted equity issues imposed additional barriers.

9.4.1. Legal and Government Restrictions

Prior to deregulation in 1993, the maximum amount of free shares in Finnish companies could amount to only 20 % of share capital. The Ministry of Trade and Industry could grant a permission up to 40 %. Amer had a permission to issue free shares up to 28 %, while in 1991 the amount of its free shares outstanding represented 21.4 % of the equity capital. In 1993 all shares in Finland became freely transferable to foreign investors. Towards the end of 1992, the price premium on free shares fell gradually and the price of restricted shares rose.

Until Fall 1992 Finland was one of the very few European countries where the liquidity and the attractiveness of the stock exchange was damaged by a 1 % turnover tax. Both the buyer and the seller paid 0.5 % tax on the value of the transaction. SEAQ benefited from the tax in increased turnover at the expense of the Helsinki Stock Exchange.

The third institutional barrier in Finland was the tax system that discriminated against equity investments, especially against dividend income. Dividends were taxed at the marginal tax rate whereas interest income was taxed at a fixed rate of 15 % (withholding tax). In 1993, all capital income and gains became subject to a 25% tax.

9.4.2. Ownership Structure

Dual class share structures were and still are typical in Finland. The ordinary shares are entitled to ten or twenty times more votes than the preference shares. The critical ownership mass of most Finnish stock exchange listed companies is in safe hands preventing any hostile takeover. Such an ownership concentration distorts the true value of the share, making it uninteresting to independent investors.

Most free shares were preference shares. Finnish investors disliked preference shares in the late 1980's. They were willing to pay for voting power when the restructuring process in the economy was on the way. There was a market for corporate control. Foreign investors might also have appreciated equal voting power. In addition, there was hard critique in Finland against targeted share issues priced at a discount that discriminated against existing shareholders who had pre-emptive rights. The international market practice in Europe was to price international equity offerings at a 2-3 % discount to market prices.

9.4.3. Investor Perception

Foreign investors' perception of Finland and Amer can create barriers to further internationalisation of the cost of capital. Foreign investors might not choose to invest in Amer because of the small market size. The market capitalisation of the Helsinki Stock Exchange at the end of 1990 represented 0.8 % of the total market capitalisation of the European stock exchanges and 0.19 % of the world.

Amer has actively worked to promote the company among international institutional investors since 1984. Its strategy has been to focus on a small group of investors. Over the years Amer has learned to know the investors and has personal relationships with them. Investors and investment researchers are met regularly in Finland and abroad. They are also invited to visit the company.

Amer publishes the annual report and the half-year report in English. It supplies the financial statement applying both the Finnish and the IAS accounting standards. However, foreign investment researchers find the Finnish accounting standards much more informative. Listing in London and SEAQ quotations have improved the liquidity of the shares and reduced the degree of market segmentation. Foreign investors have become more aware of the company after the Wilson and MacGregor acquisitions. With 50 % of net sales abroad, Amer has become an international company which reduces its risk exposure to Finland.

In early 1992, Amer already had plans for the next step in the process of internationalising its capital structure, provided the development program in Wilson was effectively implemented and satisfactory profit levels achieved. At the time, it was thought that the strategic decision then to be made was whether to list the well known subsidiary Wilson or the parent company Amer in the United States.

However, by the end of 1995 Amer had not succeeded in restoring Wilson's profitability, although as a group it returned back to profits in 1992. There was disagreement among the four founding parties. They then engaged themselves for several months in negotiations to sell the company to an international sporting goods company. The uncertainty of the company's future was reflected in the share price development. No buyer was found. Simultaneously Amer underwent a strategic reorientation process. It chose to focus further on sporting goods and had acquired the Austrian ski manufacturer Atomic. It sold its publishing and printing division and the Japanese motor vehicle import operations.

In the beginning of 1996 Amer's financial performance collapsed. The first four months of 1996 were heavily under water, while the stock market had anticipated improving profits. MacGregor was divested. Amer had a long restructuring period ahead. With the newly-appointed managing director Roger Talermo it seemed to be regaining credibility among investors.

10. Nokia: Two Directed Issues, One Private Placement and One Euroequity Issue

Kaisa Vikkula

10.1. Introduction

It is July 2, 1994. Jorma Ollila, Nokia's CEO and Olli-Pekka Kallasvuo CFO, congratulated themselves. For the last two weeks they had been on the road introducing Nokia, the new leading telecommunications company of the world, to American, European, and Japanese investors. The work bore fruit.

Nokia's debut on Wall Street with a FIM 2.5 billion (USD 484 million) stock issue the day before had been an immediate big hit. The issue was oversubscribed. Nokia became the first Finnish company to be listed on the New York Stock Exchange. Furthermore, the issue was the biggest ever issued by a Finnish company. Nokia was the first Finnish company to price the issue without any discount, at the closing price of the Helsinki Stock Exchange on July 1, 1994

The leading financial press had discovered the new high-tech superpower. Within the next three months papers were filled with articles about corporate fairytale, how an ugly parochial conglomerate turned into a hi-tech swan. "One of the hottest companies on the New York Stock Exchange, sounds Japanese, comes from Finland and used to make toilet paper and rubber boots. Nokia has overcome its obscure name, remote location and uninspiring past to emerge as a key player in wireless communications", wrote *USA Today*. "Motorola lost its technology lead to Nokia last year", commented the editor of *Telecomeurope*. "Nokia is an example of a smokestack company that has fought its way out of its old skin. Nokia emerged in the past year as a high-tech superpower and will end this year as the market leader in Europe", wrote *The Wall Street Journal*. "Nokia has fulfilled its managers' dream of transforming an obscure Finnish conglomerate into a world beating telecommunications company" continued *International Herald Tribune*.

10.2. History

In 1985 Nokia was a dull Finnish conglomerate, making boots, tires and toilet paper. In fact, it was one of Europe's largest suppliers of toilet paper. Nokia's operations consisted of electronics, Salora-Luxor TV's, cables, machinery, metal products, engineering, forest industries, chemicals, rubber industries and plastics. By 1994 Nokia had transformed itself to become the world´s second-largest manufacturer of mobile phones and the world's second-largest supplier of GSM/DCS cellular networks, with only 11% of sales in Finland. In addition, Nokia had become a significant European supplier of colour televisions and computer monitors, and the world's largest supplier of cable manufacturing machinery.

Nokia's rapid growth in telecommunications not only astonished the securities markets, but also far exceeded the most revolutionary thoughts of Nokia's management. In mobile phones Nokia was and still is the market leader in Europe with a 35% market share and second after Motorola in the Americas and Asia. In all markets Nokia was growing fast and challenging the leadership of Motorola. In cellular systems and infrastructure Nokia was number two after the Swedish Ericsson. Nokia had proven that with today's digital-electronics markets moving at warp speed, even small, relatively new players can, if they are agile enough, seize strategic positions from multinationals.

Nokia's remote location in Finland worked to the company's advantage. Being a country with 5 million people and long distances Finland had always been one of the most open phone markets in the world. There were dozens of different phone companies and phone company suppliers. In 1994 Finland had more mobile phone users per capita than any other country, with 10% of the population using the phones, compared with 6% in the U.S. and 3.5% in Great Britain. In the Nordic countries mobile phones had shaken off their yuppie image and were seen as essential items.

Nokia got its break through already in the late 1970s, when the telecommunications authorities of Sweden, Norway, Denmark and Finland decided to build the world's first international cellular system. Nokia understood the potential of this opportunity. In 1981, when the system was turned on, Nokia was there with both equipment and phones. Nokia introduced base stations for use in connection with the NMT 450 cellular system. Nokia's cellular system product introductions included NMT 450 and NMT 900 analogue cellular systems, as well as both GSM and DCS digital cellular systems.

In 1983 when the U.S. commercial cellular service was switched on, Nokia joined forces with Tandy Corp. and got its products into over 6,000 Radio Shack stores under the Tandy brand. From Tandy Nokia learned what cost consciousness really meant. Joint manufacturing plants, which Nokia later took over, were built in Korea and Texas. Through other retailers in the U.S. Nokia phones were usually sold under the cellular carriers' names- the Bell companies, McCaw Cellular and GTE Corp.

Competition made Finland first, along with the other Nordic countries, to adopt a mobile-phone standard and to switch from analogue to the more data-friendly digital systems. Nokia seized the opportunity while more established telecommunications players such as Alcatel from France, Siemens from Germany, and the firms from Japan were wedded to fixed-based communications. Deregulation and growing competition had started to open up new opportunities for Nokia in the traditional monopoly-dominated countries. In 1994, Nokia made handsets in Finland, Germany, the United States, Hong Kong and South Korea to service 90 national markets.

Nokia had also been fortunate. Telecommunications had experienced one of the greatest business booms of the decade. The world market had been growing by 50 % a year. However, Nokia had grown even faster. In 1993, the percentage of Nokia's net sales from phone-related businesses totalled 45% – up from 12% four years earlier, and reached 60% by April 1994. Furthermore, Nokia surprised just about everyone by parlaying its pioneer status into that of industry leadership. Since 1981, 35 million cellular phones had been sold worldwide, and Nokia had sold over 5 million of them. Its world market share had grown to 20%.

10.3. Strategy

In 1983 Kari Kairamo, the former CEO, saw that the mainly domestic bulk businesses that Nokia was in were not going to grow. The company's only long-term chance of survival lay in electronics. Telecommunications had until then been a minor business for Nokia. Although knowing nothing about computers and consumer electronics, in 1988 Nokia bought for FIM 2 billion a bleeding computer business from the Swedish Ericsson and a loss-making TV and stereo business from the German Standard Elektrik Lorenz. Nokia became the third largest TV manufacturer in Europe after Philips and Thomson and the largest Nordic information technology company.

Exhibit 10.1: Nokia (IAS), FIM millions.

	1989	1990	1991	1992	1993	4 months 1994
Net sales	22,795	22,130	15,457	18,168	23,697	8,565
Operating profit	978	1,083	−96	288	1,465	854
Profit before tax, minority interest & items	604	711	-324	−158	1,146	969
EPS	4.43	5.47	-9.6	−6.84	12.96	11.49
Dividend per share	2.8	2.8	2	2	2.8	−
Return on capital employed, %	8	10	3.8	6.4	14.2	
Return on equity, %	2.5	5.5	neg.	neg.	11	
Equity ratio, %	33.8	36.6	40.6	37.2	33.5	
P/E ratio, common	58	12	−8.4	−16.1	23.6	
Total Assets	22,386	21,694	20,153	21,238	22,647	22,546
Shareholders' equity	7,308	7,501	7,393	6,727	6,511	7,048

The acquisitions turned out to be unsuccessful. The Asian TV manu-facturers were entering Europe with lower prices. Overcapacity became a problem. Philips started to lay off people. Investors became alert. Nokia's stock prices fell 14-32 % (there were four different types of stock) in 1988, although the Helsinki Stock Exchange general index rose by 26 %. Nokia's operating profit tumbled from FIM 969 million in 1990 to a loss of FIM 81 million in 1991 (Exhibit 10.1). Between 1988 and 1993 the consumer electronics division ran up almost USD 1 billion in losses, restructuring charges and writeoffs.

The difficulties and financial pressures encountered during the reces-sion of 1991-1992 forced Nokia to restate its corporate mission and rede-fine its strategy. Nokia made a clear decision to become a leading interna-tional telecommunications company. It meant disposal of all non-core activities, however traditional or profitable they were, and to concentrate totally on telecommunications.

In 1992, Jorma Ollila, 41, head of the mobile phones division, took over as CEO. He promoted entrepreneurial and high-tech culture and plucked from inside Nokia a group of younger new managers. The average age of board members dropped by 10 years overnight to 43. Ollila saw the need to sharpen the focus further. He sold out dozens of other product lines and focused on Nokia's core strength, the mobile phone technology that it had pioneered in the 1980s. The strategy in telecommunications would be internal growth, no more acquisitions.

Ollila was convinced that Nokia had the expertise to become a major player – if it moved fast enough. Nokia's rapid rise in digital cellular phones began. Nokia decided to go global. When the world market for digital mobile phones took off, Nokia was ready to conquer the market with its hot products and low-cost manufacturing. The Nordic countries, Nokia's home base, were where the cellular phones first took off. In order to keep the low-cost commodity producers away from the market, Ollila aimed for 20 % annual productivity gains.

After two years of losses Nokia reported an operating profit in 1993. For the first four months of 1994 Nokia's pre-tax profits soared to FIM 969 million (USD 180 million) compared to just FIM 154 (USD 29) million during the same period in 1993.

10.4. Products

Nokia had four business divisions: Nokia Telecommunications, Nokia Mobile Phones, Nokia Consumer Electronics, and Nokia Cables and Machinery (Exhibit 10.2).

10.4.1. Nokia Telecommunications

Nokia Telecommunications supplied advanced telecommunications infrastructure systems and equipment for use in fixed and mobile networks and has delivered such equipment in more than 40 countries throughout the world. The product line consisted of cellular systems, transmission sys-

Exhibit 10.2: Nokia, 1993: Key Data.

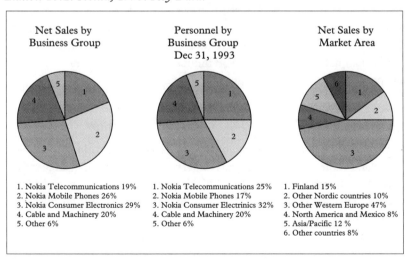

Net Sales by Business Group	Personnel by Business Group Dec 31, 1993	Net Sales by Market Area
1. Nokia Telecommunications 19%	1. Nokia Telecommunications 25%	1. Finland 15%
2. Nokia Mobile Phones 26%	2. Nokia Mobile Phones 17%	2. Other Nordic countries 10%
3. Nokia Consumer Electronics 29%	3. Nokia Consumer Electrinics 32%	3. Other Western Europe 47%
4. Cable and Machinery 20%	4. Cable and Machinery 20%	4. North America and Mexico 8%
5. Other 6%	5. Other 6%	5. Asia/Pacific 12 %
		6. Other countries 8%

tems and switching systems. Nokia supplied cellular systems and equipment based on NMT and GSM standards and was one of the few companies with the capacity to supply complete GSM and DCS cellular systems. Nokia had supplied equipment to 21 PTTS and private operators in 16 countries. In 1993, Nokia Telecommunications had net sales of FIM 4,578 million (19% of Nokia's net sales) and operating profit of FIM 983 million.

10.4.2. Nokia Mobile Phones

Nokia Mobile Phones began operations in 1979 and became in 1993 the largest European, and the world's second largest, manufacturer of mobile phones. Nokia manufactured a complete range of cellular phones for all major analogue and digital cellular systems. The phones were sold in more than 90 countries. Nokia's brand names were Nokia, Technophone and Mobira. In 1993, Nokia Mobile Phones had net sales of FIM 6,314 million (27 % of Nokia's net sales) and operating profit of FIM 950 million.

10.4.3. Nokia Consumer Electronics

Nokia Consumer Electronics was one of the leading European suppliers of colour televisions, computer monitors and car loudspeaker systems. The group also manufactured picture tubes, electronic systems for the automotive industry and satellite receivers. The group incurred operating losses in 1991-93 resulting mainly from a significant deterioration in the market for colour televisions and picture tubes throughout Western Europe. Nokia had initiated a major restructuring of the group and was planning to discontinue to manufacture picture tubes. In 1993, Nokia Consumer electronics had net sales of FIM 6,938 million (29% of Nokia's net sales) and an operating loss of FIM 747 million.

10.4.4. Nokia Cables and Machinery

Nokia Cables and Machinery manufactured telecommunications and power cables and cable manufacturing machinery. It was the world's largest supplier of cable machinery. In 1993, Nokia Cables and Machinery had net sales of FIM 4,933 million (21% of Nokia's net sales) and an operating profit of FIM 261 million.

In early 1994 Nokia defined its primary business objectives as further development as a leading international telecommunications group. In order to achieve this objective, Nokia decided to pursue the following strategies: targeting high growth segments of the telecommunications industry; focused pursuit of international opportunities; emphasis on technological development through the efficient use of Nokia's research and development resources; creating enhanced consumer recognition of the Nokia brand name; and business rationalisation, particularly in Nokia's consumer electronics operations.

The strategy chosen involved risks. The telecommunications industry is highly competitive and Nokia's competitors like Motorola and Ericsson had substantially greater resources. In order to achieve the technological advances necessary to supply products which reflect the latest technology, Nokia must make significant investment in R&D. In 1993 Nokia spent 17 % of sales on R&D. Given Nokia's relatively small size, its R&D expenditure in absolute terms was much smaller than those of its competitors, which could put Nokia into a competitive disadvantage. This is why gaining financial strength through new equity issues has been crucial for Nokia's overall strategy.

10.5. Ownership at the Time of the 1994 Equity Issue

Nokia had a dual class share structure. Each common series K share was entitled to 10 votes at the shareholders' general meeting whereas each preference series A share was entitled to just one vote. The preference shares had a preferential treatment in terms of dividend payment. They were paid cumulative dividends of 10% of the nominal amount prior to common shares. The nominal value of each share was FIM 20. Any shareholder that increased its ownership to 33 1/3% of votes or 50% of shares was obliged to purchase the shares of all other shareholders.

At the end of 1993, there were 41,098,266 common shares and 27,789,299 "preference" shares outstanding. The common shares represented 59.7% of the shares outstanding and 93.7% of the votes, whereas the preference shares stood for 40.3% of shares outstanding but only 6.3% of votes.

Altogether Nokia had 31,486 shareholders. The major shareholders with voting rights were Kymmene, a Finnish paper company, Pohjola insurance group from Finland, and the Union Bank of Finland group. The aim of Nokia was to make the preference share a liquid share series. In 1993 Nokia had issued 6,000,000 new series A shares to international investors and invited investors to change their common shares to "preference" shares. At the end of 1993, the proportion of foreign ownership of the total number of shares outstanding was 46.2%, up from 13.3% the year before. However, since foreign investors mainly held "preference" shares, they only accounted for 27% of all votes.

10.6. Finance strategy

Nokia's finance strategy has been closely linked to the corporate strategy. When Nokia in the 1980s was to become a major European electronics company, new capital was needed to finance the major acquisitions. Nokia wanted to internationalise its cost and availability of capital and to reduce its dependence on traditional bank loans. It turned to lower margin securitized lending and acquired the necessary ratings for name recognition. It extended its financing and capital sourcing to Euromarkets. It established a group finance center, Nokia Finance, in Geneva, Switzerland.

Nokia was among the first Finnish companies to launch a USD 300 million Eurocommercial paper (ECP) program in 1988. It issued Eurobonds in Swiss francs, Sterling and German marks, and floating rate notes (FRN) in Dutch guilders and Finnish markka. In 1987, to reduce funding cost, Nokia was the first Finnish company to issue bonds with warrants in the Euromarkets and among the first ones to introduce the instrument in FIM to the domestic capital markets. The interest rate of both bond issues was 5% p.a. while the market yields were several percentage points higher.

Since Nokia's line of business, first electronics and later telecommunications, was riskier than that of conglomerates or mature industries, it had to keep its equity/assets ratio on an acceptable level. Since the mid-1980s the ratio had always been over 33%. To achieve this, and to finance simultaneously internal growth as well as acquisitions in the 1980s, Nokia needed more equity. Between 1980 and 1993 Nokia launched five rights issues to existing shareholders, two targeted equity issues to international investors, one issue to the State of Finland, one private placement abroad, and two bond issues with warrants. Furthermore, Nokia issued shares to finance some smaller acquisitions. Nokia raised over FIM 1.4 billion through targeted share issues alone. The share capital was increased six-fold from FIM 234 million to FIM 1,378 million. Investments between 1986 and 1993 equalled FIM 14 billion.

Already in 1987, Nokia had initiated an American Depositary Receipt (ADR) program in the United States. However, the program remained relatively passive. In 1993 Nokia took advantage of lifted regulations on foreign ownership in Finland to issue 6,000,000 preferred shares to international investors at FIM 159 per share or USD 28.07 per ADS. The US offering consisted of 2,088,000 shares offered in the United States and Canada to qualified institutional buyers under Rule 144A for direct placements. The total proceeds of the issues were FIM 954 (USD 165) million. The proceeds were used to restructure the consumer electronics division and to finance growth in telecommunications and cellular phones.

Due to the most severe recession in Finland since 1945, with GDP declining 6.5% and with rising unemployment, the Finnish markka was devalued by 12.3% on November 15, 1991. On September 8, 1992 the Bank of Finland let the Finnish markka float freely against other currencies. It quickly depreciated some 14%. In 1992, GDP declined a further 3.5%. By the end of March 1993, unemployment had reached 17%. The weaker currency boosted exports and attracted foreign investors to Finland. Nokia became their favourite share.

Nokia also listed its shares abroad, partly to support its businesses in the local markets, and partly to extend its ownership base. Both Nokia's share series were already listed on the Helsinki Stock Exchange in Finland. "Preference" shares were also listed in Stockholm (1983), London (1987), Frankfurt (1988) and Paris (1988). Nokia shares have been traded on the SEAQ system in London since 1987. The main markets for Nokia shares have been London and Helsinki. In 1993, the number of shares traded in Helsinki was 25.4 million, up 21.3 million from 1992, and in London 31.8 million, up 26.6 million from 1992. However, as was previously mentioned, in the SEAQ turnover all transactions are reported twice, by the buyer and the seller. Turnover in Stockholm, Frankfurt and Paris was some hundreds of thousands a year.

By the beginning of 1994, Nokia had outgrown its domestic market. It had quickly become Finland's largest publicly traded company, with a market capitalisation totalling FIM 29.8 billion (USD 5.6 Billion) as of April 30, 1994. That was 25% of the total market capitalisation of the Helsinki Stock Exchange. Nokia's shares represented alone one third of the daily stock exchange turnover. There was hardly any more capital available from Finland as the capital market of the country was small. The limits of the domestic mutual funds had been reached, since they were not allowed to invest more than 10% of their funds in a single company.

Nokia had outgrown the London market as well. Most fund managers placed Nokia under Finnish exposure and all the Finland limits in London were full. Nokia, whose dependence on the Finnish economy was minimal, wanted to become classified and priced as a telecommunications company with its peers like Motorola and Ericsson.

To finance its future growth Nokia had to turn to the U.S. capital markets which was the home for high-technology companies. The United States was also the largest single market for telecommunications and Nokia had to strengthen its market position there. Yet very few U.S. investors recognised Nokia's name although they might have been using Nokia's products. A New York Stock Exchange listing was seen as an important tool to improve Nokia's visibility in North America. The U.S. GAAP and disclosure norms were not a problem for Nokia, because for years it had been publishing results according to IAS. The additional work to meet GAAP requirements was small.

Nokia's stock price had been rising along with ever improving earnings and even higher expectations. Still Nokia's stock was cheap, cheaper than the shares of competitors. Motorola shares traded at 22 times estimated 1994 earnings, Ericsson at 25 times, but Nokia at 14 times. It was time to seize the opportunity.

10.7. NYSE listing and Global Offering

Nokia made a strategic decision to list its "preference" shares on the New York Stock Exchange. In addition, it decided to seize the opportunity to raise capital. Nokia decided to issue 5,250,000 "preference" shares, of which 3,5 million in the form of ADS, to the U.S. market and to international investors. Each ADS was to be equal to half a share of Nokia preferred stock. In case of oversubscription there was an option to issue an additional 750,000 shares, totalling 6 million shares i.e. 22% of the outstanding preferred stock. The issue size was FIM 2.6 billion (USD 485 million), the largest ever done by a Finnish company. Nokia anticipated it would use one-third of the proceeds to finance working capital needs, one-third for its capital expenditure program, primarily in the telecommunications business, and the balance to repay debt. Lead managers of the issue were CS First Boston, Goldman, Sachs & Co. and Morgan Stanley & Co. Exhibit 10.3 presents the "tombstone" for the prospectus.

The listing plan in New York was announced April 1, 1994. The stock exchange reaction was initially negative (Exhibit 10.4). The price of the preference stock fell from FIM 395 to FIM 387, but turnover increased from 69,000 to 132,000 shares. The following day the price recovered to FIM 399. The announcement of the FIM 2.6 billion issue and NYSE list-

Exhibit 10.3: The Nokia 1994-Tombstone

Global Offering of
5,250,000 Preferred Shares

3,500,000 Preferred Shares, in the form of
American Depositary Shares or Preferred Shares

As Part of the Global Offering

Nokia Corporation (the "Company") is offering hereby, through the several U.S. Underwriters, Preferred Shares, nominal value FIM 20 each (each a "Preferred Share"), of the Company, in the form of American Depositary Shares ("ADSs"), each representing the right to receive one-half of one Preferred Share, or Preferred Shares. The ADSs are evidenced by American Depositary Receipts ("ADRs"). See "Description of American Depositary Receipts". This offering is part of a combined offering of 5,250,000 Preferred Shares (the "Combined Offering") consisting of 3,500,000 Preferred Shares, in the form of ADSs or Preferred Shares, being offered in the United States and Canada (the "U.S. Offering") and 1,750,000 Preferred Shares being offered outside the United States and Canada (the "International Offering").

The Preferred Shares being offered as part of the Combined Offering will rank pari passu with the existing Preferred Shares of the Company and will be entitled to any dividend declared in respect of the financial year ending December 31, 1994 and any dividends declared thereafter. Preferred Shares rank equally with the Company's common shares of nominal value FIM 20 each ("Common Shares") with respect to dividends, except that Preferred Shares are entitled to receive, out of available profits, a cumulative dividend of 10% of the nominal value of the Preferred Shares prior to any dividend being paid on the Common Shares. Preferred Shares rank equally with Common Shares in the event of a winding-up of the Company. Each Preferred Share is entitled to one vote and each Common Share is entitled to ten votes at meetings of shareholders.

The existing Preferred Shares of the Company are listed on the Helsinki, London, Stockholm, Paris and Frankfurt stock exchanges. The ADSs have been approved for listing on the New York Stock Exchange and application will be made to list the Preferred Shares being offered as part of the Combined Offering on the Helsinki, London, Stockholm, Paris and Frankfurt stock exchanges. On July 1, 1994, the closing price on the Helsinki Stock Exchange of the Preferred Shares was FIM 432 per share and of the Common Shares was FIM 430 per share. See "Market Information" for historical price information relating to Preferred Shares and Common Shares.

See "Risk Factors" for a discussion of certain factors that should be considered by prospective investors.

THESE SECURITIES HAVE NOT BEEN APPROVED OR DISAPPROVED BY THE SECURITIES AND EXCHANGE COMMISSION OR ANY STATE SECURITIES COMMISSION NOR HAS THE SECURITIES AND EXCHANGE COMMISSION OR ANY STATE SECURITIES COMMISSION PASSED UPON THE ACCURACY OR ADEQUACY OF THIS PROSPECTUS. ANY REPRESENTATION TO THE CONTRARY IS A CRIMINAL OFFENSE.

	Price to Public	Underwriting Discounts and Commissions	Proceeds to the Company(1)
Per Preferred Share	FIM 432	FIM 13.954	FIM 418.046
Per ADS	$40.375	$1.304	$39.071
Total(2)	$282,625,000	$9,128,000	$273,497,000

(1) Before deduction of expenses payable by the Company estimated at $1,750,000.
(2) Assuming that all the Preferred Shares offered hereby are sold in the form of ADSs. The Company has granted the U.S. Underwriters and the Managers an option, exercisable by CS First Boston Corporation, for 30 days from the date of this Prospectus to purchase a maximum of 750,000 additional Preferred Shares to cover over-allotments. If the option is exercised in full, the total Price to Public will be $343,187,500, Underwriting Discounts and Commissions will be $11,084,000 and Proceeds to the Company will be $332,103,500. See "Underwriting".

Global Coordinator
CS First Boston

The Preferred Shares and the ADSs are offered by the several U.S. Underwriters when, as and if issued by the Company and accepted by the U.S. Underwriters and subject to their right to reject orders in whole or in part. It is expected that the Preferred Shares and ADRs evidencing the ADSs will be available for delivery on or about July 11, 1994.

CS First Boston
Goldman, Sachs & Co.
Morgan Stanley & Co.
Incorporated

The date of this Prospectus is July 1, 1994

ing was published May 25, 1994. The share price of the preference share fell from FIM 438 to FIM 410, but the turnover peaked from 89,000 to 198,000 shares that one day. The share price started to rise steadily from June 14, 1994 onwards. That day Nokia announced a £ 100 million deal with NYNEC, one of the UK's largest cable communications operators.

Exhibit 10.4: Nokia, Helsinki Stock Exchange. February 1, - August 31, 1994.

June 16 1994, Nokia confirmed its record results for January-April 1994. Preliminary results were published already on June 2.

The global offering was priced at the closing price of the Helsinki Stock Exchange, i.e. at FIM 432 (USD 40.375 per ADS), on July 1, 1994. The very same day American depositary shares of Nokia started trading on the NYSE. The first trading day in Helsinki after the issue Nokia's share closed at FIM 452, up FIM 20 or 5% in one day. Trading volume rose from 40-60,000 shares a day to 292,000 shares the day after the issue. On July 6, Nokia announced that the underwriters had exercised their option to purchase an additional 750,000 shares. The additional preferred shares were offered at the same subscription price. The next day the Nokia share price reached FIM 475 in Helsinki and on July 22, it pushed through FIM 500, i.e. a price increase of 16% in just three weeks. At the end of August the price was FIM 555, up 29% within two months.

Within three months Nokia's ADS had surged 45% vs. a 2% gain for the NYSE composite index (Exhibit 10.5). The price formation had clearly shifted from the Helsinki Stock Exchange to New York. The share was now priced in US dollars, which increased the daily price volatility in Helsinki.

The six million new preference shares or ADSs were initially placed with some 80 institutional investors. Two-thirds of the issue was placed in the United States, mainly on the East coast. All the major investment banks had published a buy recommendation and despite the astonishing

Exhibit 10.5: Nokia, ADS, New York Stock Exchange. July 1, 1994 - Feb. 13, 1996.

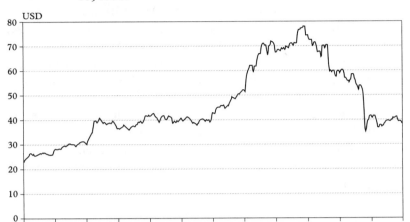

start they still believed in a further rise. In fact, because of a continual stream of positive earnings surprises, Nokia's share price had already appreciated by over 1200% since 1992. Could it still be cheap?

On August 24, 1994, Merrill Lynch reiterated an intermediate and long term buy recommendation stating that Nokia shares at FIM 525 and a P/E of 14.8 are significantly undervalued. The following day, Alfred Berg, a leading Nordic stockbroker company, issued an outperform investment recommendation with a FIM 620 price level obtainable in the short-term. On August 26, 1994, CS First Boston wrote "Nokia continues to offer best value of the three global cellular equipment plays. Nokia should achieve a 25% return on capital employed in 1994 and 1995, the highest of any company we cover. Trading at less than 14 times prospective 1995 earnings, Nokia has potential to reach FIM 650 (USD 65 for ADR) by the late 1995." On October 4, 1994, Lehman Brothers raised its earnings projections for Nokia and issued a buy recommendation with moderate risk. "Nokia should achieve at least 20% EPS growth per annum over the next three years and hence the share was undervalued and trading at a discount to Ericsson and Motorola". On September 19, 1994, UBS Global Research believed Nokia's future prospects would remain strong and the share price at FIM 556 had 10-20% upside potential relative to its peer group.

The January-August interim results, published October 19, 1994 were excellent and better than expected. Investment banks subsequently upgraded their forecasts. The following day Alfred Berg, at the price of FIM 689, retained its outperform investment conclusion. On October 24, 1994, at the price of FIM 677 (USD 71.75), Morgan Stanley saw potential upside of around 20% in the stock price. Two days later Merrill Lynch reconfirmed its buy recommendation as it still believed the stock was undervalued.

Just in two years, by the end of 1994, Nokia's "preference" share had risen 195% compared with a 51% rise at the same time of the Helsinki Stock Exchange General Index. The closing price at the end of the year was FIM 698. The highest price for the year was FIM 712, a more than 18 times increase from the lowest quotation in 1992.

10.8. The Aftermath to the 1994 Global Equity Issue

Nokia's future lies in its ability to select growth sectors in telecommunications, in successful product implementation, and in competitive R&D expenditure. It has to be a good listener to its clients' needs and to be able to produce products that meet those divergent needs. Nokia has continued to focus on mobile phones and to build on Nokia's digital expertise. Digital cellular phones are expected to conquer the US market in 1997-98, increasing sales by 20-30% a year. According to the most aggressive forecasts the number of mobile phone subscribers in the whole world is expected to grow by 35 million in 1996, by 45 million in 1997 and by 55 million in 1998. By the year 2000 there would be 350 million subscribers in the whole world compared to the present 80 million.

Nokia will also have to enter into strategic alliances to overcome its own lack of resources. It has already leaped onto the information superhighway with an initiative to develop intelligent network systems together with the computer maker Hewlett-Packard.

In early 1996, Olli-Pekka Kallasvuo was looking back at the New York listing. The listing had achieved all the strategic objectives. Nokia's name recognition in the U.S. market had improved substantially. Through traditional advertising Nokia would never have obtained such results, and even ignoring the expenses of such a campaign. The press coverage of the NYSE listing, the share offering, and the subsequent price development had been overwhelming.

Nokia had name recognition as one of the world's leading telecommunication companies and its stock was priced comparably to its peers, Ericsson and Motorola. The share was liquid. Nokia's ownership structure had changed dramatically. Nokia has become a mid-Atlantic company. A total of 61.4% of the shares were held by foreigners, mainly by U.S. investors. It had 60,000 U.S. shareholders compared to 28,000 in Finland. Some 10% of the shares were held by other Europeans.

Nokia had become one of the largest non-U.S. companies on the NYSE. A couple of times it has been the most traded single company on the NYSE. Nokia sees the limited capital base of Finland as a potential cap on the future. Therefore it will seek to become more American and to increase the number of its U.S. shareholders, with a target of 250,000. That would involve further management commitment and time for investor relations and communications, as well as investment in Nokia's brand recognition in the US market. From the beginning of 1995, Nokia already had an investor relations office for the U.S. market, stationed in Dallas, Texas.

In April 1995, Nokia's preferred share was renamed an A-share and the common share a K-share. The par value of Nokia's shares were divided by four, i.e. from FIM 20 to FIM 5. The value of one ADS was split, after which one ADS was equivalent to one A-share. The change simplified the share structure and lowered the unit share price closer to typical share prices in the United States. This is part of the reason for the decline in the ADS price on the New York Stock Exchange as shown in Exhibit 10.5.

11. Huhtamaki (Finland) and Procordia (Sweden): A Strategic Alliance

Kaisa Vikkula

11.1. Background

On June 29, 1993, Huhtamaki of Finland and Volvo's subsidiary, Procordia of Sweden, announced their plans of industry rationalisation and strategic cooperation in the areas of confectionery products and pharmaceuticals.

According to the signed agreement Huhtamaki took over Procordia United Brands European confectionery business, an unit with annual revenues of SEK 1,050 million (USD 150 million, FIM 880 million) and 1,300 employees. The divestment made Procordia a pure pharmaceutical and biotechnology company.

The other part of the Procordia and Huhtamaki transaction was to establish in January 1994 a joint venture between Procordia's pharmaceutical company, Kabi Pharmacia, and Huhtamaki's Leiras division. The new company, Pharmacia-Leiras, would market two innovative gynacological products in European countries, excluding the Nordic countries: Kabi Pharmacia's Estring, a vaginal ring for estrogen delivery, and Leiras' contraceptive hormone spiral Levonova.

11.2. History and the Evolution of Huhtamaki's Strategy

11.2.1. Product Development

In 1993, Huhtamaki was a Finnish-based consumer products group with worldwide operations. In 1992, the group's net sales amounted to FIM 6.4 billion (USD 1.2 billion), of which 82 % originated from abroad. The group employed some 9,700 people in 26 countries. Exhibit 11.1 presents key figures at the time of the alliance.

Exhibit 11.1: Key Figures for Huhtamaki 1989-1993.

FIM million	1989	1990	1991	1992	1993
Net sales	5,489.1	5,799.0	6,029.1	6,582.0	7,935.2
Increase in net sales, %	23.6	5.3	4.3	9.2	20.6
Foreign net sales	3,745.7	4,028.1	4,322.0	5,385.9	6,836.6
Operating profit before depreciation (FAS)	695.8	687.8	719.1	912.3	1,067.6
Operating profit before depreciation/net sales (FAS), %	12.7	11.9	12.2	14.2	13.5
Operating earnings	425.4	402.8	399.2	561.1	649.3
Operating earnings/net sales, %	7.7	6.9	6.6	8.5	8.2
Profit after financial items	201.8	239.3	244.8	399.1	505.5
Profit after financial items/net sales, %	3.7	4.1	4.1	6.1	6.4
Profit before appropriations and taxes (FAS)	175.6	195.6	245.0	371.1	567.7
Net income	29.4	107.3	144.5	249.1	347.7
Return on invested assets, %	11.9	12.6	11.0	13.6	12.5
Return on shareholders' equity, %	7.7	8.0	7.1	11.6	12.0
Solidity, %	35.1	40.6	36.8	36.9	41.4
Debt to equity	1.06	0.90	1.03	0.95	0.63
Current ratio	1.36	1.30	1.12	1.25	1.63
Times interest earned	3.18	3.53	4.79	6.93	7.84
Capital expenditure	299.6	443.9	455.4	618.2	467.2
Equity	1,033.2	2,045.6	2,023.0	2,419.1	3,651.0
Number of shareholders (December 31)	29,744	29,404	29,161	28,931	20,424
Personnel (December 31)	9,047	10,088	9,994	9,405	11,180

Note: Figures for 1989 are based on FAS and figures for 1990-1993 are according to IAS, unless otherwise indicated.

P/E ratio =
Issue-adjusted share price at Dec 31
Earnings per share

Return on shareholders' equity =
100 x (profit after financial items ./. actual taxes)
Equity + minority interest (average)

Current ratio =
Current assets
Current liabilities

Market capitalisation =
The number of shares issued in the different share series at Dec 31 multiplied by the corresponding share prices on the stock exchange

Debt to equity =
Interest bearing net debt
Equity

Times interest earned =
Operating earnings + depreciations and amortisations
Net interest expenses

Return on invested assets =
100 x (profit after financial items + interest expenses + other financial expenses)
Balance sheet total ./. interest-free liabilities (average)

Solidity =
100 x (equity + minority interest)
Balance sheet total ./. advances received

At the time of the alliance the Huhtamaki Group consisted of three lines of business; confectionery, pharmaceuticals, and food packaging (see Exhibit 11.2. The largest subsidiary, *Leaf,* was the 10th largest confectionery company in the world with its sugar confectionery, sugar-free chewing gum and chocolate products. *Polarcup* was the leading producer of packaging for catering, dairy, and fast food industries in Europe and Asia-Pacific region and number three worldwide. It produced single-use food and beverage containers. *Leiras* was a Finnish pharmaceuticals company with several internationally successful products in reproductive health care, supportive cancer therapy, and opthamalics.

Exhibit 11.2: Huhtamaki's Distribution of Sales and Growth 1984-1993.

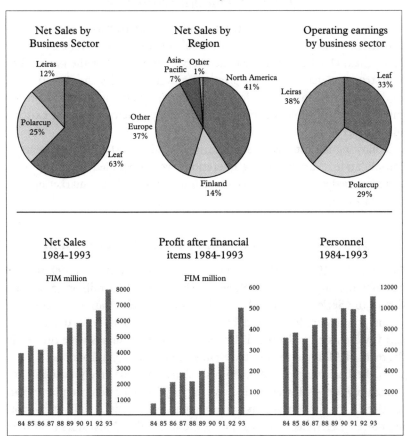

In the early 1980s Huhtamaki was a completely different company than in 1992. It was engaged in 15 different industries in Finland. At that time Huhtamaki decided to undergo a major strategic change process. Its new goal was to become a leading international manufacturer of a few narrow product segments in the chosen fields of industry. The chosen industries were confectionery, packaging and pharmaceuticals. In a ten-year reorientation process, Huhtamaki was transformed from a multibusiness Finnish conglomerate into a multinational enterprise. Altogether between 1983-1989, 65 units were acquired, established, divested or discontinued. Consequently, over 40 percent of the business portfolio of 1980 was divested and the remaining 60 percent represented only 35 percent of the company sales in 1990.

11.2.2. Organisation Structure

The organisational and legal structure of Huhtamaki was changed. Product divisions were incorporated into subsidiaries. The parent company, Huhtamaki Oy (Ltd), only provided service functions for the group. The new structure enabled flexible strategic moves in entries and divestments, e.g. strategic alliances with local or major international partners on the subsidiary level, while retaining parent company control with the existing shareholders.

Following the intensive restructuring decade, 1990-1992 were years of consolidation. Manufacturing operations were upgraded and simplified, and increased investments were made into brand building, marketing, and focused R&D.

11.3. Ownership & Share Price Development

At the end of 1992 the share capital of Huhtamaki was FIM 490 million. The outstanding amount of Series K shares was 12.5 million (51%) and that of the Series I shares 12.0 million (49%). Their relative shares of the voting power were 95.4 % and 4.6 %, respectively. Both types of shares, K and I, were listed in Helsinki. In addition, Series I shares were quoted in the form of ADRs in the United States and on SEAQ in London.

In the beginning of 1993, Finnish shares became freely available for foreign investors. However, due to company issuance policy and previous restrictions on foreign ownership foreign investors tended to hold low voting power preference I shares. Domestic institutional investors held high voting power ordinary K shares. The estimated foreign ownership of Huhtamaki was 29.4 percent in June 1993, but grew to 36 percent by the end of the year. Huhtamaki free shares were trading in the 1980's at a 20-40 % price premium to restricted shares, but in 1991-1992 free shares were trading at a discount to restricted shares. The market was discounting the abolishment of foreign ownership restrictions in 1993.

In 1992, Huhtamaki's shares had, in value terms, the second highest turnover on the Helsinki Stock Exchange and in volume terms the Huhtamaki I share was the second most traded Finnish share series at SEAQ.

The ownership structure of Huhtamaki was well diversified. At the end of 1992 the company had 29,000 shareholders and some 24.5 million shares. (By the end of 1993 the number of shareholders had been reduced to 20,400 and the number of shares outstanding raised to 29.4 million).

Exhibit 11.3: Huhtamaki's Share Price Development.

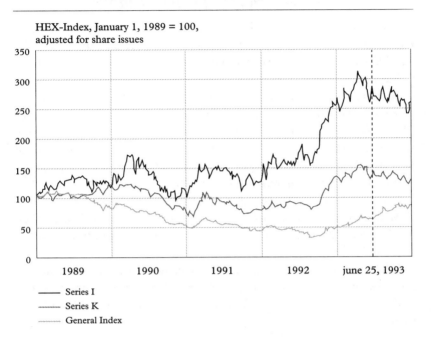

HEX-Index, January 1, 1989 = 100,
adjusted for share issues

——— Series I
------- Series K
········· General Index

The dual-class share structure effectively protected the company from any takeover. Friendly Finnish foundations and insurance companies held more than 50 % of the votes. At the end of 1992, the market capitalisation of Huhtamaki was FIM 4,338 million (USD 810 million).

The stock prices and trading volumes on the Helsinki Stock Exchange had been deteriorating since April 1989. In September 1992, the Bank of Finland abandoned the currency band and let the Finnish Markka float freely. That marked a turnaround in the stock exchange development. By the end of the year the currency had depreciated about 13 % against other currencies. The short term domestic interest rates had fallen from 17 % to the 10 % level. The stock market index rose by 53 %. However, the primary market for equity issues remained untouched until Spring 1993. The Huhtamaki share price development relative to the general index is shown in Exhibit 11.3.

11.4. Financial Performance in 1992

Despite a deep recession in Finland and recession in the global economy, Huhtamaki was able to improve its financial performance (Exhibit 11.1). In 1992 its profits after financial items reached FIM 399 million, a 63 % rise from the previous year.

Huhtamaki had publicly committed itself to very challenging performance goals. The company had set a long-term target annual growth rate for EPS at 10 %. Return on equity capital had to exceed 15 % and debt to equity should not exceed one. In 1992, Huhtamaki was well on target in terms of EPS growth rate (+72 %) and gearing (0.95), but, despite a major improvement, it lagged behind in terms of return on equity capital (11.6 %).

During the consolidation phase of 1990-92 Huhtamaki had invested FIM 1.5 billion to improve its manufacturing efficiency and FIM 1 billion into brand building. This process depressed its equity/assets ratio temporarily under 40 %.

While the stock price development remained relatively stagnant, the improved financial results lowered Huhtamaki's P/E ratio from 16.4 in 1992 to 13.8 in 1993 for Series K shares and from 15.8 to 13.3 for Series I shares.

11.5. The Growth and Strategy of Leaf

In 1983, as part of its strategy of focusing on a few niche industries, Huhtamaki acquired three mid-sized U.S. confectionery companies with 14 manufacturing plants. They were:

Leaf Confectionery Inc., the confectionery units of Beatrice Foods Co., and the Donruss division of General Mills. These units were joined together under Leaf, Inc. Within the next 10 years the Leaf Group grew 2.5 times, doubling the size of the Huhtamaki Group. Also the structure of the Leaf Group changed dramatically due to many acquisitions and divestments (see Exhibit 11.4).

Leaf had built its strategy on strong core brand names, on organic growth through innovations and on external growth through international acquisitions. Leaf's organic growth had consistently outperformed the industry. Outside the core market areas, Leaf was open to joint-ventures and other forms of cooperation. Accordingly, it had a successful chewing gum venture in China and newly started confectionery and gum plants in Mexico and Poland.

Exhibit 11.4: Dynamic Evolution of Leaf 1984-1993.

1983	Major Acquisitions in the USA: Leaf Confectionery Inc., the confectionery units of Beatrice Foods Co. and the Donruss division of General Mills.
1985	Acquisition of Ford Gum (USA); Divestment of Richardson Mint (USA)
1986	Acquisition of Maple Leaf (Holland)
1987	Hellas (Finland) incorporated under Leaf
1988	Leaf worldwide headquarters moved to Amsterdam; A joint venture was established in China
1989	Acquisition of Hollywood Brands and Heath (USA) and a minority in Elizabeth Shaw (UK); Divestment of plants in Brooklyn and Long Island
1990	Acquisition of the remainder of Elizabeth Shaw; Acquisition of Gepro N.V., a distributor in Belgium
1991	Establishment of Dulsa, a Mexican joint venture with PepsiCo's sabritas snack division; Divestment of the Clark factory (USA)
1992	Acquisition of Merijal division from Rettig (Finland) in exchange for Marli (food products, Finland); Closing of small plants in Sweden, Canada and Chicago
1993	Project Bravo completed (a four-year, USD 100 million enterprise to consolidate the US manufacturing operations to dedicated, state-of-the-art facilities); The Polish plant starts manufacturing; Acquisition of Procordia's confectionery units.

Leaf had invested heavily in focused R&D and had proprietary expertise in areas such as chewing gum, sugarfree products, low-calorie products and xylitol technology. Innovations such as sugarless chewing gum, XyliFresh 100, and LO Light chocolate bars had given Leaf the first mover advantage vis-à-vis its competitors. XyliFresh brand was the world's most researched chewing gum, and its dental benefits had been officially endorsed in many countries. Furthermore, the xylitol technology had been successfully applied to child medication by Leiras, Huhtamaki's other subsidiary.

In 1993 Leaf had manufacturing operations in 13 countries. Its products were sold in almost 100 countries. The group employed 6,500 people (see Exhibit 11.5 for Key Figures). Its share of the Huhtamaki Group's sales was over 60 %, but only 50 % of operating earnings. In the process of transforming Leaf from a US company to an international one the worldwide headquarters were moved from Chicago to Amsterdam in 1988.

Leaf concentrated on segment leaderships instead of competing head-on in the mainstream product categories, such as solid chocolate bars. The key brands were complemented with locally strong products. With a critical mass for efficient production and distribution in most of its key mar-

Exhibit 11.5: Key Figures of Leaf (FIM million).

	1993	1992	1991	1990	1989
Net Sales	5,013	3,857	3,248	2,908	2,760
North America	63 %	66 %	66 %	67 %	72 %
Europe	37 %	34 %	34 %	33 %	28 %
Operating Earnings	207	312	238	241	242
Capital Expenditure	278	429	254	157	113
Personnel	6,119	5,218	4,862	5,221	4,162

kets, the company now pursued expansion of its presence through a step-by-step "multilocal" approach. In Europe, Leaf continued to focus and consolidate its activities while its network and brands gradually spread further across the Continent.

In Europe, sales promotion was targeted for products that had potential for Pan-Nordic or Pan-Europe brands. Leaf's Eurobrands were sugar-less chewing gum, XyliFresh 100, (Leaf had 25 % of the market), throat lozenges with dental benefits, Xylitol Plus, and Chewits fruity toffee. It also had a strong market share in pastilles. Local best-selling brands included Sportlife in Holland, Elizabeth Saw chocolate in the UK, ML stick gum in Germany and Xylitol Jenkki and Tupla in Finland.

In North America, Leaf was the overall number two in non-chocolate candy, with several segment leaders such as Jolly Rancher, PayDay, Heath, Milk Duds, Good & Plenty and Whoppers among its brands. Collectible baseball and NHL ice hockey cards played an important role in sales growth.

To enjoy economies of scale in production most plants specialised in the production of a single brand. Investments were made to modernise and enlarge production facilities. Outdated plants were shut. In most key markets, Leaf had its own sales force. In the United States, it relied on a strong network of independent food brokers.

The size of the European confectionery industry was about FIM 200 billion (USD 40 billion). The major multinationals such as Mars, Nestle and Hershey, competed mainly in the chocolate candy business (2/3 of the market) which was a relatively concentrated segment. The other segment, sugar confectionery, was still very fragmented. Most competitors were local producers. Thus Leaf encountered a number of different competitors based on the product segment and the country in question. Only the Norwegian Freia-Marabou (acquired by Philip Morris in 1993) followed an European strategy. In Finland, Leaf had one fourth of the FIM 2,6 billion

(USD 0.5 billion) market and had several brand names among the top 10 selling candies.

11.6. The Growth and Strategy of Leiras

Until the late 1980's, Leiras was mainly manufacturing pharmaceuticals for the Finnish market and for the neighbouring countries. Between 1985-1987, Leiras acquired three other Finnish pharmaceutical companies and obtained a dominant position in the oligopolistic domestic market. Relative to its size it obtained a wide and partially overlapping product range.

For years Leiras had been manufacturing a wide range of common drugs in Finland. The manufacturing was based on its own patented process methods that were different from those used by the holders of the original product patents for the same drugs. In 1995, however, process patents would lose their importance in Finland, as they had already lost elsewhere in Europe. For production the owner of a process patent would then need a license from the holder of the original product patent, or the process patent holder had to wait until the product patent protection expired.

In the late 1980's, Leiras had some 80 process patents, but no product patents. In order to prepare itself for the changing and accelerating international competition of the 1990's Leiras had to formulate a new strategy. At the time of the alliance in 1993, many international industry leaders and competitors believed that in the future the pharmaceutical industry would consist of two main types of companies; (1) large, international, research-intensive companies continuously identifying and developing effective new substances for important therapeutic areas, and (2) generic drug companies manufacturing and marketing preparations and substances for which the patent protection had expired. (Generic drug companies sell low-price copies and depend entirely on the research industry for their supply of products).

Neither one of the future scenarios was tempting. Leiras was not large and strong enough to finance the time-consuming and long-term research efforts necessary for the development of new preparations and to convey them to all large markets speedily, simultaneously and effectively. Nor did it want to become a generic drug producer. Leiras chose to specialise and concentrate its R&D into narrow speciality areas and aim for international leadership in these product segments. In international distribution and marketing it would look for foreign alliances.

Consequently, the yearly R&D expenditure was expanded to 15 % of

Exhibit 11.6: Key Figures of Leiras (FIM million).

	1993	1992	1991	1990
Net sales	933	744	674	682
Exports	518	358	259	282
Operating Earnings	243	148	84	65
Capital Expenditure	39	48	46	69
R&D Expenditure	145	108	95	93
Personnel	1,260	1,237	1,211	1,278

net sales. R&D work was concentrated on four areas; (1) reproductive health care (RHC) and hormone replacement therapy (HRT), (2) bone metabolism, (3) opthamalic drugs, and (4) inhalation technique for respiratory drug dosage.

The domestic strategy of Leiras was to focus on holding its strong market position in Finland in prescription products and in OTC drugs for self medication. Due to product rationalisation, some 70 products were delisted and an inexpensive AO-product family of OTC drugs was launched to the domestic market.

Internationally Leiras was a relatively small company with 1,260 employees (see Exhibit 11.6). In 1993 its net sales amounted to FIM 933 million (USD 170 million) of which 56 % were exports. However, thanks to the new strategy and increasing exports it was growing fast. Between 1992 and 1993, net sales grew by 25 %, exports by 45 % and operating profits by 64 % to FIM 243 million (26 % of net sales). The main export markets were North America, Southeast Asia, and Scandinavia.

At the time of the alliance, three of Leiras's original preparations had made it or had potential to make it into international or global distribution. *Norplant* was a contraceptive implant which already had a sales license in 38 countries and had some 2 million users. *Levonova* was a contraceptive hormone spiral. *Bonefos* was a preparation for treating cancer-related disturbances in bones and had potential for treatment of osteoporosis, an illness suffered by millions of people. It had a sales license in 35 countries.

To obtain necessary strength in international marketing and distribution Leiras had been active in promoting cooperation with foreign parties. In the United States it worked with the Population Council to develop Norplant for industrial production. The product was successfully launched to the US market in 1991. The UK market was entered in 1993 and in Canada the sales license was obtained in January 1994. In 1993, Leiras had agreed with a leading international reproductive health care (RHC) company on the global distribution of Norplant. In 1992, Leiras entered into a joint research agreement with Kissei Pharmaceutical Co. in order to launch Bonefos to the Japanese market. The US subsidiary of Leiras was relocated to Washington D.C. close to the Food and Drug Administration FDA, which over the next few years would decide on several drug registrations presented by Leiras.

11.7. Procordia (Sweden)

In 1985, Procordia had acquired the 100-year old Swedish family confectionery company Ahlgrens. It expanded the group into Procordia United Brands through acquisitions in Germany, Denmark and Finland. All the acquired foreign firms were over 100-year-old family companies. Procordia was in the process of implementing one cohesive "We in Procordia" culture, when major changes in the Procordia corporate structure and business portfolio took place. Procordia became a major foods and pharmaceuticals company. For some time the contents of the business portfolio was very mobile and the future of the confectionery business in the portfolio uncertain.

In 1992, Procordia's Confectionery business showed a loss of SEK 40 million (USD 6 million, FIM 28 million). It was expected to be under pressure for some time. It was ripe for an alliance or joint venture which could finance expansion and rationalise production.

11.8. The Strategic Alliance

On June 29, 1993, when the strategic alliance was first announced, it was expected to provide significant operating and financial synergies for both parties.

11.8.1. Benefits for Leaf

According to Huhtamaki President and CEO Timo Peltola the acquisition suited Leaf perfectly with respect to brands as well as geographic structure. The Procordia products would add to Leaf's confectionery range, although the assortment was likely to be cut. Procordia's best selling product was Läkerol, which was the leading cough drop in Sweden, Denmark, Norway, and Switzerland.

Procordia's confectionery business strengthened Leaf's position in Europe. In 1992, the sales of Leaf Europe amounted to FIM 1.3 billion

(USD 240 million). As a result of this transaction sales in Europe would increase by 60 % and Europe would represent 40 % of the total sales of the Leaf Group. The Leaf Group's share of the Huhtamaki Group sales were expected to rise from 59 % in 1992 to 63 % in 1993.

Procordia's production units were located in Sweden (Ahlgrens), Denmark (the former Evers and Benzon Brands), Germany (Villosa) and Spain (Damel), whereas Leaf's production units were located in Finland, United Kingdom, Ireland, Holland, Poland, United States, Canada, Mexico and China. Procordia's sales units were located in Sweden, Denmark, Finland, Norway, Holland, Belgium, Germany, Switzerland, and Spain, whereas Leaf's were located in Germany, Belgium, and Sweden. After the transaction Leaf would have 12 production plants in Europe. The number was likely to be cut down due to synergies to be gained from rationalisation and economies of scale. Each plant would in the future specialise in producing a particular brand. Leaf would design an individual product portfolio for each country and focus sales promotion efforts accordingly.

As mentioned earlier, the other part of the Procordia and Huhtamaki transaction was the establishment of a joint venture between Procordia's pharmaceutical company Kabi Pharmacia and Huhtamaki's Leiras division in January 1994. The new company, Pharmacia-Leiras, would market two innovative gynaecological products in European countries, excluding the Nordic countries: Kabi Pharmacia's Estring, a vaginal ring for oestrogen delivery, and Leiras' contraceptive hormone spiral Levonova. The headquarters of the venture would be located in Amsterdam.

The venture provided Leiras with a marketing channel for Levonova, a product with a great potential in the area of contraception. The drug was likely to be registered in the EU area during the year 1994. Kabi Pharmacia had already an existing sales network in Europe which provided a quick start for the penetration of the European market for Levonova. The joint venture would incur start-up costs in 1994, but Levonova's impact on the future results of Leiras was expected to be substantial.

With USD 3 billion (SEK 21 billion) sales and 18,000 employees, Kabi Pharmacia ranked as the eighth largest pharmaceutical company in Europe and the 18th largest in the world. Its global market share was about 1.5 %, compared with the market share of Merck & Co., the world's largest company in the industry, just over 3 %. In 1992, Kabi Pharmacia's operating income amounted to USD 370 million (SEK 2,597 million).

Kabi Pharmacia's goal was to become one of the leading pharmaceutical companies in the world. It already had a leading position in oncology (cancer), ophthalmic surgery, growth disorders, nutrient solutions for intravenous infusion and in vitro allergy diagnostics. Its R&D expertise was in biotechnology and synthetic chemistry. Its research team consisted of 3,000 persons. The research budget amounted to USD 430 million (SEK 3 billion), representing 14 % of sales. The company had production plants in 13 countries, own sales companies in about 40 countries, 2,500 medical representatives, of which over 1,500 were based in Europe, and distribution channels in more than 100 countries. Its major markets were Italy, United States, Sweden, Japan and Germany. In 1992, 67 % of sales originated in Europe and 2 % in Finland.

Out of Kabi Pharmacia's 10 largest-selling products none was in the field of gynaecology. However, the company would have 19 important product launches during the next five years, two of which were in the field of gynaecology and four in the field of oncology or cancer diagnostics.

11.9. Financial Synergies

The financing of Huhtamaki's acquisition of Procordia's confectionery business was done through a targeted share issue. Procordia bought three million new shares of Class I in Huhtamaki for SEK 900 million. The transaction price per share was about FIM 210 compared to FIM 190 paid on the stock exchange. Thus, Procordia paid a premium of some 10 %. The issued amount of new shares was equal to 10,9 % of Huhtamaki's capital stock. According to the agreement Procordia's share of the capital stock and votes in Huhtamaki would be limited to a maximum of 21 %. No restriction on the sale of the shares was set. In return, Huhtamaki would pay SEK 900 million for Procordia's European confectionery business.

The transaction would strengthen Huhtamaki's balance sheet. Since the acquired unit had no interest-bearing debt, Huhtamaki's equity to total assets would rise above 40 %. However, the transaction would have a slightly negative effect on earnings per share. The 1994 EPS, which would be diluted by the increase in the number of shares, was expected to drop from FIM 16 to FIM 14.40.

Procordia President & CEO Jan Ekberg regarded the shareholding in Huhtamaki primarily as a financial investment, but stated that it should also be seen as an expression of an alliance between two successful pharmaceutical companies that may very well result in new forms of cooperation. The transaction was finalised September 13, 1993. At the Annual

Shareholders' Meeting of Huhtamaki in April 1994, Jan Ekberg was elected a member of the Supervisory Board of Huhtamaki.

11.10. Stock Market Effects of the Announced Alliance

The stock market's reaction to the announced alliance and agreed transactions between Huhtamaki and Procordia was positive. Huhtamaki I shares had closed at FIM 190 the day before but jumped to FIM 200 (+5.3 %) after the announcement. The ordinary K share jumped from FIM 194 to FIM 205 (+5.7 %). The general index rose only by 0.3 % that day.

The turnover in Huhtamaki Series I shares reached 48,275 shares the day after the announcement compared to 15,600 shares the day before the announcement, and to the daily average turnover of 30,500 shares in June, 1993. In Series K shares the volume remained at a couple of thousands a day.

The positive effect on share price was not permanent. In fact, the announcement broke only temporarily the stagnant or slowly declining share price development of Huhtamaki shares, which continued until August 1993.

11.11. An Update on Huhtamaki as of December 1996

On February 13, 1996, Huhtamaki announced that negotiations on the sale of the pharmaceutical division Leiras to an international pharmaceutical company were underway. According to CEO Timo Peltola, Huhtamaki's basic strategy of pursuing world leadership in closely defined segments was unchanged. Huhtamaki would concentrate on foods-related business, Leaf in confectionery and Polarcup in food packaging. The sale of Leiras would significantly strengthen Huhtamaki's balance sheet, enabling further development of the core businesses. This would enhance the company's strategic position, earnings potential and, ultimately, shareholder value.

"The rapid consolidation within the global pharmaceuticals industry has changed Leiras's operating environment. A wave of mergers has swept the top 40 pharmaceutical companies and will extend to smaller firms as well. High research and development costs, downward pressure on drug prices and health-care cost cutting have forced the industry to seek economies of scale from larger unit sizes," CEO Peltola commented. The international marketing of new products also required substantial resources.

In 1995, Leiras's net sales amounted to FIM 857 (USD 200) million, 11% of Huhtamaki's total. Operating earnings were FIM 135 (USD 30) million. A decline of 22% from 1994 was mainly attributable to low contraceptive implants sales. Leiras's R&D expenditure was in excess of 20% of its net sales. According to Peltola, Leiras's potential would be best realised as a specialised unit within a major international pharmaceutical company.

Huhtamaki did not disclose the name or names of the companies with which it was currently negotiating. A solution was expected during the spring 1996. The security analysts tipped Pharmacia & Upjohn, a newly merged Swedish-American pharmaceuticals group, as a likely buyer. Pharmacia & Upjohn was one of Huhtamaki's largest shareholders with 10.2% of shares and 1.1% of votes. Its Chairman Mr. Jan Ekberg was a member of Huhtamaki's Supervisory Board. Other likely candidates cited were American Bristol-Myers Squib and British SmithKline Beechham. The deal could be worth between FIM 1.5 billion and FIM 2 billion (USD 333-435 million). The announcement boosted Huhtamaki's stock price by 5.1%.

On July 16, 1996, Huhtamaki announced that the German Pharmaceutical company Schering AG would purchase Leiras for a consideration of FIM 1,425 million (USD 315 million) including assumed debt. The deal excluded Leiras's ophthalmologic business, some 15 % of Leiras's sales. Schering had always been Leiras's supplier of hormones, and had successfully marketed Leiras's intrauterine devices worldwide for more than 20 years. In a related transaction Huhtamaki's finance company repurchased three million Huhtamaki shares from Pharmacia-Upjohn and purchased Pharmacia-Upjohn's shares in their joint marketing company for female healthcare products.

On December 23, 1996, the final transaction in the divestment process of Huhtamaki's pharmaceuticals business was brought to an end. Santen Pharmaceutical from Osaka Japan, the world's second largest manufacturer of ophthalmological products, had acquired Leiras's ophthalmologic business, Star Ltd, with annual net sales of FIM 110 million (USD 24 million). The purchase price was FIM 430 million (USD 93 million), twice the market expectations. Santen's net sales in 1995 were FIM 2,5 billion (USD 0.6 billion). The company was listed on the Tokyo Stock Exchange. Until 1996 Santen had been a very domestic company, until it opened a development unit in Napa Valley, California. With its modern manufacturing plant Star would become the center for Santen's European operations.

The complete divestment of Leiras resulted in an extraordinary profit in excess of FIM 1 billion (USD 220 million). The stock market's reaction was positive. On December 23, 1996 the price of both Series of Huhtamaki shares rose by 3 percent, Series I from FIM 208 to FIM 214 and Series K from FIM 203 to FIM 209. Huhtamaki's P/E ratio was 28, in line with international competitors.

Earlier during the year Huhtamaki had sold its U.S. confectionery business to Hershey and acquired Hershey's factories in Europe. The sales proceeds from Leiras and Leaf North-America strengthened Huhtamaki's cash position by FIM 4 billion (USD 1 billion).

Part VI

Strategies of
Norwegian Corporations

The 1980s and the first part of the 1990s represented a transition period for internationally-oriented Norwegian companies. As illustrated by the three case studies, Norwegian companies used a number of ways to reduce their cost of capital. On the issue of international access to capital, Norwegian public policy was trailing innovations in the capital market. The oil price shock (decrease) of 1986 created an increased public awareness of the need for a diversified and internationally-oriented Norwegian economy. Eventually deregulation became a political goal in itself. As was shown in Chapter 2, the final step of deregulation came with Norway's membership in the European Economic Area (EEA) Agreement, implemented on January 1, 1994. This made Norway a *de facto* member of the EU as it relates to corporate finance. It implied that all nationality restrictions on stock ownership were abandoned.

Our three Norwegian case studies illustrate some of the financial innovations that companies took in order to succeed in the international marketplace. Companies, such as Norsk Data and Hafslund Nycomed, understood the necessity of accessing internationally-priced equity. During the second half of the 1980s the annual average growth of Norwegian foreign direct investments (FDI) abroad was an impressive 35.8% per year.[1] In 1982 the net outflow of Norwegian FDI was NOK 1.9 billion. The same figure had increased to NOK 8.8 billion by 1989, after peaking at NOK 11.9 billion in 1986. It was essential that these foreign investments could be financed at an international price of capital, and not restrained by a limited Norwegian equity market. These FDIs were driven by strategic motives such as: access to complementary resources and capabilities in foreign markets, improved economies of scale and scope, and improved utilisation of firm-specific capabilities and products.[2] The increased emphasis on internationalisation was driven by a change of business strategy. Companies that used to have a domestic focus, such as Elektrisk Bureau, understood the need for a much larger global market share. Commonly a change to a "global" strategy was motivated by cost concerns (particularly in research and development costs) and the desire for improved distribution access. Better access to new technology and complementary products, as shown in the case of Elektrisk Bureau, was also an important promoter of internationalisation.

1. Central Bureau of Statistics in Norway.
2. See Randøy, T. (1997). "Toward a Firm-Based Model of Foreign Direct Investment" in I. Björkman & M. Forsgren (eds.) *The Nature of the International Firm*, Copenhagen: Copenhagen Business School Press, pp. 257-280.

Our three cases show that the different financial strategies promoted the overall internationalisation of these companies. The Norsk Data case is an example of internationalising capital in the early 1980s, whereas, the Elektrisk Bureau case is from the mid-1980s. The Hafslund Nycomed case provides an example of internationalisation of the cost and availability of capital from the late 1980s to the early 1990s. The cases of Norsk Data and Hafslund Nycomed provide interesting illustrations of how sourcing international capital made these companies able to compete head-on with large U.S. or European rivals. These firms were able to sell their equity abroad at a higher P/E-ratio than on the domestic equity market. Norsk Data was able to sell its shares at a similar P/E-ratio to other comparable computer companies on the international equity market. The case of Norsk Data reveals how the injection of fresh capital enabled the firm to manage an average annual sales growth of 40 %. In July 1981 Norsk Data listed on the London Stock Exchange. During 1981 the stock price increased by 700%. In March 1982 Norsk Data made its first foreign equity issue in London, providing the company with NOK 100 million. A second successful issue was made in September 1984 in the United States, providing the company with NOK 396 million.

By the end of the 1980s the degree of market segmentation in Norway had decreased substantially. However, Hafslund Nycomed's large market capitalisation relative to the Norwegian equity market, made the company less attractive to domestic investors. In 1991, Hafslund Nycomed represented 11% of the total value of the Oslo Stock Exchange. Another important fact was that the U.S. equity market was much more experienced in assessing pharmaceutical companies. Hafslund made two successful international stock issues, one on June 22, 1989 in London, and the second one in New York on June 22, 1992.

Elektrisk Bureau was able to make a strategic alliance with ASEA, later known as ABB. Through a 20% targeted issue towards ASEA in September 1986, Elektrisk Bureau was able to obtain NOK 370.5 million in new equity. ASEA paid NOK 200 per B-share at the same time as the existing shareholders could use their preemptive rights to buy B-shares at NOK 145. Elektrisk Bureau's stock price increased 18% within two weeks after the announcement of the strategic alliance.

12. Norsk Data A/S: Two Directed Issues[1]

Trond Randøy

12.1. Introduction

During the period 1981-1984, Norsk Data (ND) financed its phenomenal growth by a creative international financial strategy. First it crosslisted on the London Stock Exchange in July 1981. Then it floated a directed equity issue in the United Kingdom in March 1982. ND created an ADR (American Depositary Receipt) system in the United States in January 1983 and crosslisted its ADSs on NASDAQ in May 1983. ND crosslisted on the Stockholm Stock Exchange in 1983. In 1984, it floated a S.E.C.-registered B-share equity issue directed at U.S. investors, but also sold heavily to European and Japanese investors. During the first half of 1981, just prior to all these transactions, ND had been "discovered" by foreign investors in a similar manner to Novo Industri's earlier experience in 1980. As a result of the demand from foreign investors, ND's B-share price had risen 700 % in the first half of 1981. This created the opportunity for ND to internationalise its cost and availability of capital during the subsequent three years.

12.2. Historical Development

Norsk Data was established in 1967 by a group of three scientists from the Norwegian Defense Research Establishment. The company developed, produced and sold 16-bit and 32-bit computers, or mini-computers. This was supported by extensive associated software systems with particular emphasis on the development of on-line operating systems. The firm's proprietary hardware and software provided the basis for the company's successful growth.

1. Valuable comments and suggestions from Terje Mikalsen, the former chairman of Norsk Data, are acknowledged.

Initially, ND concentrated on developing systems for Norwegian customers. A major breakthrough came in 1973 with a large order from CERN, the European Organisation for Nuclear Research. This helped to create a platform for further export. It gave ND a reputation that might not otherwise have been enjoyed by a small company selling in the European market. Since 1973, CERN followed up the initial purchase with a steady flow of new orders. These in turn led to a number of orders from national and international research organisations.

From 1974, priority was given to strengthening the marketing organization both in Norway and abroad. The first overseas operation was established in France near Geneva in 1973. Subsequently, in 1975 the company set up a subsidiary in Sweden. Thereafter subsidiaries were established in Denmark (1976), West Germany and the United States (1978), and the United Kingdom and Switzerland (1980).

In addition to the orders from CERN, Norsk Data won several contracts which were particularly significant in the company's development. In 1976, the company won a contract from the Norwegian State Railways worth NOK 11 million for a turnkey system for the control of all Norwegian freight rolling stock. In 1977, the company won the contract from the Link Division of the Singer Company in the United States for the supply of computers for a flight simulator for the F-16 fighter aircraft. By 1981, the total sales under the F-16 program amounted to around NOK 60 million.

In 1977, the company established its NORTEXT division to supply turnkey computer systems for the newspaper industry. In 1979, Norsk Data received NOK 30 million from Mobil Exploration Norway Inc. for two research programs which were carried out during 1980-82. These programs overlapped with part of the company's long term general research and development program, and provided computer systems tailored for use by the oil industry.

Although in the early 1970's sales of Norsk Data's computer systems tended to be for scientific and technical applications, from 1975 onwards the company increasingly concentrated on administrative applications, in particular on-line data-base systems. By the end of the 1980s, about half the company's turnover derived from commercial or managerial applications.

In 1983, Norsk Data was the leading computer company in its category in the world in terms of profit margin, return on equity and operating result per employee. 1983 was also the year when Norsk Data received the

Exhibit 12.1: Total Turnover for Norsk Data 1974-1990.
Mill. NOK

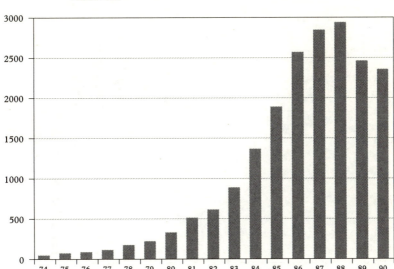

prize as the "Norwegian company of the year", which was awarded by the "Næringsrevyen".

From 1973 on, until the time of the U.S. equity issue, ND's turnover increased by approximately 40 % per year, while the profit increased by 50 % per year. During the same period, the company developed a considerable international organisation, and exports stabilised around 50% of total turnover. Sales to the Nordic countries accounted for approximately 18 % of sales while the rest of Europe, including the United Kingdom, accounted for another 20 %. With few exceptions, the international operations did not provide much profits, as opposed to the home-market.

In retrospect, 1986 turned out to be ND:s most profitable years. After that Norsk Data suffered a rapid decline until its eventual demise. Exhibits 12.1, 12.2, and 12.3 show total turnover, operating profits, and employment, respectively, for the period 1974-1990. These exhibits illustrate the spectacular rise and fall of an information technology company in a fast-changing technological landscape.

Exhibit 12.2: Operating Profits for Norsk Data 1974-1990.
Mill. NOK

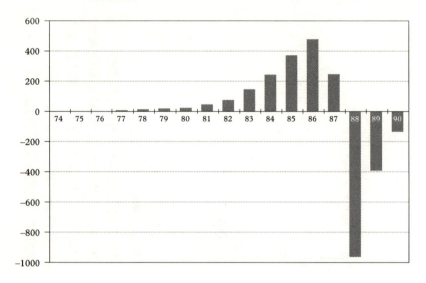

Exhibit 12.3: Number of Employees in Norsk Data 1974-1990.

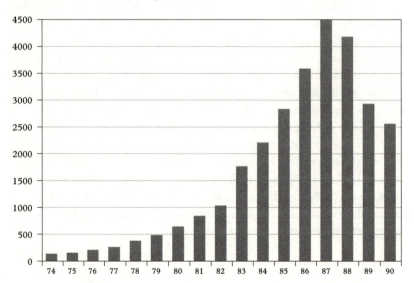

12.3. Competition

From the start, ND competed against international competitors. ND's international breakthrough came with the CERN contract. Other producers of minicomputers were first and foremost large, U.S.-based manufacturers. In the early years, Digital Equipment was the strongest competitor, especially in the markets outside Norway. Later on, IBM became stronger and in 1982 it was viewed as the main competitor in Norway. WANG Laboratories was also strongly present in the Norwegian market, while Prime Computer and Hewlett Packard provided much of the competition ND faced in the international arena.

In the 1970s the computer market could best be described as an oligopoly. Eventually the number of producers increased substantially as the barriers to entry decreased over time. At the same time, the number of competing products increased. In the Norwegian market, ND faced less competition than abroad. Later on, a number of companies started to serve the Norwegian market. The new companies were mainly software companies, with no hardware capabilities. Some of these software companies used ND's operating system (SINTRAN) when making new software solutions.

12.4. Success Factors

Following the contract from CERN, ND entered a phase with continuous growth and prosperity, which lasted from the early 1970s to the mid-1980s. ND seemed to succeed in every aspect. The products were among the best in its category. Part of the secret was that ND managed to utilise their smaller size to circumnavigate the larger U.S. competitors. By using new technology before the competitors were able to react, ND could draw more profits out of equipment which could be sold at a premium price. ND was also better at keeping a compact and closely knit product range, something which was closely tied to profits. The production of minicomputers and other hardware involved a large amount of fixed cost. Economies of scale in production were therefore important to achieve. Finally, ND had a lead in terms of software, which made it easier to sell at a premium price.

ND's human resource policy was regarded as a substantial contribution to its success. Its employees were highly motivated, and they could freely use their ideas and ambitions. The relationship between employees and management was loose and informal. Few market opportunities were lost, and the company was constantly looking for new areas, much like a teenager willing to try everything.

Research and development were activities of high priority to the founders and managers of ND, and subsequently constituted a focus of the operations. The R&D-efforts were often rooted in a bundle of creativity and innovative thinking. Despite substantial technological and marketing-related boldness, ND landed on its feet every time. The customers were enthusiastic and helpful, but also demanding in terms of after-sale services, software/hardware-suitability and quality demands.

ND was also very creative and innovative with respect to its financing strategies. While the Norwegian market was still heavily regulated they found a path to escape dependence on the segmented and illiquid Norwegian financial market.

12.5. The Path Toward Internationalising Norsk Data's Cost of Capital

The founders of ND established the company with an equity of NOK 194,000. The growth of the company was closely tied to its successful financial strategy. Part of the business philosophy was that the employees should own shares in the company. In 1980, almost 15 percent of the existing two million shares were owned by the employees. As many as 74 % of the employees owned shares in the company.

The company was listed on the Oslo Stock Exchange's secondary (B-list) in 1975 and in 1979 on the major list (A-list). By the end of 1980, ND had 785 shareholders.

12.5.1. Crosslisting in London

The decision to apply for a listing on the London Stock Exchange was made in 1980. The company's stated objective was to finance a considerable portion of the future growth by a strong operating cash flow. Access to new share capital was, however, necessary in order to finance the exceptional strong growth the company was expecting.

On July 3, 1981, Norsk Data's shares were listed on the official list of the London Stock Exchange. This marked an important milestone in the internationalisation process of the company. The London listing, together with a growing international interest for the company's shares, helped to drive up the total value of ND from NOK 16,485,000 in the beginning of

1980 to NOK 593,187,712 by the end of 1981. A successful stock issue in London of 295,000 shares was made in March, 1982. In addition, 50,000 shares were issued to employees. The London issue provided the company with NOK 100 million in new equity. The introduction of the shares on the London Stock Exchange enhanced the financial flexibility of ND. Such a flexibility was previously only available to the large U.S. competitors.

12.5.2. Crosslisting in the United States and Sweden

Until 1983, ND had only one class of shares. The shares were divided into two classes; A-shares with voting rights and B-shares without voting rights. On January 11, 1983, American Depositary Receipts (ADRs) for A-shares were listed on the U.S. "over-the-counter" market and quoted in the NASDAQ-system on February 15, 1983. From May 27, 1983, American Depositary Receipts for B-shares (B-ADR) were listed on the National Market System (NMS) in the NASDAQ-system with the symbol NORKZ. The company was also listed on the Stockholm Stock Exchange in 1983 in the form of Swedish depositary receipts.

12.5.3. A Directed Issue of B-shares in the United States With Secondary Sales in Europe and Japan

In September, 1984, Norsk Data offered its second issue of B-shares. It sold 1,250,000 B-shares for the price of NOK 335 per share. This provided the company with a net capital inflow of NOK 396 million. The offering was organised as a public subscription in the United States and registered by the US Securities and Exchange Commission. It was, however, emphasised that non-American investors also were able to participate. More than half of this issue was sold in Europe, and about 200,000 shares were sold in Japan. In 1984, the company started the initial preparation for both the A-shares and the B-shares to be listed on the Stock Exchanges in Frankfurt and Hamburg.

Only two shareholders owned more than 20 % of the share capital in 1980. These were A/S Norsund (controlled by Terje Mikaelsen) with 31 % and Th. Brøvigs Rederi with 21,9 %. 14.2 % of the shares were owned by employees of ND. Four years later, in 1984, no single shareholder owned more than 20 % of the company. However, Terje Mikalsen, the Chairman of ND, controlled 28.2 % of the votes. Employees owned 8 %.

12.5.4. Foreign Ownership

Foreign ownership of shares was, according to Norwegian law, limited to 33 % prior to 1981. In 1981, The Ministry of Industrial Affairs granted ND the right for up to 40 % of the A-shares to be owned by foreign investors. This permission was extended in 1982, to 45 %, and again in 1983 to 49 %. The A-shares could be converted to B-shares in the relation 1:1. In 1984, the Government gave up the restrictions of foreign ownership of B-shares and foreign ownership of the total number of shares. The only remaining restriction in 1984 was that foreigners were not allowed to own more than 49 % of A-shares, and that the A-share capital had to exceed NOK 100 million. The dismantling of the restriction on B-share ownership enabled ND to finance its future growth with full flexibility. The company was able to choose among the most attractive capital markets and means of financing.

By the end of 1981, 20.6 % of ND's shares were owned by foreign companies or individual investors. Of the 1,678 shareholders ND had by the end of 1981, 255 were foreign.

By the end of 1984, after the U.K. and U.S. equity issues in 1982 and 1984, ND had 6,331 shareholders. Of these 2,290 were foreign owners of A-shares and 221 were foreign owners of B-shares. Of the A-shares, 36.6 % were owned by foreigners, and more than 90 % of the B-shares were in foreign ownership. Exhibits 12.4 and 12.5 show the ownership distribution of all shares and A-shares, respectively, as of December 31. 1984.

12.6. Share Price Development

The development of the share price is shown in Exhibit 12.6. During the period 1976-1980, the share price showed a stable increase. It had a sudden boost in the first half of 1981, and another large increase in the beginning of 1983. After this, the share price increased steadily until the last quarter of 1987, when it experienced a dramatic drop. This drop was related to problems in the industry, the global stock market crash in 1987, and standardisation of the minicomputer market.

Looking at 1981, which was the year when ND first listed on the London Stock Exchange, one can see a clear increase in the value of the shares. The price went from just over NOK 5 (adjusted) to NOK 40 in the first six months of 1981, implying an increase in the value of some 700 %. There was a dramatic increase a few days prior to the London listing in July, 1981 and

Exhibit 12.4: All Shares (December 31,1984).

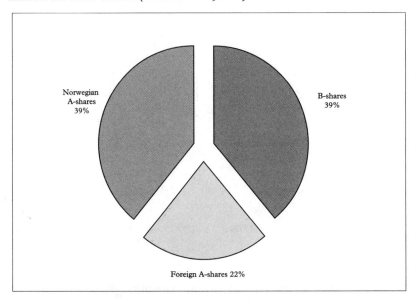

Exhibit 12.5: A-shares Only (December 31, 1984).

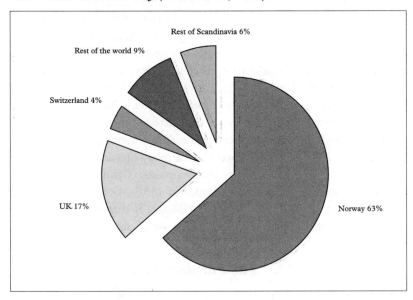

Exhibit 12.6: Stock Price Development.

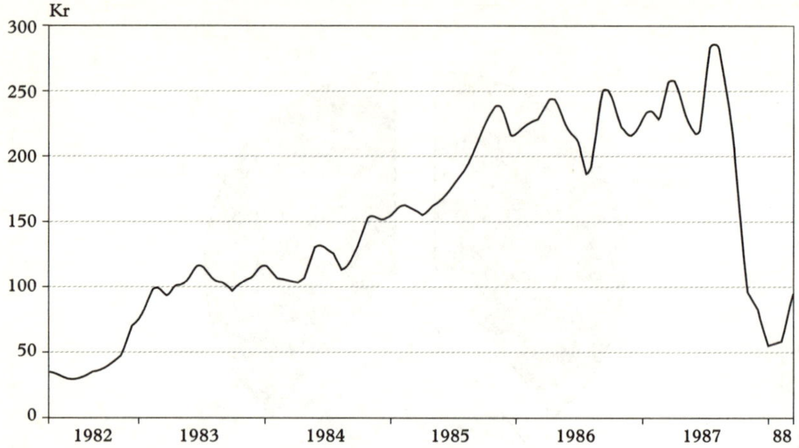

Source: Annual Report, 1987.

thereafter, a slight drop in the value. In the 3 months following the London listing, the value dropped 40 %. It increased again towards the end of the year. The value by the end of 1981 was 600 % above that of the first days of January, 1981 and 12 % below the price at the time of the London listing.

1982 started with a moderate volatility in the share price, but again, there was a sharp price increase towards the end of the year. The first few months of 1983 were marked by great volatility, as well as an overall growth of some 200 % in value. On January 11th, the day when ND listed ADSs for A-shares on the over-the-counter market in New York, the price increased by 13.5 %. When the shares were listed in the NASDAQ-system (February 15th), the share price experienced only minor changes. The last six months of 1983 were also a period with many ups and downs, but the value ended the year 160 % above the beginning of the year. 1984 was a year with an overall increase in the value of 133 %. During the year, the volatility was relatively high. The second issue of B-shares on the US market in September, 1984 did not result in any significant price movements.

12.7. The Failure of ND

Norsk Data was a company whose success had no comparison in Norway. Hardly any other Norwegian company had enjoyed more publicity and attention. The company was acknowledged for its pioneering-spirit, outstanding management, clear and focused share-policy, great product planning and marketing. Later, ND also received considerable attention, but then as the loser that did not fit the new competitive environment. The company went through a dramatic restructuring process.

Towards the middle of the 1980s, the market for minicomputers collapsed. The introduction of open computer standards (Unix) and ND's inability to attract new customers for its proprietary technology, were the main reasons behind ND's demise. The customers demanded more flexible solutions, both in terms of future extension possibilities and in terms of possible supplier-switching. The customers demanded more standardisation and increasingly they preferred network-connected PCs.

Increasingly ND had to compete on price/performance alone. The outcome was that the past gross margins of 60-80 % could not be sustained. According to chairman Terje Mikkelsen the firm had the inappropriate competencies, the wrong kind of organisation, and hardly any general purpose products.

Norsk Data published a press release on Friday, October 16, 1987, announcing that the expected result of 1987 would not be reached. This was due to decreasing sales in India and in the United States. The following "Black" Monday, the share price plunged from NOK 240 to NOK 180 before lunch. Later on the same day, when the news arrived from the United States about the New York stock market crash, the share price decreased a further NOK 60, and ended at NOK 120 (see Exhibit 12.6).

Norsk Data still continued their initial strategy of being a minicomputer manufacturer until Spring, 1988. At this time, all new employment was stopped, and the research and development department was reorganised into project-teams. The rationale behind this reorganisation was to bring ND into the world of standardised products. Financially, 1988 ended with a considerable loss, and the share price continued to fall. In the Summer of 1989 the price stabilised around NOK 55. A considerable number of people were made redundant in 1989. This coincided with the sale of some parts of the company. There was a total reorganisation of the remaining parts, new management, and a separation of the company into business units.

The 1990s commenced with further downscaling of the operations and the reduction of number of employees. Significant parts of the company were sold off to other companies. ND Comtec, the newspaper section, was sold to the British news-magnate Robert Maxwell. ND's buildings were also sold. The remaining parts of ND were split in three. One unit was sold later to Siemens/Nixdorf. What was left was a domestic computer service company with no production of its own, and no export or foreign operations. Four years later, ND was no longer in existence. The remaining parts of the company were sold in 1992/93, to Telenor Comma.

13. Hafslund Nycomed A/S: Directed Share Issues

Trond Randøy[1]

13.1. Introduction

During the period 1989-1992, Hafslund Nycomed (HN) internationalised its cost and availability of capital by aggressively targeting foreign investors. In June, 1989, HN listed on the London Stock Exchange and floated an international share issue, which netted NOK 761 million. In June, 1990, HN launched an ADR program in the United States and was quoted on NASDAQ. In June, 1992, HN listed its B-shares on the New York Stock Exchange and floated an issue of B-shares in the United States, which netted USD 74.7 million. This case will emphasise challenges related to the U.S. equity issue of 1992.

13.2. Historical Development

Hafslund Nycomed was formed in 1985 when Hafslund (established in 1898) acquired Actinor (former Norgas A/S), that previously had acquired Nycomed (established in 1874). In the 1960's Nycomed changed its focus from import substitution (based on licensing technology) to independent development of pharmaceutical products. Nycomed's present major source of income, non-ionic image diagnosis products, was first introduced in 1974.

A major restructuring took place in 1985 with the Hafslund Nycomed merger. Hafslund's engineering activities were sold. Developing Nycomed's pharmaceutical activities became the core strategy of the new company. Terje Mikalsen, the Chairman of the Board between 1985 and 1996, was very influential in forming this new strategy. By restructuring the company was able to increase R&D efforts and at the same time build a global distribution network.

---

1. Valuable comments from Chairman Terje Mikalsen are acknowledged.

The success of HN was very much due to diagnosis enhancement products. In the 1950s and 1960s the company was producing ionic image enhancement products, but these products gave undesired side effects to the patient. In 1970 Torstein Almen (at that time not employed by Nycomed) was able to make a non-ionic image enhancement and persuaded Nycomed to continue his research effort. By 1974 the patented Amipaque products were released, giving the company an important head start in the competition. The first equivalent competing product was released in 1980/1981. In 1982, HN was able to introduce the second generation product – Omnipaque. A few years later competitors were able to launch similar products.

From an international perspective, Norwegian doctors represented sophisticated buyers. The Nordic countries were well-known for innovative use of radiology. The demanding regulations for accepting pharmaceutical products in Norway made Norwegian approval an international quality certificate.

One of the key competencies used by HN was organic chemistry, but radiology and pharmacy were also important. The University of Oslo had a strong faculty in these areas. Until 1987, all the major R&D investments were located in Norway. Because of the significant growth of HN during the 1980s, well qualified researchers were in short supply. In 1987, the company extended its primary research network to include Sweden (at Lund University).

Successful development of new products and improvement of existing products continued during the 1980s and early 1990s. These were financed from internal cash flow as well as the two foreign equity issues mentioned earlier.

13.3. HN's Products in 1992

Just prior to the U.S. equity issue in June, 1992, HN was operating in three primary product areas: medical imaging drugs, therapeutical drugs and energy production. These are summarised in Exhibit 13.1. The pharmaceutical business was conducted through two major business units; Nycomed – focused on contrast agents for medical imaging and Nycomed Pharma – focused on therapeutical pharmaceuticals. During the 1980s the imaging products, particularly Omnipaque, contributed most to both revenues and profits.

In 1991, revenues from the *medical imaging* products were NOK 2,085

Exhibit 13.1: Main Product Areas at the End of 1991.

Divisions:	Nycomed Imaging	Nycomed Pharma	Hafslund Nycomed Pharma[1]	Hafslund Energy
Main area of business	Medical imaging diagnostics (contrast media)	Prescription/non-prescription drugs, medical equipment, consumer products	Prescription/non-prescription drugs	Hydroelectric energy
Major markets	International, but with a focus on the triad; the US, Europe and Japan	Nordic markets	German speaking Europe, the former USSR and the Japanese markets	Norway and the US
Employees 31.12.91	947	1,138	750	310
Operating revenues	NOK 2,085 million	NOK 1,599 million	NOK 953 million	NOK 645 million

[1] HN Pharma was integrated with Nycomed Pharma from January 1, 1992.

million. The operating profit from medical imaging was NOK 1,317 million in 1991. The world-wide price for such contrast media did not change significantly during 1991-1992. Imaging diagnostics allowed physicians to detect and pinpoint defects. The contrast media enhanced the diagnostic ability of X-ray, MRI and ultrasound technologies by improving the contrast of pictures.

The operating revenues in the *therapeutics* business area (Nycomed Pharma and Hafslund Nycomed Pharma combined) was NOK 2,552 million in 1991, compared to NOK 1,812 million in 1990, an increase of 36%. Part of the sharp increase was due to the acquisitions of two Danish companies. HN's sales of therapeutical products shifted from a strong reliance on the Norwegian market, 61% of sales in 1989, to one with 78% of sales outside Norway in 1991. 34% of total sales in 1991 was in Nordic countries, except Norway, and 31% was in European countries outside the Nordic area.

In 1991 the *energy* operations (Hafslund Energy) accounted for 12% of HN's operating revenues and 15% of operating profit. The company owned waterfall rights along the Glomma and Laagen waterways in Norway, as well as three smaller power plants in the United States. Hafslund Energy provided HN with a very stable and attractive cash flow.

13.4. Market Characteristics

In 1990, the world *diagnostic imaging* market represented approximately 320 million examinations, of which 70% were based on X-ray, 22% on ultrasound, 3% on MRI and 5% on other methods. The trend was towards increased use of MRI and ultrasound, although the total market volume of

X-ray was still growing. HN estimated that the total diagnosis enhancement market was NOK 12 billion in 1990, and that it would expand to
NOK 24 billion by the year 2000. From 1990 until the year 2000 the market share of X-ray based image enhancements was estimated to decline
from the present 70% to around 50%. Within the next few years the
amount of MRI machines were expected to double. The tremendous
investments in the installed base of X-ray and MRI machines suggested a
very slow conversion rate to possible new technologies. From 1980 to 1990
(see Exhibit 13.2) the non-ionic contrast media took over the contrast
media market. The product benefits characterising non-ionic products
were its negligible side-effects. Ionic contrast media tended to be painful
and also produced side-effects. The price of non-ionic contrast media was
approximately 5-7 times the price of ionic contrast media.

In 1990 the estimated world penetration of non-ionic contrast media
was 42% in terms of volume, with a peak of approximately 90% in Scandinavia, 80% in Japan, and 60% in North America. Since non-ionic contrast
media was significantly more expensive than ionic, the value-based world
market share was 86% in 1990.

Exhibit 13.2: World X-ray Contrast Media Market by Value.

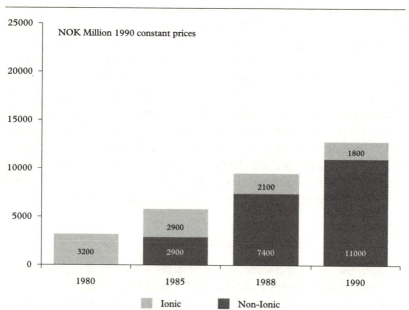

Source: HN presentation in New York, Boston and Chicago, November 12-14, 1991.

In the *therapeutics* drug business Nycomed Pharma was the largest supplier of pharmaceuticals to the Danish and Norwegian markets, and the fourth largest in Nordic markets as a whole. The pharmaceutical products included a broad line of prescription drugs, over-the-counter (OTC) drugs and medical consumer products. In 1990 HN increased its European presence considerably through the acquisition of CL Pharma AG of Austria (renamed HN Pharma). HN's recent acquisitions in Norway and Denmark had significantly expanded HN's distribution network, product portfolio and R&D capabilities in the pharmaceutical drugs business.

13.5. Corporate Strategy and Strategic Direction

In the early 1990s, the main income source and strategic focus of HN was on medical image diagnosis and the secondary focus was on therapeutical drugs. In October, 1991 HN President Svein Aaser explicitly pointed out that *"Our ambition is to be the leading company in medical image diagnosis. This vision is firmly in our minds continuously"*.[2] In order to maintain world-class R&D the company had to be focused on a narrow range of products and technologies. The total research spending in 1991 amounted to approximately NOK 600 million, up from NOK 290 million in 1989. From 1985 until 1991 the R&D expenditures had been in the range of 13-15% of total operating revenues.

The *acquisitions* of therapeutical drugs had provided HN with a wider product portfolio and a stronger distribution network. The competitive advantage of HN's therapeutical business was secured by concentrating marketing and R&D effort on a selected number of drugs meeting specialised health care needs. The synergy between the image diagnosis and therapeutic areas was most evident in relation to marketing and distribution.

In the early 1990s, HN was following three major strategic directions: (1) downward integration towards end-user by building an international distribution network; (2) horizontal integration on the Nordic home market; and (3) upward integration by acquiring and developing new technology for medical image diagnosis. These strategic directions are summarised in Exhibit 13.3.

The first strategic direction implied that the firm expand its international network. During the late 1980s HN had very much depended on its

2. A remark quoted in the main Norwegian business newspaper *Dagens Næringsliv* on October 28, 1991.

Exhibit 13.3: Major Strategic and Financial Actions During 1988-1992.

	Strategic or financial action	Intention
1988		
	Agreement with MBI, USA	Access to technology
July	Acquisition of pHarma-medica a.s. (Denmark) for NOK 32 million.	Access to distribution and as well as an expanded product line.
1989		
February	Acquisition of Laboratoire Ingenor SA, France, for NOK 40 million.	Access to technology
March	HN and Instrumentarium OY (Finland) agree to collaborate on the development of new technology for low-field MRI (magnetic resonance imaging).	Development of new technology for low band MRI.
April	HN exercises its option to purchase all shares in Salutar, Inc. (USA) for NOK 375 million.	Strengthen position in medical image diagnostics.
June	International share offering nets NOK 761 million. HN shares listed on London Stock Exchange.	Provide competitively priced funding for further expansion as well as reduce the long-term cost of capital.
July	HN and SmithKline Beecham (USA) agree to cooperate on the development of a new therapeutical product for use in conjunction with cancer treatment.	Development of new drugs for use for cancer patients.
December	HN agrees to sign an agreement to purchase CL Pharma (Austria) for NOK 871 million. The acquisition gives HN marketing outlets in Austria, West Germany and Switzerland.	Strengthen market presence and distribution capacity in Europe.
1990		
April	Sold Hafslund engineering activity	Divest activities outside of core strategy.
June	Acquisitions of Collett-Marwell Hauge in Norway for NOK 197 million.	Extend the product-line to get access to distribution channels for OTC and generic products.
June	ADR program launched in the USA.	Reduce cost of equity by increasing marketability of stocks to US investors.
July	Renegotiating of license agreement with Schering AG, Germany	Strengthen long-term relationship with distribution channels.
1991		
January	Acquired DAK AS, Denmark for NOK 630 million.	Access to distribution in Denmark as well as a number of finished products.
July	Acquired Benzon Pharma AS, Denmark for NOK 223 million. Option trading started on Oslo Stock Bourse on NH shares	
December	Acquired Kebo Care's hospital division (Denmark) for NOK 12 million.	Access to distribution of medical-technical equipment.
	Establishing of Nycomed East Europe in Vienna	Develop and coordinate HN activities towards East Europe and ex-Soviet.
1992		
April	Acquisition of Hydro Pharma a.s. for NOK 128.	Strengthen pharmaceutical product line
May	75% of HN shipping activity was given to shareholders	Reduce debt in HN and divest activities outside core strategy.
June 24th	NYSE listing of HN B shares and simultaneously a targeted issue of 2.75 million B-shares at US$ 27.175 per share (equivalent to NOK 166.60 per share). The issue gave HN a gross cash contribution of US$ 74.7 million.	Provide funds for future expansion as well as reduce the cost of capital through internationalisation.

Sources: HN annual and quarterly reports and Kjell Grønhaug (1992) "The pharmaceutical industry – an industry report for the project: A Competitive Norway", Research report no. 72/92, Centre for research in Economics and Business Administration, Bergen, Norway.

major distributive partners. Schering from Germany performed much of the distribution in Europe, and Sterling in the U.S. served the U.S. market for HN. One major problem was that Schering was also developing competing products to the one they distributed for HN. In order to respond to this challenge HN made a twofold strategy. First, HN made various acquisitions in Europe in order to build up its own distribution network. Second, a new product – Imagopaque – was developed to compete against Schering, which had a long-term contract for distribution of HN's own Omnipaque in a number of markets. The outcome was that HN's own distribution in major European markets went from almost nothing in 1987 to approximately 90% in 1996. Chairman Terje Mikalsen emphasises that without this strategic manoeuvre, HN would have lost most of its European market share to Schering.

A similar threat was evident in the U.S. market where Sterling was in the process of developing its own products. The 1994 acquisition of Sterling was therefore a paramount strategic move in order to survive in the U.S market. HN was able to perform the acquisition rather swiftly, as HN prior to the offer was actively looking for ways to increase its distributive leverage in the U.S. market. HN's "strategic contingency" provided the firm with significant lead time over other potential buyers when Sterling suddenly was offered for sale. According to Chairman Terje Mikalsen, HN was able to buy Sterling before Schering was finishing their assessment of Sterling.

The second direction implied that HN was strengthening its position as a full line pharmaceutical distributor in the Nordic market. This strategy focused on scale economies in distribution and the capability to develop differentiable products for the high-priced Nordic market.

The third strategic direction implied that HN would aggressively pursue development of new technology. X-ray was the only medical imaging equipment in the 1960s. The MRI was introduced in 1980 and by 1990 Ultrasound and OMRI (Overhauser MRI) were also on the market. X-ray examination was still the dominating technology. According to Vice President Mikkelborg, HN was not able to develop these new technologies from scratch. Therefore, HN had aggressively used acquisitions in order to give the firm a head start. The 1989 acquisition of Salutar Inc. from the US was one such example. It gave HN access to MRI technology. Cooperation with Instrumentarium OY of Finland was one alternative way of getting access to new technology (OMRI technology).

13.6. Research, Development, and Production

HN's competitive advantage stemmed from its ability to assess research and development, build alliances and undertake acquisitions. Alliances were built with distributors in order to serve global markets. Important technological alliances were being built with universities and other research-based entities. HN also considered the ability to spot the effect of market trends and technical developments to be one of its firm-specific skills. These invisible assets were a result of years of building a research organisation and monitoring market development. Since new products typically take 8-12 years from a breakthrough in research to being saleable, an important strategic opportunity for HN was to speed up the conversion of research results into new business development. For example, the acquisition of CL Pharma of Austria created an important opening to the emerging markets in eastern Europe.

In 1991, more than 80% of the pharmaceutical products HN produced were manufactured at one of HN's ten production plants located in Norway, Denmark, Germany and Austria. HN's strategy was to reduce the number of production sites to seven by 1997. This was mainly due to overlap in the European production lines because of acquisitions.

13.7. Competition

At the time of the U.K. and the U.S. equity issues, there were only three direct competitors in the X-ray non-ionic contrast media market. Bracco of Italy was the largest with a market share of almost 35%. HN had a slightly smaller market share. Schering of Germany had around 10% and Mallinckrodt had 15%. Within MRI the same pattern of competition was about to emerge. Eventually new (mostly U.S.) competitors were expected to enter into the market. Ultrasound represented a mass market since the contrast media was not sold to hospitals but to individual doctors. The main competitor in this market was Schering. There were only negligible product and price differentials between the different X-ray non-ionic contrast medias. The competitive outcome was primarily determined by being first on the market, and secondly by having access to distribution channels.

HN was well positioned in alternative emerging technologies. Although the company did not expect any totally unknown technology to be present in the market place before the year 2000.

Some of HN's major patents were about to run out in the 1990s. The first one expired in 1992. Even as patents expired there were still very considerable barriers to entry because of costs in product development, inertia in market acceptance, and slowdown due to governmental certification. The most likely new competitors were large pharmaceutical companies or one of the existing licensees.

It is the physician who chooses to use the contrast media for diagnosis. Doctors have few incentives to switch to new products when the present treatment is satisfactory, unless given considerable product benefits (of which price is not a major concern in most western countries). Governments can be tempted to intervene in the market since a large part of the medical bill is being paid by taxpayers. Governments can intervene either through utilising their bargaining power or through regulation of an oligopolistic industry. Therefore HN was monitoring EU directives very closely.

13.8. Finance

In order to attain its corporate objectives HN needed to accomplish its financial strategy. Some of the main objectives of the financial strategy were to maintain a high degree of liquidity, uphold the equity ratio during a time of high growth, build long-term shareholder satisfaction and trust, and reduce HN's cost of capital. Financial highlights for 1990 and 1991 just before the U.S. share issue, are presented in Exhibits 13.4, 13.5, and 13.6.

13.8.1. New Share Issues

In order to take advantage of possible acquisitions, a high degree of liquidity had been necessary. The equity-ratio had been maintained at the desired level due to a positive cash flow from operations as well as new equity issues. The divestment of highly leveraged activities, such as the shipping activity in May, 1992, had considerably reduced HN's long-term debt. As mentioned earlier, HN made two major international stock issues, one in London on June 1, 1989 and one in New York on June 22, 1992. Both issues had been a part of a long-term strategy of internationalising HN's shares and thus reducing HN's cost of capital and increasing its liquidity.

Exhibit 13.4: Financial Highlights.

Million NOK, except per share data	1986	1987	1988	1989	1990	1991
Turnover	2,525	2,113	2,610	2,971	4,340	5,519
Turnover outside Norway	1,600	1,400	1,780	2,200	3,042	4,249
%-turnover outside Norway	63%	66%	68%	74%	70%	77%
Results						
Oper.result before R&D	497	651	1,001	1,241	1,562	2,192
R&D	119	164	211	290	479	617
Result before extraordinary items	52	222	705	962	1,042	1,310
Result after tax	28	174	570	801	838	1,035
Operating margin	15%	23%	30%	32%	25%	29%
Return on total assets	7.8%	11.7%	21.4%	20.2%	16.5%	16.0%
Return on equity (100% of untaxed reserves)	2.2%	13.4%	41.4%	35.3%	24.5%	23.7%
Capital per 31 December						
Total assets	4,322	4,540	5,257	7,338	9,297	11,556
Fixed assets	2,591	3,175	3,652	4,415	6,258	8,399
Acid test		1.0	0.8	1.3	1.0	0.9
Equity in % of total assets	29.4%	27.1%	29.1%	40.1%	41.2%	42.3%
Shares, NOK per share (adjusted)						
Earnings per share	0.50	3.09	10.71	14.37	14.24	17.06
Cash-flow per share	4.41	6.85	14.29	19.88	20.68	25.50
Dividend payments per share kr.	0.52	0.52	0.75	1.25	1.75	2.50
P/E ratio	86	24.3	14.94	9.39	10.57	13.89
A shares at December 31st	43	75	160	135	151	237
Free A shares at December 31st	–	–	172	164	160	259
B shares at December 31st	–	–	165	163	153	249
Market capitalisation at December 31st	2,437	8,595	8,595	8,560	9,102	14,914
Employment at year end	2,698	1,726	1,878	2,029	2,735	3,333

Exhibit 13.5: Income Statement.

NOK million	1991	1990
Operating Revenues and Expenses		
Operating revenues	4,940	3,879
Royalties	579	461
Total operating revenues	5,519	4,340
Raw materials, goods and services	1,145	978
Wages, etc.	1,039	881
Other operating expenses	1,216	992
Ordinary depreciation	544	406
Total operating expenses	3,944	3,257
Operating profit	1,575	1,083
Financial Income and Expenses		
Financial income	390	295
Financial expenses	683	359
Net Financial Items	–293	–64
Minority interests in results	–293	23
Results Before Year End Adjustments and Taxes	1,310	1,042
Taxes	275	204
Result after Tax	1,035	838
Year end adjustments	–640	–570
Net Result for Year	395	268

Exhibit 13.6: Balance Sheet.

NOK million	1991	1990
Assets		
Cash and equivalent	656	470
Shares and bonds	933	638
Accounts receivable	621	469
Other short term receivables	289	339
Inventories	657	509
Total Current Assets	3,156	2,425
Long Term Receivables and Investments	573	614
Intangible assets	1,907	1,178
Fixed assets	5,920	5,080
Total Fixed Assets	7,827	6,258
Total Assets	11,556	9,297
Liabilities and Equity		
Total Current Liabilities	2,683	1,887
Total Long Term Liabilities	3,983	3,388
Minority Interests	0	195
Untaxed reserves	3,084	2,445
Total equity	1,075	1,382
Total Equity and Untaxed Reserves	4,890	3,827
Total Liabilities and Equity	11,556	9,297

13.8.2. Ownership and Control

There were three classes of Hafslund Nycomed shares in 1991: ordinary A-shares, B-shares, and Free-A shares (commonly referred to as F-shares). As of December 31, 1991, just prior to the U.S. share issue, HN had 60,824,568 outstanding shares. They were divided between 31,523,641 ordinary A-shares, 15,452,272 F shares and 13,848,655 B-shares. There were two classes of voting shares: ordinary A-shares and F-shares. The ordinary A-shares could only be owned by Norwegians and the F-shares had no nationality restrictions. The B-shares did not have any voting rights. The ownership of the B-shares was not restricted as to nationality. In 1991 the turnover of HN shares was 79 million, or 1.33 times the amount of outstanding shares. 42% of the trading took place in London. Exhibit 13.7 shows the composition of the main shareholders as of year-end 1988, before the London share issue; 1991, before the U.S. share issue, and 1992 after the U.S. share price issue.

Throughout the period HN was controlled by Chairman Terje Mikalsen, Mosvold Fursund, and Board Member Tharald Brøvig, both from Farsund, Norway. In 1988, they controlled 18.7% of the ordinary A-shares, 13.6% of the F-shares and 1.8% of the B-shares. The second largest owner in 1988 was Orkla Borregaard, a Norwegian industrial conglomer-

Exhibit 13.7: Main Shareholders all classes of shares as of Year-end 1988,
Year-end 1991 and Year-end 1992:

Ranking as of Dec. 31,1988	%- of shares	Ranking as of Dec. 31, 1991	%- of shares	Ranking as of Dec. 31, 1992	%- of shares
1. Mosvold Farsund	12.7 %	1. Mosvold Farsund	11.9 %	1. Mosvold Farsund	9.4 %
2. Orkla Borregaard	10.1 %	2. UNI Storebrand	9.4 %	2. UNI Storebrand	9.2 %
3. Tharald Brøvig	6.0 %	3. Orkla Borregaard	7.0 %	3. Orkla Borregaard	7.0 %
		4. D.A. Invest and			
4. Aktivum Invest	5.6 %	Udvikling a/s	4.4 %	4. Folketrygdfondet	5.6 %
		5. Morgan Guaranty		5. D.A. Invest and	
5. Per Berg-Andersen	4.2 %	Trust	3.7 %	Udvikling a/s	4.1 %

ate, with 12.9% of the A-shares and 3.3% of the F-shares. The largest foreign owner in 1991 was the Danish company D.A. Invest og Udvikling a/s with 13.7% of the F-shares. D.A. Invest og Udvikling became a major foreign owner of HN shares after HN paid DKK 470 million and transferred to them 446,769 F-shares and 580,000 B-shares for the acquisition of DAK Labratoriet A/S on January 1, 1991. During 1991, Invest og Udvikling had increased its holdings of F-shares to 2,126,619 shares.

13.9. Internationalising the Cost of Capital

It had been the explicit goal of the firm to internationalise the cost and availability of its capital. The first important steps in this process took place in 1988 when the allowed number of shares owned by foreign citizens was increased from 20% to 33%. During the same year HN made the first issue of non-voting B-shares with no restrictions on foreign ownership. During 1988 most of the new investors were foreigners.

13.9.1. The London Equity Issue

As mentioned earlier, in 1988 the B-shares became listed on SEAQ in London, the international electronic exchange, and simultaneously a number of stockbroker firms in London agreed to make a market in HN shares. On April 5, 1989 plans for a London issue were made public. On June 2, 1989 HN F-shares and B-shares were admitted to the official list of The Stock Exchange in London. On June 1, 1989 HN realised net proceeds of NOK 761 million from the London offering, which substantially strengthened its financial position and thus enabled the company to make a number of strategic acquisitions. Approximately NOK 670 million of the 1989 B share issue was sold to foreign investors.

Exhibit 13.8: Share Price Development 1988-1992.

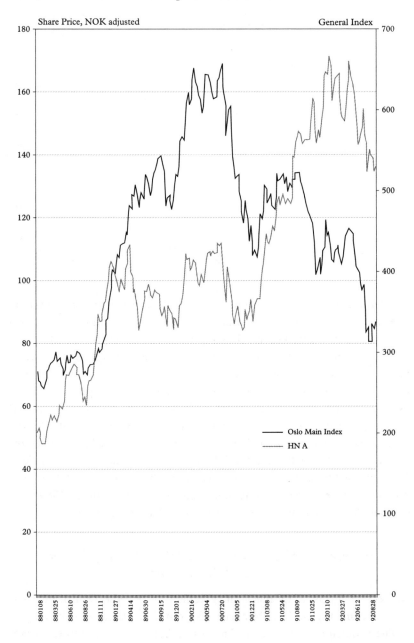

Exhibit 13.9: Hafslund Nycomed B.

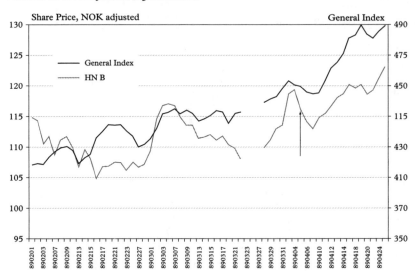

Even though the issue itself was successful, the stock performed poorly after the issue. The sell-out of major stockholders, including some board members, gave the wrong signal to the market. In retrospect, Chief Financial Officer Øyvin Brøymer now considers that the London issue was overpriced. It took some time to regain shareholder confidence after the 1989 issue. The 1989 prospectus focused on the need for new capital in order to expand the pharmaceutical activity. Consequently the market reacted quite negatively to a 5% share purchase in Orkla Borregaard just after the London issue. The Orkla stock purchase was only intended as an attractive cash placement, but the market did not support the move. Nevertheless, HN kept the Orkla stocks for half a year and achieved a profit of NOK 140 million. The perceived dilution in earnings per share from the 1989 issue of 4,350,000 million new B-shares was also a depressing factor.

13.9.2. DAK-Labratoriet – Both a HN Acquisition and a HN Investor

In December 1990, HN made an agreement to buy the Danish pharmaceutical company DAK-Labratoriet AS from D.A. Invest og Udvikling a/ s. The acquisition price was DKK 470 million in cash and 974,769 HN shares (446,769 F-shares and 580,000 B-shares) in HN's possession, which

Exhibit 13.10:   Share Price Movements November–December 1990.

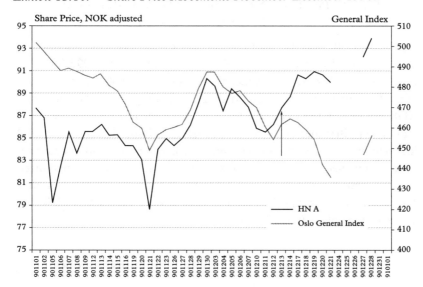

were priced at approximately NOK 150 per share at the time[3]. The DAK acquisition provided HN with complementary products, as well as strong R&D resources. DAK was quite profitable. Its 1990 earnings were close to DKK 200 million, indicating that HN was able to buy the company at a very low P/E-ratio of only 3. By partially financing the acquisition with HN shares in its own possession, one could argue that D.A. Invest og Udvikling's investment was comparable to a NOK 150 million targeted issue. As an industrial investor with superior ability to assess the value of HN, D.A. Invest og Udvikling was willing to pay a premium price for HN's shares. Interestingly, D.A. Invest og Udvikling increased its holdings of HN shares during 1991 and by the end of 1991 it was the fourth largest owner of HN shares. The market effect of the DAK acquisition announced December 14, 1990 was quite measurable. From December 13, 1990, to January 1, 1991 the HN ordinary A-shares increased from NOK 88 per share to NOK 94 per share. At the same time the general Oslo index was down 1%.

3. According to Norwegian law it was illegal for a company to buy back its own shares, but in 1988 HN acquired 90% of Aktivum AS, an investment company, and subsequently became the indirect owner of 3.2 million of its own shares.

13.9.3. The U.S. Share Issue and Crosslisting on the NYSE at the End of 1991

On October 28, 1991 President Svein Aaser announced the intention to make a regular listing on the New York Stock Exchange by 1992. The first intention of such a listing was mentioned as early as 1990 with the release of the HN 1989 Annual Report. It stated that HN planned to establish an ADR program in the US as the first step to a regular listing in New York. CFO Øyvin Brøymer pointed out that the individual effects of increased internationalisation of the shares were very hard to trace. On February 6, 1992, simultaneously with the release of the 1991 results, HN announced that the company was making a 4,000,000 B-share issue (ADS) in New York at the same time as the NYSE regular listing. The New York listing and issue took place June 22, 1992.

13.10. The Aftermath of the U.S. Equity Issue

13.10.1. Highlights

Hafslund Nycomed AS continued to grow after the U.S. share issue. Revenues in 1994 amounted to NOK 7.8 billion, up from 6.6 billion in 1993. The operating profit before R&D expenditures was NOK 2.4 billion in 1994, up from NOK 2.3 million in both 1992 and 1993. In 1994, HN's contrast media drugs for X-ray imaging enhancement represented 71% of the firm's profit before R&D expenditures, and 41% of its revenues. Even though the company continued to expand, its profit margins were slipping. The stock market reaction to this was that the firm was valued, more or less, at the same amount at the end of 1994 as it was three years earlier. The total market capitalisation of HN as of October 7, 1995 was NOK 17.7 billion, up from NOK 14.1 at the end of 1994. Financial highlights for 1993 and 1994 are presented in Exhibit 13.11.

13.10.2. Strategic Moves

According to President Aaser, pursuing globalization was still the paramount focus of the firm in 1995. This related to areas such as distribution, research, and financing. On October 3, 1994 HN acquired its U.S. distributor, the contrast media division of Sterling Winthrops, for US$ 450 million. The two major strategic objectives for the acquisition were to increase

Exhibit 13.11: Hafslund Nycomed Financial Highlights for 1993 and 1994.

NOK million	1994	1993
Operating Revenues and Expenses		
Operating revenues	7,153	5,776
Royalties	666	803
Total operating revenues	7,819	5,843
Raw materials, goods and services	2,136	1,396
Change in finished goods	–57	–92
Wages etc.	1,771	1,551
Other operating expenses	1,829	1,671
Ordinary depreciation	610	514
Total operating expenses	6,289	5,041
Operating profit	1,530	1,538
Financial Income And Expenses		
Financial income	834	883
Financial expenses	1,043	846
Net Financial Items	–209	37
Minority interests in results	–7	–5
Results Before Year End Adjustments and Taxes	1,350	1,570
Taxes	413	458
Year-end adjustments	0	0
Result after Tax	901	1,112

Balance Sheet	1994	1993
Assets		
Cash and equivalent	475	441
Shares and bond	1,329	2,169
Accounts receivable	1,294	852
Other short term receivables	749	395
Inventories	1,460	1,023
Total Current Assets	5,307	1,023
Long Term Receivables And Investments	1,254	800
Intangible assets	5,100	2,889
Fixed assets	5,182	4,515
Total Fixed Assets	10,282	7,404
Total Assets	16,843	13,084
Liabilities And Equity		
Total Current Liabilities	4,422	3,709
Total Long Term Liabilities	6,210	3,668
Minority Interests	25	13
Total equity	6,186	5,694
Total Liabilities and Equity	16,843	13,084

control over distribution (in the United States) and get access to an advanced research organization. The acquisition was financed by a bond issue targeted towards U.S. insurance companies. Another important strategic move was the establishment of a Chinese joint venture in Shanghai. By the end of 1994 the company had operations in 36 countries with a total of 5,609 employees, of which 4,482 worked abroad.

13.10.3. Ownership Control and Internationalisation of Capital

Due to the Norwegian implementation of the European Economic Area (EEA) the past nationality restrictions on stock ownership were abandoned as of January 1, 1994. This implied that the F-shares, or free A-shares, and the restricted A-Shares were merged into one class of A-shares. In 1995, two stock classes remained: A-shares with voting rights and B-shares without voting rights. 33% of the stock turnover in 1994 took place in London, and at the same time ADS's represented 11% of all B-shares.

13.10.4. Separation of Hafslund and Nycomed

In 1996 Hafslund Nycomed was separated into one pharmaceutical company (Nycomed ASA) and one energy supplier (Hafslund ASA). Another important change was that Chairman Terje Mikalsen (1985-1996), one of the architects behind HN's rapid internationalisation, left the Board of Directors and sold out a substantial number of shares. This split-up was initiated by the Board, and Chairman Terje Mikalsen left the Board in accordance with his own wish.

14. Elektrisk Bureau A/S /ASEA AB: A Strategic Alliance

Trond Randøy

14.1. Introduction

On September 29, 1986, it was announced that Elektrisk Bureau A/S (EB) and ASEA AB (ABB) would form a strategic alliance[1]. The cooperative scheme initially involved a targeted 20% equity issue sold to ASEA AB by EB. In terms of operations, the coordination was limited to certain R&D projects and some common international marketing. After ABB increased its equity stake in EB to 63% in August, 1987, EB became in effect the Norwegian part of ABB. By the beginning of 1992, ABB controlled more then 98% of the shares in EB, then considered a wholly-owned ABB subsidiary. It was EB that took the initiative for the initial formation of the strategic alliance. The case is written with EB's perspective in mind. This case is particularly focusing on the background and the formation of the first phase of this strategic alliance taking place in 1986.

14.2. The Situation Just Prior to the Alliance

EB's adjusted (using 1989 as a base year) profit per share had fallen from NOK 23.30 in 1982 to NOK 11.50 in 1985. During the same time period the revenues had increased by 48% to NOK 2,881 million. The decline in profit margin was a serious threat to the future growth of EB.

In 1985, international sales accounted for 32% of revenues, up from 30% in 1982. Nevertheless, growth in international revenues was not satisfactory and EB had to reconsider its international strategy. During 1985 EB divested most of its domestic activities related to cable television and office equipment. The strategy was to focus the resources of the company on fewer areas and then seek international leadership in those product areas.

---

1. ABB was the new company formed after the merger between ASEA of Sweden and Brown Boveri of Switzerland.

Until 1983, EB had been one of the major suppliers of electronic equipment to the Norwegian telecommunication authorities. The domestic "monopoly" of EB was lost after Standard Kabel Fabrik (STK) got an important contract. In order to develop products for the international market, EB needed to divest unprofitable products and strengthen its technological competence.

The technologically-advanced products of EB made it necessary to make considerable investments in ongoing product development. In 1985, the company used 6.5% of revenues for research and development (R&D), which amounted to NOK 240 million. The necessary restructuring also included acquisitions. These increased the need for competitively-priced equity and debt capital.

14.3. Main Activities of EB

In 1986, EB was among the larger privately-owned companies in Norway. The company was established in 1882. It became an important pillar of the industrial sector in the country. Historically, the company had focused on telecommunications, energy and energy-related industry. In 1986, the EB-group was concentrated mainly in three areas: public communication products, cable products, and other electronic communication products. In 1986, the total revenues of the company were NOK 3.2 billion, up from NOK 2.8 billion the year before. Exhibit 14.1 presents the breakdown of sales and profits derived from EB's main subsidiaries for the years 1985 and 1986.

In 1985, the public communication products (EB Telecom) represented 48% of EB's revenues and 75% of its operating income. In 1986, compara-

Exhibit 14.1: Sales and Profits from Main Subsidiaries.

Figures in NOK millions	1986		1985	
	Revenues	**Operating profit**	**Revenues**	**Operating profit**
EB Telecom	1,583	124	1,333	107
EB Norsk Kabel	726	82	677	53
EB Nera	520	13	448	(4)
EB Forsvar	142	8	95	6
EB Engineering	117	5	116	(2)
EB Eurocom	132	2	124	3
EB Asean	64	2	70	(18)
Internal sales	(80)		(61)	
EB group	3,207	235	2,802	142

ble figures were 48% of EB's revenues and 52% of operating profit. The proportion of international sales from this division increased from 14% in 1985 to 16% in 1986. International cooperation with ASEA was already going on before the equity issue was announced in September, 1986. The strategic alliance helped EB to speed up internationalisation of communication products and reduce R&D costs.

In 1985, the cable products (EB Norsk Kabel) represented 24% of revenues and 37% of operating profit. The comparable figures for 1986 were 22% and 35%, respectively. The cable division's sales from abroad increased from 24% in 1985 to 27% in 1986.

The special communication products division (EB Nera) delivered microwave communication. In both 1985 and 1986 the division accounted for 16% of revenues. This division was very R&D intensive. As much as 72% of its 1986 sales were abroad, up from 65% the year before. The division had a negative operating profit in 1985, that changed to 5% of EB's operating profit in 1986.

In addition to the three main product areas EB had four more main businesses: defence, engineering, Eurocom and Asean. These four business units all had positive profit margins and sales abroad between 44% and 80% of their total sales.

In 1985, EB's international sales amounted to 32% of revenues, which increased to 34% in 1986. In 1985, the international revenues of NOK 918 million were divided between: Western Europe outside the Nordic area (44%), the Nordic countries except Norway (20%), Africa and the Middle East (19%), United States and Canada (8%), ASEAN 8% and other countries 3%.

EB's main competitors in the telecommunication market were STK (later Alcatel STK) of Norway and NEC of Japan. In the cable market NEK Kabel (Norwegian) and Alcatel (French) were the largest competitors. EB's market share in Norway just prior to the alliance is shown for selected products in Exhibit 14.2.

Exhibit 14.2: EB's Market Share in Norway 1985.

	Market Share
Public switches	10%
Private switches	50-60%
Special communication products	50%
Phones	80-90%
Cable products	30-40%

14.4. The Strategic Response to the 1985 Challenges

EB's strategy was to strengthen its core activities in electronic communication, and electric equipment for the electric utility industry. In October 1986, EB acquired Elektro Union. EB became the fourth largest privately-controlled company in Norway.

In 1985, EB was only listed on the Oslo Stock Exchange. On December 23, 1986 a dual stock issue was made, one public and one targeted. The public offering gave preference to the old shareholders. It gave the company an increase in equity of NOK 153.5 million. The targeted issue was towards ASEA of Sweden. It provided EB with an additional NOK 370.5 million. After that deal ASEA had a 20% stake in EB.

To gain international leadership with the technologically intensive products of EB, it was necessary to make considerable investments in ongoing product development. By narrowing the technological focus and utilising the alliance with ASEA, EB was able to increase revenues without any increase in R&D expenditure. R&D as a percentage of sales came down from 8.3% in 1985 to only 3.4% in 1987.

14.4.1. The Choice of a Strategic Partner

In 1986, EB was looking for a large international partner. ASEA was one of several potential companies that EB considered. The candidate needed to have complementary products, with an emphasis on electronics, as well as a strong international marketing network. The potential strategic partner should also be able to provide EB with competitively priced new funds. Companies like AEG, Alfston and General Electric were considered before ASEA was chosen. One of the main factors favouring ASEA was the fact that ASEA was a well-known company to EB. Geographical and cultural closeness to the Swedish company was also considered important. EB had for quite some time been having cooperative projects with ASEA in the area of power station communication. ASEA was also a major customer for one of EB's subsidiaries – AS Norsk Kabelfabrikk. The new equity funds from ASEA made the acquisition of Elektro Union possible. Elektro Union had for quite a long time been cooperating with ASEA.

In 1986, ASEA was the largest electronics and electrical equipment company in Sweden. The company had as many as 71,000 employees and approximately 100 subsidiaries in 36 countries. In 1986, ASEA's sales amounted to NOK 50 billion, or 15 times that of EB. To ASEA, EB represented access to certain technologies and an increased position in Norway. In the area of electrical installation there was some overlap between the two companies, so that restructuring the companies could increase scale advantages.

14.4.2. Benefits from the EB-ASEA Alliance

The 1986 ASEA deal was not intended to effect the daily operations of EB, but it should strengthen the cooperative ties in R&D and marketing. The strategic alliance was a step in building a larger Nordic electronics group. ASEA's eventual take-over of EB was not an implicit part of the first 20% equity position.

Internationalisation of equity capital was also considered to be an important element for the alliance. In 1986, ASEA's shares were widely traded on international exchanges. Another stated reason for the alliance was that EB was increasing its reliance on export, import, and foreign production, as well as cross-national product and technology development.

When the strategic alliance with ASEA was announced on September 29. 1986, EB's stock price increased 18 % from the adjusted price of NOK 114 on September 28th to NOK 135 pr share on October 17th, as shown in Exhibit 14.3. Most of the increase took place within the three first days

Exhibit 14.3: EB Share Price: September-October 1986.

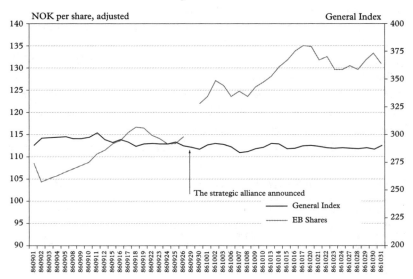

after the announcement. Within the same time frame the Oslo stock market index decreased slightly.

14.5. Share Capital and Investor Relations

At the end of 1985, Investa A/S (Norway) was the majority owner of EB shares. Investa was an investment company that started to buy into EB during 1985. At the same time, the former main shareholder, L M Ericsson (Sweden), had reduced its position in the company from 25.1% at the end of 1984 to 10.1% at the end of 1985. Investa's stated reason for its position in EB was its intention of build a larger, internationally-competitive, Norwegian-based electronics company. To most of the management of EB, Investa was considered a short-time owner, not focused on the long-term well-being of the company. The main stockholders in EB as of year-end 1985 and 1986 are shown in Exhibit 14.4.

On September 29, 1986 it was announced that EB was to make a targeted equity issue to ASEA in addition to the previously announced public issue. The public issue at NOK 145 per share, was made so that old shareholders could be given the right to buy one new share for every six old shares. NOK 153.5 million was gained from this issue. The targeted issue towards ASEA of Sweden was priced at NOK 200. This issue gave the company NOK 370.5 million in new equity. ASEA received 20 % of the voting shares, but A/S Investa controlled 50.3% of the voting shares at this time. ASEA did not have any shares in EB before the issue.

In August 1987, ASEA bought Investa's EB shares and agreed to sell its enlarged stake in EB for NOK 350 per share. This transaction was announced simultaneously with a merger between EB, NEBB and ASEA. Before the announcement the EB shares were trading at NOK 200-220 per share. Within some few weeks the share price increased to more than NOK 300 per share. However, this was at a time with a considerable increase in the Oslo Stock Exchange Index.

The annual report for 1986 pointed out that an international listing of

Exhibit 14.4: Main Shareholders as of Year-end 1985 and Year-end 1986:

Ranking as of Dec. 31st, 1985	%- of shares	Ranking as of Dec. 31st, 1986	%- of shares
1. A/S Investa	59.4 %	1. A/S Investa	50.3 %
2. L M Ericsson	10.1 %	2. ASEA AB	20.0 %
3. UNI Forsikring	4.6 %	3. AB Patricia/L M Ericsson	8.0 %
4. Årdal og Sunndal Verk A/S	3.9 %	4. UNI Forsikring	4.0 %
5. Nimbus A/S	1.5 %	5. Bergen Bank	0.8 %

EB was desirable. The official rationale for the foreign listing was to get the benefits from access to a larger equity market. This indicated that the intention was to reduce the cost of capital by going beyond a small segmented capital market. Because of the large ASEA position in the company, an international listing was in effect achieved through the international listings of ASEA. EB's shares were never introduced on any foreign exchange, but its cost of capital had become internationalised through its strategic alliance with ASEA.

14.6. The Alliance in Retrospect

The EB-group changed considerably after 1986. The initial investment of ASEA was the first step towards total ownership control by ABB. As of the beginning of 1991 ASEA had became ABB. ABB owned 63% of the shares in EB. On June 3, 1991, ABB offered the remaining shareholders NOK 330 for each share. The offer was successful and by January 1, 1992 ABB controlled 98.19% of EB. In 1991, the EB-group had sales of NOK 10,071 million and net profits of NOK 365 million.

The operations of EB did not change much during the first year after the 20% equity alliance. However they changed very much in 1987, when EB became the Norwegian part of ABB. ABB was restructured so that the activities were divided into 30 main business areas. EB was made worldwide responsible for telecommunication, hydroelectric power equipment,

Exhibit 14.5: Financial Highlights for EB-group.
All numbers in NOK million.

	1982	1983	1984	1985	1986	1987	1988	1989
Turnover								
Turnover	1,957	2,294	2,609	2,881	3,326	6,771	10,095	9,370
Sales abroad	584	918	801	918	1,140	2,350	2,743	3,537
Result								
Operating profit	170	129	122	142	235	373	395	406
Net profit after exceptional items	154	98	81	68	182	277	384	602
Total Assets								
Total assets	1,967	2,203	2,326	2,519	3,519	5,974	8,484	8,865
Return on assets	10.7%	7.6%	6.6%	7.7%	10.2%	11.6%	10.7%	8.8%
Return on equity	18.1%	9.9%	7.1%	11.3%	7.1%	13.8%	12.9%	13.5%
Equity in % of total assets	32.8%	33.2%	32.7%	32.7%	41.3%	25.9%	20.9%	23.7%
Shareholder Information								
Share capital	144	159	159	159	232	232	232	291
Dividend per share, NOK	3.75	3.00	3.00	3.00	3.60	3.60	3.60	4.50
Earnings per share, NOK adjusted	23.30	13.50	7.60	11.50	19.50	18.00	18.00	21.00
Share price year end, NOK	39.00	91.50	98.50	106.00	128.00	149.00	136.00	210.000
P/E – year end	1.7	6.8	13.0	9.2	6.6	8.2	7.6	10.0
Employment at year-end	5,001	4,960	4,809	4,587	4,638	9,802	14,251	13,155
Research and Development expenditure	90	130	190	240	230	230	400	440

Exhibit 14.5 (continued).

Income Statement

NOK million	1986	1985
Operating Revenues And Expenses		
Operating revenues	3,206	2,802
Royalties and other operating income	119	78
Total operating revenues	3,326	2,880
Raw materials, goods and services	1,545	1,299
Wages etc.	911	813
Other operating expenses	605	555
Ordinary depreciation	77	74
Change in inventory	(61)	(20)
Loss on accounts receivable	14	16
Total operating expenses	3,091	2,738
Operating Profit	235	142
Financial Income and Expenses		
Financial income	94	65
Financial expenses	151	105
Exceptional items	4	(34)
Results after Exceptional Items	182	68
Taxes	20	10
Minority interests in results	1	3
Year end adjustments	(95)	(54)
Net Result For Year	66	2

Balance Sheet

NOK million	1986	1985
Assets		
Cash and equivalent	791	99
Accounts receivable	795	677
Other short term receivable	78	67
Inventories	723	604
Total Current Assets	2,388	1,447
Long Term Receivable and Investments	327	324
Intangible assets	2	2
Fixed assets	801	746
Total Fixed Assets	1,131	746
Total Assets	3,519	2,519
Liabilities and Equity		
Total Current Liabilities	1,117	820
Total Long Term Liabilities	715	669
Minority Interests	19	15
Total Equity And Untaxed Reserves	887	327
Total Liabilities And Equity	3,519	2,519

marine equipment, and oil- and gas related equipment. EB benefited from the restructuring that took place during the period of 1986-1988.

Exhibit 14.5 shows the financial highlights for EB from 1982-1989. This covers the period before and after the strategic alliance with ASEA.

Exhibit 14.6: EB Share Price, 1985-1990.

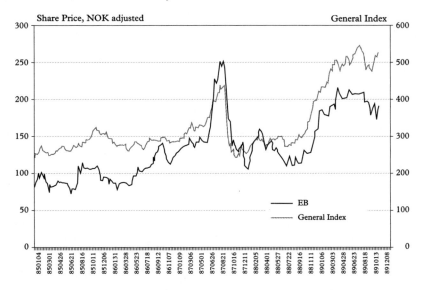

Part VII

Strategies of
Swedish Corporations

The three Swedish cases – Fortia, L M Ericsson and Electrolux – were chosen from a much larger sample of cases (see Chapter 4) in order to illustrate typical directed share issues prior to deregulation, as well as a post-deregulation Euroequity issue. All three cases reinforce our earlier findings in Chapter 5 that Nordic companies sell equity issues abroad not only because of the potential for higher share prices and liquidity, but also to enhance the company's image with customers, suppliers, the news media, and the financial community.

The Fortia case was particularly important because in November 1981 Sweden was still a very segmented equity market. Fortia followed in the footsteps of Novo Industri with similar favourable results for its share price. Its directed share issue in the U.S. market raised about $51 million at a share price almost 50% higher than had been achieved earlier in the year with an equity issue sold to Swedish investors. The equity issue to Swedish investors was motivated by the requirement at that time that foreigners own no more than 40% of a Swedish company's equity capital and no more than 28% of its voting power. Restricted shares were sold only to Swedish investors and unrestricted to anyone including foreigners. Thus an artificial price gap existed between restricted and unrestricted shares. There was more foreign demand for Fortia's shares than could be legally supplied, whereas the domestic Swedish market was in equilibrium with respect to the demand and supply of Fortia's restricted shares.

Apart from enjoying the share price premium abroad, Fortia's equity issue was motivated by a desire to gain more credibility in the worldwide pharmaceutical industry to help market its products. Fortia also planned to make some future acquisitions and needed an equity infusion to reduce its existing high debt ratio, while still funding more intensive research and development expenditures.

Despite what must have seemed like a high share price premium abroad, investors were rewarded over the next 15 months by a further increase in share price to SEK 500 compared to SEK 93.50 for the U.S. share issue.

The L.M. Ericsson $240,000,000 directed share issue in the United States in May, 1983 presents another example of the advantages of escaping from dependence on a segmented market. In this case, similar to Novo Industri, foreign investors had already discovered an "undervalued" L.M. Ericsson in 1982 and driven its share price up to world levels for the telecommunication industry. The share issue, which was the largest foreign stock issue in the United States up to that time, was partly opportunistic. It took advantage of L.M. Ericsson's favourable share price compared to other Swedish companies that were still mired in a segmented market, with prices determined by demand and supply for restricted shares.

As was the case for Fortia, L.M. Ericsson was partly motivated by a desire to increase its credibility and image as a technology leader. It felt that success with the U.S. news media and financial community would enhance its worldwide reputation. Further motivation came from the need to improve its debt ratio, provide funds for expansion, and fund an expected increase in working capital levels.

Unlike Fortia, L.M. Ericsson's operating results during the year following its equity issue did not live up to the investors' somewhat inflated expectations. Although the large initial equity issue was sold out, many of the shares flew back to Stockholm, a segmented and illiquid home market. The result was a drop of 32% in the unrestricted share price by March 1984. This illustrates the potential downside of a foreign equity issue.

Finally, the AB Electrolux Euroequity issue of $275 million in June 1986 illustrates what could happen after Sweden had in essence deregulated its equity market. Unlike Fortia and L.M. Ericsson, the shares of AB Electrolux were not originally undervalued by world standards. The Euroequity issue was priced at the closing price on the Stockholm Stock Exchange just before the subscription period. It was sold mostly to investors in the U.K., Spain, Italy, and other European countries. It was not sold in the United States, even though it was listed on NASDAQ in 1987 as a convenience to all investors.

Although an undervalued share price was not a motivation for AB Electrolux, the Swedish market was still not totally unsegmented. By law up to June 10, 1986 Swedish companies had to raise capital abroad to fund foreign operations. An alternative was to sell other Swedish securities it held. Since AB Electrolux pursued a growth-by-acquisition strategy, it became necessary eventually to undertake a foreign equity issue to meet these foreign exchange restrictions. The acquisitions of Zanussi in Italy and White in the United States were financed in part by an unusually high level of debt. An equity issue was necessary to lower the resulting debt ratio. The Swedish equity market was too small and illiquid to provide the equivalent of $275,000,000, the amount raised by the Euroequity issue.

Similar to Fortia and L.M. Ericsson, AB Electrolux was also motivated by a desire to enhance its corporate image and credibility with customers, suppliers, and the worldwide financial community. By 1986, this could be done without having to go to the U.S. market, with its costly S.E.C. registration requirements and listing requirements.

15. Fortia AB (Pharmacia-Upjohn): A Directed Issue

Lars Oxelheim and Arthur Stonehill

15.1. Background

On November 19, 1981, Fortia[1] raised SEK 258 million (USD 51 million) (net) in the U.S. capital market. This followed on the heels of a SEK 147 million (net) equity offering through preemptive rights to Swedish investors on November 13, 1981.

At the time of the international issue, Fortia was engaged in the development, production, marketing and sales of medical science products – pharmaceuticals, diagnostics, separation products and techniques, and proprietary products. In 1980, sales of medical science products accounted for 72% of Fortia's net sales; 86% of net sales of medical science products were to customers outside Sweden. Fortia also provided marketing services in the Nordic region to a number of non-Nordic companies for both pharmaceutical and general consumer products.

15.1.1. The Swedish Issue

On August 21, 1981 Fortia announced, in detail, a financing program which included a five-for-one stock split applicable to all of its capital stock, a 10% stock dividend and two rights offerings to non-U.S. stockholders. The dividend and rights offerings were based on post-split stock ownership.

The subscription period for the rights offerings expired on November 13, 1981. Trading in the rights had ended on November 6, 1981. Fortia received net proceeds from the rights offerings of approximately SEK 147 million. The rights offerings were underwritten by two Swedish banks, Svenska Handelsbanken and Uplandsbanken.

In one of the rights offerings, each stockholder was entitled to subscribe

---

1. Fortia eventually changed its name to Phamacia and merged with Upjohn (U.S.), becoming Pharmacia-Upjohn today.

Exhibit 15.1: The Fortia 1981 Tombstone.

All of these Securities have been sold. This announcement appears as a matter of record only.

AB Fortia
(A Swedish Corporation)

3,000,000 American Depositary Shares
Representing

3,000,000 Non-Restricted B Shares
Nominal Value Skr. 10 each

MORGAN STANLEY & CO.
Incorporated

GOLDMAN, SACHS & CO.   MERRILL LYNCH WHITE WELD CAPITAL MARKETS GROUP
                              Merill Lunch, Pierce, Fenner & Smith Incorporated

BACHE HALSEY STUART SHIELDS   BEAR, STEARNS &CO.   BLYTH EASTMAN PAINE WEBBER
      Incorporated   *Incorporated*

DILLON, READ & CO. INC   DONALDSON, LUFKIN & JENRETTE
                                                   Securities Corporation

DREXEL BURNHAM LAMBERT   E.F. HUTTON & COMPANY INC.   KIDDER, PEABODY & CO.
      Incorporated   *Incorporated*

LAZARD FRERES & CO   LEHMAN BROTHERS KUHN LOEB
                                                       Incorporated

L.F. ROTHSCHILD, UNTERBERG, TOWBIN   SALOMON BROTHERS INC

SHEARSON / AMERICAN EXPRESS INC.   SMITH BARNEY, HARRIS UPHAM & CO.

WARBURG PARIBAS BECKER   WERTHEIM & CO. INC.
      Incorporated

November 26, 1981

for shares of the same series and type (A-shares or B-shares, restricted or non-restricted) as those held prior to the stock dividend on the basis of one additional such share for each ten such shares held.[2] In the other rights issue, each stockholder was entitled to subscribe for one non-restricted B-share for each ten shares held prior to the stock dividend.

The subscription prices in both rights offerings were SEK 65 per non-restricted share and SEK 50 per restricted share.

15.1.2. The U.S. Issue

The issue to the U.S. capital market represented a value of SEK 280 million. Three million American Depositary Shares (ADS) were offered to the market. Each ADS represented one non-restricted B-Share. The subscription price in the offering was SEK 93.50 per non-restricted share. It was the first post-World War II Swedish equity offering in a foreign capital market. However, prior to the issue, some foreign ownership of Fortia's shares existed.

The pricing was done by the lead underwriting bank, Morgan Stanley & Co., together with Fortia's management, based on the market price of the shares on the Stockholm Stock Exchange. The tombstone is shown in Exhibit 15.1.

In the United States the shares were not listed until November 20, 1981. At that date, the shares (ADS) could be traded on the over-the-counter market in the United States. Contemporary rules prohibited Fortia from being listed on the New York Stock Exchange because of the differential voting rights in the shares (A-shares and B-shares)[3]. Exhibit 15.2 shows the calendar for major events up to the time of the issue.

Exhibit 15.2: Calendar for Major Events up to the 1981 US Issue.

Date	Events
January, 1981	Internal discussions started
May, 1981	Decision was made (unofficially)
August, 1981	Information was released
September, 1981	Decision was made by the extra ordinary meeting of stockholders
October 21, 1981	Preliminary Prospectus was officially released
November 19, 1981	The pricing ceremony. The pricing was made by Fortia and Morgan Stanley & Co.
November 19, 1981	Final Prospectus was officially released
November 19, 1981	The issue was released, and sold out in one hour
November 20, 1981	ADS could be traded over-the-counter

2. Restricted shares were limited to Swedish ownership at this time (see Chapter 2).
3. The difference between A- and B-shares was that all A-shares had one vote per share but B-shares had one-tenth of a vote per share.

15.1.3. Expected Benefits from the Equity Issues

What were the expected benefits from the two kinds of equity issues? Why was the offering to the Swedish capital market not sufficient?

Benefits from the U.S. Issue

The new issue directed to the U.S. capital market was made because of five essential reasons.

- To benefit from the great interest in the United States for biotechnical companies like Fortia. This was clearly shown by the reception to Novo Industri A/S (See Chapter 6).
- The United States was one of Fortia's most important export markets. The publicity received by the offering would make it easier to find potential partners in the United States.
- To raise funds and provide a liquid secondary market when shares are used to pay for local acquisitions.
- Offerings to the American capital market were traditionally made at market price. In this case each share yielded SEK 93.50 per share, to be compared to SEK 65 per share in the new issue to the Swedish capital market.
- In the line of biotech, commercially, most things happened in the United States. The most important connections were in the United States and the most important researchers and research activities were in the United States.

Benefits from the Domestic Issue

The only exclusive benefit was to make the foreign issue possible. Under Fortia's Articles of Association, not more than 40% of the entire share capital and not more than 28% of the voting power of all shares could be held by non-Swedish persons. To be able to issue non-restricted shares, Fortia simply had to issue more restricted shares.

Use of Proceeds

The net proceeds from the sale of the ADSs offered to the American capital market were estimated to be SEK 258 million. Together with approximately SEK 145 million which Fortia received from the rights offerings to the Swedish capital market, such proceeds were applied to repay a substantial portion of Fortia's short-term indebtedness, which at September 30, 1981 was SEK 179 million. On December 31, 1981, the short-term indebtedness was down to SEK 70 million.

The remaining proceeds were placed in short-term investments pending future use. Over time the proceeds permitted Fortia to accelerate certain of its research and development activities, to fund further capital expenditures internally, to strengthen Fortia's international marketing activities, and to facilitate possible acquisitions of enterprises in research and production which complemented Fortia's medical science business.

15.2. Company History

The origin of Fortia's business dates back to 1911, with the organisation of a Swedish pharmaceuticals company named Pharmacia. In the 1940's, the introduction of Azulfidine and the dextran infusion solution Macrodex led to Fortia's expansion into non-Nordic markets. In 1950, Fortia moved to Uppsala in order to benefit more closely from research relationships with the University of Uppsala. In the early 1960's Fortia began to increase emphasis on separation products and processes for use in research in the biotechnology field. As a result of research and development in biotechnology, Fortia was able to introduce in the early 1970's a line of immunoassay tests to be used for the diagnosis of various diseases, particularly allergic disorders. Fortia's medical products were by then sold worldwide; 86% of 1980 medical science products sales were to customers outside Sweden.

15.3. Ownership

As shown in Exhibits 15.3 and 15.4, HB Lundberg & Malmsten's total ownership of A- and B-shares represented a great part of the total voting rights before as well as after the issue. HB Lundberg & Malmsten was a partnership of two individuals, Mrs. I. B. Lundberg and Mr. Erik Malmsten, a Fortia director. Shares owned by Mr. Malmsten in his individual capacity equalled less than 0.5% of total Fortia shares. Mrs. Lundberg owned less than 0.5% in her individual capacity.

Fortia's largest stockholder was not in total control of the company before the issue, but after the issue there was an obvious dilution effect. However any direct shift of power did not occur because of the issues. Most of the foreign owners were funds that were not interested in voting power. At the time the U.S. funds just wanted to make a profit on the investment.

Exhibit 15.3: Ownership before the 1981 Equity Issues.
                    August 25, 1981.

Name	Percentage of voting rights	Percentage of share capital
HB Lundberg & Malmsten	42.2	12.2
Fjärde AP-fonden	3.5	8.8
Trygg Ömsesidig Livförs.	2.5	7.1
AB Custos	5.3	3.5
Skand. Bankens Pensionsstift.	0.8	2.0
S-E-Bankens Aktiesparfond	0.8	1.4
Livförsäkring AB Skandia	0.4	1.2
Other stockholders (app 7,400)	44.5	63.8
Total	100.0	100.0

Exhibit 15.4: Ownership, after the 1981 Equity Issues.
                    February 25, 1982.

Name	Percentage of voting rights	Percentage of share capital
HB Lundberg & Malmsten	35.5	8.7
Fjärde AP-fonden	3.1	6.7
Trygg Ömsesidig Livförs.	2.3	5.6
AB Custos	4.8	2.2
Skand. Bankens Pensionsstift.	1.2	1.6
Svenska Handelsbanken	0.6	1.4
S-E-Bankens Aktiesparfond	0.8	1.3
Other stockholders (10,000)	51.7	72.5
Total	100.0	100.0

15.4. Major Products and Competition

The structure of Fortia's organisation is shown in Exhibit 15.5. The general health care and medical market in which Fortia operated was characterised by a large number of pharmaceutical and health care companies. Many of these had established international markets for their medical science products. Most of such companies were larger, more diversified, and had greater financial, technical and marketing resources than Fortia.

In addition, the fields in which Fortia competed, particularly in diagnostics and separation products and techniques, had been characterised by a rapid technological change. Fortia's future was affected by new techniques developed by others.

Fortia's competitive strategy in the health care and medical fields was to concentrate its efforts on the development of a selected number of products which met specialised health care needs. Exhibit 15.6 shows its major products and sales during the period 1980-1982, which bracket 1981, the year of Fortia's U.S. equity issue. Exhibit 15.7 shows sales by geographic market.

Exhibit 15.5: The Structure of Fortia's Organisation at the Time of the US Issue.

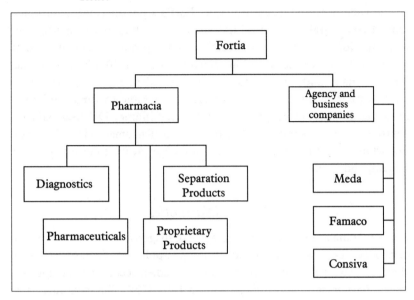

Exhibit 15.6: Major Products.

Sales in million SEK.

Product groups	1980	1981	1982
Medical science products			
Pharmaceuticals	433	489	641
Diagnostics	271	340	439
Separation Products	166	214	324
Proprietary Products	18	23	31
Agency and business companies			
CONSIVA	242	265	291
MEDA	89	105	132
FAMACO	18	24	30

Exhibit 15.7: Sales by Geographic Market 1980-1981*.

Sales in million SEK.

Countries and regions	1980	1981
Sweden	115	126
Western Europe	411	433
USA and Canada	251	330
Japan	54	106
Other countries	57	71

Note: In 1982, Fortia's foreign sales were 1,291 million SEK, or 90 % of the total sales
* Agency and business companies are not included.

15.4.1. Pharmaceuticals

At the time of the U.S. equity issue, Fortia's pharmaceutical products ranged from established products such as Azulfidine, which had been marketed for more than forty years, to newer products such as Healon, which was introduced in 1980. Fortia marketed 10 pharmaceuticals internationally and approximately 70 in Sweden. In 1980, 58% of net sales of pharmaceutical products were attributable to three individual products or product group. They were: Azulfidine, Debrisan and the dextran infusion solutions Macrodex and Rheomacrode. The most important export markets were the United States, West Germany, Great Britain, and Canada.

15.4.2. Diagnostics

Fortia manufactured and marketed a line of diagnostic kits which they had developed. They were the world's leading supplier of diagnostic tests for allergies. About five different products together accounted for approximately 65% of net sales of diagnostics in 1980-1982. The most important products were Phadebas RAST, Phadebas PRIST, Phadebas Amylase, and Phadebas micro test. The most important export markets were Japan, the United States, West Germany, France, and Belgium.

15.4.3. Separation Products

The most important products were Sephadex, Sepharose and Ficoll. The most important export markets were the United States, Japan, West Germany, France, and Great Britain.

15.4.4. Proprietary Products

The most important products were HTH H, HTH S and L300. The most important export markets were Finland, Norway, and Denmark.

15.5. Financial Data

As shown in Exhibit 15.8, the capital structure did change with the 1981 U.S. equity issue. Initially there was an increase in total assets from the cash infusion. The equity ratio increased from 36% (1979) to 52% (1981).

Exhibit 15.8: Capital Structure 1979-1982.

	1979	1980	1981	1982
Total assets, million SEK	1,008.2	1,184.1	1,679.6	2,092.5
Debt-Equity ratio	1.78	2.03	0.92	1

The positive changes in the capital structure gave Fortia the strategic opportunities they wanted.

As shown by Exhibit 15.9 profits improved dramatically after the equity issues. However, additional factors like the following were also important:

• Improved competitive position from the Swedish krona devaluations in 1981 and 1982.

• Healon became a very profitable product.

Exhibit 15.9: Profit and loss account 1979-1982.

Million SEK	1979	1980	1981	1982
Sales to customers	1,047.7	1,221.5	1,440.6	1,862.8
Operating profit	109.2	105.3	168.7	275.8
Income before appropriations and income tax expense	88.0	77.2	131.2	318.3

15.6. Preparations for the U.S. Equity Issue

Were there other alternatives to the U.S. and Swedish equity issues? Ralph Hammer, Chief Financial officer at the time of the issues, remembers that two more alternatives were considered.

• A convertible Eurobond issue.

Novo Industri A/S (see Chapter 6), before listing their shares in the United States in 1981, floated a $20 million convertible bond issue in the Eurobond market in 1978 and listed Novo's B-shares in London. They did it to investigate the foreign interest and for the management to acquire some experience. Fortia studied this case, but because of the great interest in biotechnical companies in the United States they concluded that they would only lose time and money, if they first checked the interest in London. Furthermore the non-restricted shares listed in Sweden were traded to such an extent that they could be sure about the interest.

- A bigger issue to the Swedish capital market.
  SEK 147 million was all the Swedish capital market could absorb. Moreover, a Swedish issue would not achieve the expected benefits of a U.S. issue that were described earlier.

15.7. The Stock Market's Reaction

The analysts were overwhelmingly positive about the issues. The interest was enthusiastic, especially in the United States. Fortia was mentioned as one of the world's leading biotechnical companies. "Success," was the word analysts used.

The analysts were right. The issue was sold out in one hour. The shares were issued at SEK 93.50. Exhibit 15.10 presents the stock market's short term reaction to the Fortia U.S. issue, compared to a Swedish stock market index. It shows that Fortia's B-share price increased in a downturning market. In fact, its risk-adjusted abnormal return was more than 10% for the three day period following the press release on August 21, 1981, as is shown in Exhibit 15.11.

Exhibit 15.10: The Development of the Fortia Share Price Compared to the Market Index.

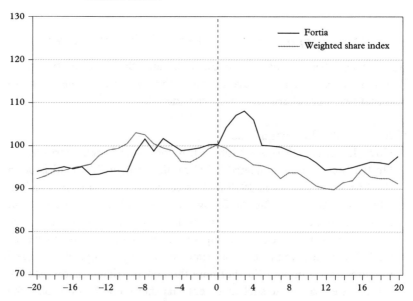

Note: The X-axis shows the number of days before and after the event day (day 0).

Exhibit 15.11: Daily Abnormal Return around the Date of Announcement of the U.S. Equity Issue.

Date	Daily abnormal return %
August 14	−0.7
August 17	1.3
August 18	0.2
August 19	−0.9
August 20	−1.5
August 21 Pressrelease date	−0.7
August 24	4.4
August 25	4.6
August 26	1.9
August 27	−0.2
August 28	−5.6

Note: The abnormal return on a particular day is the excess return after having considered the riskiness of the share and the general stock market development that very day. See also Chapter 4.

From a longer term perspective, as shown in Exhibit 15.12, Fortia's B-share price continued to increase more than the Swedish stock market as a whole. In addition to the positive impact of the U.S. issue on the share

Exhibit 15.12: The Long Term Development of the Fortia Share Price.

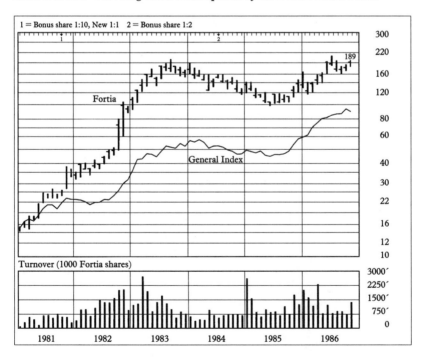

price, Fortia had an increasing operating profit, due in part to the Swedish krona devaluations of 1981 and 1982.

15.8. The Aftermath to the 1981 Equity Issue

Before the first issue to the U.S. capital market, Fortia expected to use their shares as means of payment for acquisitions. However, they did not use this alternative. Rather, they went to the U.S. market once again. In September-October, 1983, Fortia (since May 5, 1983 under the name of Pharmacia), issued new American Depositary Shares (non-restricted B shares) to the U.S. capital market. Pharmacia managed to repeat the success from 1981. (See Chapter 4). Hence in this particular case and at this point in time of the deregulation process it paid off to make a second effort to internationalise the cost of capital.

16. L.M. Ericsson: A Directed Issue

Lars Oxelheim and Arthur Stonehill

16.1. Background

16.1.1. Public Offer

On May 10, 1983, Telefonaktiebolaget L.M. Ericsson (Ericsson) issued 4,000,000 B-Shares on the U.S. over-the-counter market (OTC). At that time this was the biggest foreign issue ever made in the USA. It amounted to USD 240,000,000 (SEK 1,798,600,000), net of the issue costs.

The issue costs were USD 10,360,000. Ericsson paid USD 2.44 per share in commission, plus USD 640,000 in fixed expenses. This amounted to 4.2 % of the gross proceeds of the issue. The net proceeds were equal to 14.6 % of Ericsson's pre-issue market value.

The Ericsson issue prospectus was prepared by Price Waterhouse. The lead managers were Morgan Stanley & Co. and Dillon, Reed & Co. Inc., associated with S-E-Banken in Sweden (see Exhibit 16.1). Approximately 80 other firms took part in the sale of the shares.

The size of the issue was from the start meant to be 3,650,000 B-Shares. If demand were larger the consortium had the option to increase it to 4,000,000 B-Shares, which it eventually did.

16.1.2. Terms of Issue

Ericsson's B-Shares were quoted on the Stockholm Stock Exchange as well as on the OTC-market in the United States. The issue price was $62.50 per share. All the B-Shares offered were non-restrictive shares and had a face value of SEK 50.00 per share. Purchasers of the new U.S. shares were not to receive dividends for 1982.

A- and B-shares were entitled to an equal size of the company's equity, but a holder of an A-share had one vote per share, whereas the Ericsson B-share only had a 1/1,000 vote per share. This fact also prevented Ericsson

Exhibit 16.1: The Ericsson 1983 Tombstone.

All of these Securities have been sold. This announcement appears as a matter of record only.

ERICSSON
Telefonaktiebolaget LM Ericsson
(LM Ericsson Telephone Company)

4,000,000 B Shares
Nominal value 50 Kronor

Represented by

American Depositary Receipts

DILLION, READ & CO. INC.

MORGAN STANLEY & CO.
Incorporated

GOLDMAN, SACHS & CO.   LEHMAN BROTHERS KUHN LOEB   MERRILL LYNCH WHITEWELD CAPITAL MARKETS GROUP
Incorporated   Merrill Lynch, Pierce, Fenner & Smith Incorporated

ARNOLD AND S. BLEICHROEDER, INC.   ATLANTIC CAPITAL   BASLE SECURITIES CORPORATION
Corporation

BEAR, STEARNS & CO.   A.. G. BECKER PARIBAS   ALEX. BROWN & SONS   DONALDSON, LUFKIN & JENRETTE
Incorporated   Securities Corporation

DREXEL BURNHAM LAMBERT   HAMBRECHT & QUIST   E. F. HUTTON & COMPANY INC.
Incorporated   Incorporated

KIDDER, PEABODY & CO.   LAZARD FRERES & CO.   PRUDENTIAL-BACHE
Incorporated   Securities

ROBERTSON, COLMAN & STEPHENS   L. F. ROTHSCHILD, UNTERBERG, TOWBIN

SHEARSON/AMERICAN EXPRESS INC.   SMITH BARNEY, HARRIS UPHAM & CO.
Incorporated

UBS SECURITIES INC.   WERTHEIM & CO., INC.   DEAN WITTER REYNOLDS INC.

DAIWA SECURITIES AMERICA INC.   ROBERT FLEMING   KLEINWORT, BENSON
Incorporated   Incorporated

THE NIKKO SECURITIES CO.   NOMURA SECURITIES INTERNATIONAL, INC.   ROTHSCHILD INC.
International, inc.

SOGEN SECURITIES CORPORATION   YAMAICHI INTERNATIONAL (AMERICA), INC.   CAZENOVE INC.

ENSKILDA SECURITIES
Skandinaviska Enskilda Limited

SVENSKA HANDELSBANKEN GROUP

May 18, 1983

from the possibility of trading its shares on the New York Stock Exchange, where all shares within a company at that time must have equal voting rights. This has since been revised for non-U.S. companies.

16.2. Political and Exchange Risks

At the beginning of the 1980's, it was discovered that a lot of countries were unable to repay their heavy debt burden as a result of their increasing indebtedness during the 1970's. This caused great uncertainty politically as well as on the foreign exchange markets. For multinational companies like Ericsson, it was important to diversify their currency holdings in order to avoid large losses due to concentration of interests in a single country.

The macroeconomic situation led to devaluations in a number of Latin American countries. For Ericsson, which had big stakes in a number of these, large losses occurred. Additionally, the Falkland Islands War contributed to the problems in Argentina, where Ericsson had made some of its largest South American investments.

An important incentive for Ericsson to make the equity issue at this particular point of time was the historically high U.S. dollar value, above 7 SEK. The Swedish krona had been devalued twice, in September, 1981 and in October, 1982. Since more than 40% of Ericsson's long term debt was denominated in SEK, the inflow of a strong currency would stabilise the overall position of the company.

In 1983, interest rates in Sweden were comparatively low, but as the total indebtedness of Ericsson was at a high level, the cost of interest was a heavy burden. Ericsson wanted to pay off some of its loans. The issue gave the company, among other things, the means to do this. Exhibit 16.2 shows the chronology of events leading to the issue.

Exhibit 16.2: Calendar for Major Events up to the 1983 US Issue.

Date	Event	Comment
1979-80	Internal discussion	At first the discussions concerned an entry on the U.S. market through the commercial paper market
Fall 1982	Decision	The original idea was abandoned after the spectacular increase of the Ericsson share price on the U.S. OTC-market. Instead, the company decided to float an equity issue.
Feb. 17	Plan (leakage)	An article in the Swedish weekly magazine "Veckans Affärer" about a planned US issue.
March 16	Plan (announced)	At the time the result was reported.
April 12	Terms of the issue published	Press release about the terms.
April 29	Annual shareholder meeting	
May 10	Issue floated	

16.3. Expected Benefits From the Public Offer

16.3.1. The Reasons For Going Abroad

Why did Ericsson have to be represented in the United States? The United States was one of the largest and most important markets worldwide for Ericsson. In the beginning of the 1980's, the American telecommunication market was under deregulation and was expected to be demonopolized in the near future. In order to get a share of this lucrative market, it was necessary for Ericsson to establish quickly a position there.

For Ericsson, the public offer was also a way to improve its multinational image and to expand its equity capital stock. Håkan Ledin, Vice President, responsible for the public offer in the United States, expressed in an article in the Swedish weekly business magazine "Veckans Affärer" (39/1983), that "Ericsson wants to be acknowledged as well financially as in the media in the USA."

U.S. journalists were considered to be the best in that they possessed a great knowledge of business intelligence. This made it very important for Ericsson to be considered as a serious and technologically-advanced competitor in the US media analyses. Ericsson's credibility as a company would increase with this recognition, and its name would thereby become legitimate. Ericsson hoped that the public offer would make this possible. "If the investment in the USA turns out successfully, the whole world will be opened," said Håkan Ledin.

16.3.2. Use of Funds

One of the main points of making the public offer was to increase Ericsson's working capital. According to the prospectus, the funds would primarily be used to finance the expansion of the company's activities, first of all within its Information System and Public Telecommunication activities.

At the end of 1983, $163.7 million (68 %) of the income from the issue was used for consolidation of outstanding loans and investments within Ericsson. The remaining amount, $76.3 million was placed in interest bearing accounts. Exhibit 16.3 shows the impact of the issue's proceeds on L.M. Ericsson's balance sheet.

It goes without saying that the issue caused a rise in the company's equity. Income after financial income and expenses was SEK 892.2 mil-

Exhibit 16.3: Balance Sheet Impact.

	1981	1982	1983
Long-term liabilities (MSEK)	6,383	7,230	6,673
Untaxed reserves (MSEK)	3,251	3,617	4,333
Stockholders' equity (MSEK)	3,654	3,973	6,219
Return on equity (%)	11.0	10.0	10.9
Equity ratio (%)	28.4	26.9	31.4
Risk-bearing capital ratio (%)	35.8	33.9	38.5
Debt-equity ratio	1.4	1.5	1.1

lion in 1982 and SEK 1,662.0 million in 1983. The new capital inflow naturally improved the company's equity ratio and risk-bearing capital ratio.

16.4. Company History

In 1876, Lars Magnus Ericsson founded AB L.M Ericsson & Co. in Stockholm. After 42 years, in 1918, the company merged with Stockholm's Allmänna Telefon AB. They formed Telefonaktiebolaget LM Ericsson, a limited liability company under the Swedish Companys Act.

At the time of the issue, Ericsson had developed from a small family owned business into a multinational group. Ericsson was engaged in the manufacture and installation of automatic telephone exchanges in the international market for more than 60 years. The technological change from electromechanics into electronics made Ericsson into one of the world's leaders within this field.

The big breakthrough came about in 1977, when the AXE electronic telephone switching system was introduced. In 1982, just prior to the issue, the AXE-system had been ordered by telecommunication administrations in more than 40 countries. The AXE-system gave Ericsson the possibility to enter the market for mobile telephone systems.

At the time the issue was on the company's agenda, approximately 80% of Ericsson's sales were made to customers located outside of Sweden. It manufactured in 23 countries and operated through subsidiaries and associated companies in almost 50 countries.

By the mid-1990s the main businesses of Ericsson were design, manufacture and distribution of telecommunications systems and equipment. Main products were a broad range of telecommunications products such as public telephone and telex switching systems, information processing and communication networks for use by private businesses, telecommunications and power cable, and systems for mobile radio and telephone.

Ericsson also provided defence communication systems, network engineering, and specialised circuit components.

16.5. Organisational Aspects

A major reorganisation of the company structure was made in 1983. The high pace of growth within Ericsson called for a change as the Group began to be too rigid. A number of new business areas were created in order to increase the Group's ability to adapt to changing demands from the markets and the environment, and thus to get a more flexible organisation. The main structure of the new organisation were the eight product divisions:

- Public Telecommunication
- Radio Communication
- Information Systems
- Cables
- Defence Systems
- Network Engineering and Construction
- Components
- Other Business Activities

Between 1975-83, Ericsson reduced the number of blue-collar workers from 15,000 to 7,000. At the same time, however, the group had increased the number of white-collar workers. Ericsson had in this way moved from hardware to software production; "from the factory to the desk." In 1983, about half of the group's 70,000 employees were working outside of Sweden.

16.6. How was Control Maintained?

After the issue, Ericsson was still controlled by Swedish investors, although 40% of its shares were held by foreigners. This was due to the possibility of issuing B- shares with a voting right of only 1/1,000. Without this constraint on the voting rights, the public offer in the USA would not have been possible to carry through while still remaining a company fully controlled by Swedish shareholders. It was Ericsson's wish to stay Swedish. Exhibit 16.4 shows the ownership structure before and after the 1983 equity issue. The number of shareholders increased only slightly during 1983, from 69,600 to 69,900.

Exhibit 16.4: Ownership Structure Before and After the 1983 US Issue.

	Number of shares		Percentage of voting rights	
	1982	1983	1982	1983
AB Industrivärden	1,190,000	1,155,000	22.4	22.3
Förvaltnings AB Providentia	530,000	444,000	14.1	11.8
AB Investor	480,000	394,000	12.8	10.5
Knut och Alice Wallenbergs Stiftelse	520,626	520,626	5.5	5.5
Svenska Handelsbankens Pensionstiftelse	187,772	187,772	5.0	5.0
Allmänna Pensionsfonden	1,222,049	1,146,884	3.9	8.7
Stockholms Enskilda Banks Pensionsstiftelse	136,673	136,673	3.6	3.6
Pensionskassan SHB	136,497	136,497	3.6	3.6
Stiftelsen Oktogonen	72,246	72,246	1.9	1.9
SPP	1,879,874	1,462,199	1.5	2.6
Number of A-shares	3,728,515	3,728,515		
Number of B-shares	28,954,231	33,135,908		

Source: Ericsson Annual report, Various issues.

In 1983, the two dominating owners, each with 35% of the voting rights, were the Wallenberg S-E Bank sphere and the Handelsbank sphere. To be controlled by two such strong owner-groups was a unique situation for the Swedish engineering industry. This could easily have led to a struggle for power, but it probably gave Ericsson more advantages than disadvantages to have members belonging to two different spheres of influence on its board of directors. Those well-known powerful owners increased the credibility of Ericsson.

After the issue in the United States, 33% of the Ericsson shares were American Depositary Receipts (ADRs). The new Ericsson shares were primarily placed with U.S. institutions, mainly to avoid, as it was believed at that time, short-term speculation. The high amount of shares possessed by foreign investors constituted, however, a future risk. A flow back of shares to Sweden would cause the market value of Ericsson to fall dramatically. In the early 1983, this was not a big problem, but if the trust in Ericsson would fall, the sale of shares worldwide could cause the company difficulties.

16.7. Financial Data

16.7.1. Equity Ratio

Before the public offer in 1983, Ericsson had financed its expansion through debt financing implying a gradually decreasing equity ratio. One of the main purposes of the issue on the U.S. market was to increase this important ratio.

As was shown in Exhibit 16.3, Ericsson's equity ratio was strongly improved in 1983, mostly due to the issue, but also because of the conversions of a debenture loan ($ 4.9 million) and payment from minority owners in connection with new issues (SEK 328 million). Because of Ericsson's high pace of expansion, further issues (straight bonds, convertibles, share issues) were undertaken during the years after 1983.

16.7.2. Return on Equity

One important aspect of the issue was that the company had to pay a larger amount of total dividends if it wanted to keep the dividends per share ratio constant. The total dividend divided by stockholders' equity was targeted to be around 4 % in order to prevent the equity ratio from hollowing out. Consequently, the profitability needed to increase in order to pay the increased amount of dividends. In 1983 Ericsson raised the dividend per share from SEK 7.50 to SEK 9.00, which caused a growth of payments of SEK 87 million. In the period 1979-1982, the return on equity was a fairly constant 10 %. After the equity issue of 1983, it declined during the next four years to a range of 5-7 %.

16.8. Preparations for the Equity Issue

In order to prepare for new conditions and adjust the organization for the changing demands of the market, Ericsson had to reduce its blue collar working force and instead employ white collar labour. Within Sweden, Ericsson was the company which made the largest reduction in workers during 1975-84.

At the time of the issue, Ericsson was concentrated on two different products; cables and telecommunications. The thought was that the profitable cable products should work as the company's cash cow. The profit from this area should finance the development and implementation of the telecommunication systems. However, the economic recession in the United States made the sales of cables fall and Ericsson's old cash cow lost considerable weight. The company then changed its strategy and decided to concentrate on the field of telecommunication.

Ericsson also implemented a new organisational structure in order to be able to react faster to the changes in the market place. It changed the hierarchical structure into a matrix organisation. The company realised that it could not conduct business in industrialised and undeveloped countries at the same time with the old structure.

Two of the secrets of Ericsson's success were its endurance and long-range planning ability. While the U.S. market for telecommunication was closed to competition, Ericsson gathered knowledge and strength by working in emerging markets. The company received many orders from Middle Eastern countries and built up a strong position there. It also took its first steps into traditionally Japanese markets, such as Korea, Malaysia and Thailand. It learned to adjust its selling organisation and technology to different cultures and environments.

Together with Atlantic Richfield, Ericsson formed Anaconda-Ericsson on a 50-50 basis. This was made to pave the way for all Ericsson products in the United States. Ericsson also entered the US-market by the acquisition of Datasaab, which had built up a network of customers and distributors for its banking terminal system. In this way Ericsson bought a market share.

Later on, Ericsson also cooperated with Honeywell to reduce the high costs of market establishment. Honeywell offered a wide range of customers and a good distribution network, but Ericsson kept the intentions and rights to build up its own selling organisation in the United States.

Already three or four years before the well-known issue of new shares on the U.S. market, Ericsson's had a wish to enter the U.S. capital market. As mentioned in Exhibit 16.2, at that time the discussions were concentrated on the money market and commercial paper market. It was the rise of the price for Ericsson's shares on the U.S. OTC-market in the fall of 1982 which brought forth the idea for an equity issue.

After the announcement of the terms for the U.S. issue was made on April 12. 1983, the four top executives of Ericsson: B. Svedberg – President of the group, H. Ledin – Vice President, F. Staffas – Head of Finance, and J. Mehrling – Head of Information, made a one week "road-show" across the United States to inform investors about the company and the issue. With the help of the underwriters the issue finally took place on May 10, 1983.

16.9. Stock Market's Reaction at the Time of the Issue

In Sweden in the early 1980s, Ericsson was simply regarded as "the company which sells switchboards." Most people overlooked the great potentials within the group. Ericsson did not release much information to the market. Therefore it required professional foreign analysts to discover its capabilities. In 1982, there was a steep rise in the price of Ericsson shares, continuing right up to the time of the issue in 1983. This reflected increased interest by these analyst but mostly it reflected a bullish Swedish stock market due to the devaluation of the Swedish krona.

All signals from the company indicated self-confidence and high prospective profits. Ericsson believed that if its efforts to get into the large cities in the United States did not succeed, it would simply choose the rural areas for a start, and then move forward as it achieved greater market knowledge.

Even though the majority of the analysts expressed a positive attitude towards Ericsson, there were a few negative factors. Ericsson was one of the top companies within its field, but did it have the resources needed to stay at that position? It would take a heavy investment in research and development to maintain its position on the technological frontier. Moreover local demands in the different national markets were increasing. This reduced Ericsson's ability to standardise its products in order to gain economies of scale. This raised the question as to whether Ericsson was going to be a multidomestic or multinational company.

Exhibit 16.5 presents Ericsson's B-share price development for the period commencing 20 days before the announcement of the issue terms and ending 20 days after the announcement. After a decline on the first day following the announcement, Ericsson's share price increased by about 15 % during the next six days. However, the whole Swedish stock market was rising. Therefore, Exhibit 16.6 shows Ericsson's net share price increase after accounting for both the stock market increase and Ericsson's own riskiness. Adding up the daily abnormal returns, Ericsson's share price increased net by 1.7 % in the first six days.[1]

In the longer term, as shown in Exhibit 16.7, Ericsson's share price began a dramatic slide which continued until mid-1986. This underperformed the general development on the Stockholm Stock Exchange.

What caused Ericsson's share price to decline? One reason was that the forecast about Ericsson's future profits did not meet expectations. Furthermore, during the Summer of 1983, the interest in telecommunication companies' shares in the United States had decreased. This also affected

1. In February, when the plan to issue first leaked without further details, the stock market reaction caused small negative abnormal returns.

Exhibit 16.5: The Development of the Ericsson Share Price Compared to the Market Index.

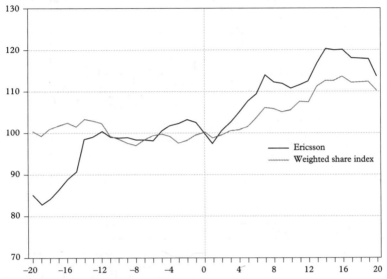

Note: The X-axis shows the number of days before and after the event day (day 0)

Exhibit 16.6: Daily Abnormal Returns at the Time the Issue was Announced.

Date	Abnormal return %
April 5	1.8
April 6	1.6
April 7	2.3
April 8	0.0
April 11	−2.0
April 12 Date of information release	−3.0
April 13	−1.5
April 14	2.2
April 15	0.6
April 18	1.9
April 19	1.5

Note: The abnormal return on a particular day is the excess return after having considered the riskiness of the share and the general stock market development that very day. See also Chapter 4.

the prices on the Stockholm Stock Exchange. As a result, Ericsson's shares flowed back to Sweden, depressing the share price.

Analysts were alarmed by the high price of the issue and the amount of shares issued. The large size of the issue put further pressure on the share

Exhibit 16.7: The Long Term Development of the Ericsson Share Price.

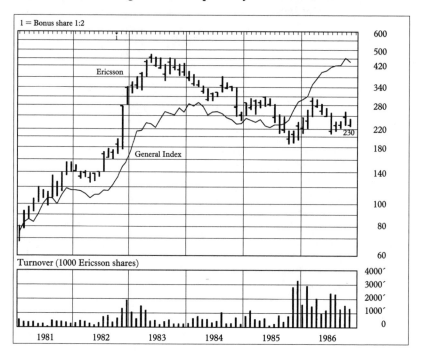

price. The size of the issue caused a high degree of dilution, which caused the old stockholders to complain.

16.10. The Aftermath to the 1983 Issue

At the time of the issue, Ericsson was in a phase of extreme expansion and internationalisation. The issue on the U.S. market had two main purposes. The first was to generate funds which could help the company to finance further expansion and development. The second reason was to get attention from the well-reputed U.S. analysts and to appear in the most respected financial press. Were these objectives reached?

The need for additional funds became urgent on January 1, 1984, when AT&T was finally demonopolized. The local telephone traffic was instead to be operated by seven regional Bell companies, which became free to choose their suppliers. Each of these Bell companies was bigger than any of Ericsson's present clients. Ericsson was established as a supplier of tele-cable to some of them and expected to receive more business in the future.

In the same year, Ericsson opened a R&D center in Dallas, Texas. Its prime task was to adapt the AXE-system to the North American market. Fiber optics also experienced a breakthrough on the U.S. market. The activities in the United States and Sweden were restructured. Less focus was put on electric cable but more on telecable. The business area "Radio Communications" had a great success with its mobile telephone in 1984, when sales increased by 100%.

1984 was also a year of disappointments for Ericsson. It experienced a fall in its earnings. This negative development was mainly caused by:

• Lack of components. This lack was not specific for Ericsson. It was a worldwide problem, but because of Ericsson's fast growth, the impact on the company was more severe.
• Increase in costs. This was caused by a technical lag and problems with Ericsson's deliveries.
• Lower than expected demand for Ericsson's products in the United States.

Growth on the U.S. market continued in 1985, especially for optic cables and the AXE-system. The major event that year was Ericsson's take-over of Atlantic Richfield's part of the jointly- owned Anaconda-Ericsson. As Ericsson gained complete control, the Joint Venture's name was changed to Ericsson Inc. However, this company made losses during the next few years. Ericsson also founded a new subsidiary in 1985, Ericsson Fibre Optics, to which all of those kind of activities were transferred from the parent company.

To conclude, at the time of the U.S. issue, Ericsson had already received recognition in the global financial community. It was since the 1960s crosslisted in London, Paris, Frankfurt, and NASDAQ (U.S.). Its shares had been analysed and priced by international investors for many years. Yet, the stock market reaction to the announcement of the U.S. equity issue indicated that some market segmentation still might have remained. However, the 1983 U.S. equity issue seems to have been the strategic move by Ericsson's management that eventually awarded the company an international cost of capital.

17. Electrolux AB: An Euroequity Issue

Lars Oxelheim and Arthur Stonehill

17.1. Background

17.1.1. Type of Activity

In June 1986, AB Electrolux floated a Euroequity issue of 8 million new free B-shares, netting about SEK 2 billion or $275 million. The international offering and the regional arrangement of management, underwriting and placing of the issue was co-ordinated by Enskilda Securities (Skandinaviska Enskilda Ltd) in London. Exhibit 17.1 shows the other lead managers and underwriters. The shares were offered to investors in a number of countries, although the major part was placed in the United Kingdom. Smaller parts were placed in Italy and in a few other countries.

17.1.2. Terms of Issue

The shares were placed at a price of SEK 278 per share and at exchange rates of SEK/ITL 0.466 and SEK/USD 7.3015. The price of the issued shares corresponded to the closing price on the Stockholm Stock Exchange on June 3, 1986. The exchange rates were the middle rate between the buying and the selling SEK spot rate as of 11.00 GMT on June 3, 1986. Exhibit 17.2 shows the key dates leading up to the issue.

17.1.3. Listing

AB Electrolux is a public company. At the date of the issue it was listed on the stock exchanges in Stockholm (1930), London (1928), Geneva (1955), Oslo (1981) and Paris (1983). At that time an ADR (American Depositary Receipts) program was established in the United States. A listing on the stock exchange of Milan was intended but heavy regulation obstructed that intention. After the Euroequity issue, Electrolux was listed on the

AB Electrolux

(Incorporated in the Kingdom of Sweden with limited liability)

International offering of 8,000,000 Free B shares
to raise
U.S. $300,000,000 equivalent

Co-ordinated by

Enskilda Securities
Skandinaviska Enskilda Limited

The management, underwriting and placing of the offering were arranged on a regional basis as follows:

Austria
Creditanstalt-Bankverein

Canada
Wood Gundy Inc.

France
Banque Paribas Capital Markets Limited

Banque Indosuez	Banque Louis-Dreyfus	Banque Nationale de Paris
Crédit Commercial de France		Crédit Industriel et Commercial de Paris
Crédit Lyonnais	Lazard Frères et Cie	Société Générale
Al Saudi Banque	Banque Française du Commerce Extérieur	Banque Hervet
Banque de Neuflize, Schlumberger, Mallet	Crédit du Nord	Hottinguer et Cie

Italy
(Italian Depository Receipts)
Mediobanca S.p.A.

Banca Commerciale Italiana	Credito Italiano	Banco di Roma
SIGE S.p.A.	Banca Nazionale del Lavoro	Credipar S.p.A.

Japan and the Far East
Singapore Nomura Merchant Banking Limited

Kokusai Europe Limited

The Nikko Securities Co., (Europe) Ltd.

Netherlands
EBC Amro Bank Limited

Algemene Bank Nederland N.V.

Nederlandsche Middenstandsbank nv

Pierson, Heldring & Pierson N.V.

Nordic countries (excluding Sweden)
Enskilda Securities
Skandinaviska Enskilda Limited

South and Central America
Merrill Lynch Capital Markets

Switzerland and Liechtenstein
Swiss Bank Corporation International Limited

Credit Suisse First Boston Limited

Union Bank of Switzerland (Securities) Limited

Banca del Gottardo	Banca della Svizzera Italiana	Bank Julius Baer & Co. Ltd.
Compagnie de Banque et d'Investissements, CBI	HandelsBank N.W. (Overseas) Ltd.	Leu Securities Ltd.
Lombard, Odier International Underwriters S.A.	Pictet International Ltd.	Swiss Volksbank

Bank Gutzwiller, Kurz, Bungener (Overseas) Limited	Banque Paribas (Suisse) S.A.	Sarasin International Securities Limited	Swiss Cantonalbanks

Bank Heusser & Cie AG	Bordier & Cie	Ferrier Lullin & Cie. S.A.	Hentsch & Cie	Rothschild Bank AG
United Overseas Bank				Verwaltungs- und PrivatBank Aktiengesellschaft

United Kingdom
Enskilda Securities
Skandinaviska Enskilda Limited

Cazenove & Co.

West Germany
Deutsche Bank
Aktiengesellschaft

Berliner Handels- und Frankfurter Bank	Commerzbank Aktiengesellschaft	Deutsche Girozentrale-Deutsche Kommunalbank
DG Bank Deutsche Genossenschaftsbank	Dresdner Bank Aktiengesellschaft	Westdeutsche Landesbank Girozentrale

Baden-Württembergische Bank Aktiengesellschaft	Bank für Gemeinwirtschaft Aktiengesellschaft	Joh. Berenberg, Gossler & Co.
Berliner Bank Aktiengesellschaft	Georg Hauck & Sohn Bankiers KGaA	Hessische Landesbank – Girozentrale –
Merck, Finck & Co.	B. Metzler seel. Sohn & Co.	Norddeutsche Landesbank Girozentrale
Sal. Oppenheim jr. & Cie.	Trinkaus & Burkhardt KGaA	Vereins- und Westbank Aktiengesellschaft
	M.M. Warburg-Brinckmann, Wirtz & Co.	

Other countries

Australia: **Cazenove Australia Pty. Limited**

Belgium & Luxembourg: **Enskilda Securities**
Skandinaviska Enskilda Limited

Greece and the Middle East: **Merrill Lynch Capital Markets.** Arab Banking Corporation (ABC). Kuwait Foreign Trading Contracting & Investment Co. (S.A.K.)

Spain: **S.I. Activos Financieros, S.A.**

June, 1986

Exhibit 17.2: Dates of Events Leading up to the 1986 Euroequity Issue.

Date	Event	Comments
Feb/March 1986	Internal discussion started	Acquisition of White
March 20, 1986	Information release	
May 22, 1986	Formal decision	Annual General Meeting
June 4, 1986	Implementation	Day of offer
June 11, 1986		Payment
June 18, 1986		Trading started

stock exchanges in Zurich (1987) and Basel (1987). Its shares were listed and traded through the NASDAQ system in New York (1987).

17.2. Macroeconomic Environment

At the time the international discussion about the Euroequity issue started, the global economic prospect looked fairly good. In January 1986, the OECD "Economic Outlook" predicted slow but stable growth for the following 18 months, and, with some restrictions, even better growth rates beyond June 1987. Except for the United States, both fiscal and monetary policies had been more restrictive than earlier. This had probably caused the slowdown, but would now contribute to more balanced and long lasting growth rates. An additional factor stimulating OECD-growth was falling oil prices.

On the negative side, the imbalance of current accounts between the United States on the one hand and Japan and West Germany on the other were a cause of concern. Another threat at the time of the equity issue was the looming industrial conflict in the Swedish labour market.

17.3. Expected Benefits From the Public Offer

17.3.1. Reasons for Issuing Equity Abroad

The main reason for approaching the international market was Swedish foreign exchange restrictions. At this time Sweden required companies to raise capital abroad if the funds were to be used in foreign operations. However, The Central Bank of Sweden made some exceptions to the rule (see Chapter 2). New shares could be purchased with funds obtained from sales of other Swedish securities, provided that no new shares were placed in Sweden. The domestic Swedish market lacked sufficient liquidity. A

◀ *Exhibit 17.1: The Electrolux 1986 Tombstone.*

successful international offering could also enhance the company's product exposure. Matts Ekman, the Corporate Treasurer, also hoped that a widely spread offering would smooth stock price performance.

17.3.2. Use of Funds

The net proceeds of the issue, approximately SEK 2,020 million after costs amounting to SEK 204 million, was intended to reduce short-term indebtedness. Any funds raised in Spain or in Italy would be used for investments in either the Group's or Zanussi's operations in those countries.

In practice, the proceeds were used to pay back foreign loans raised in connection with the acquisition of White Consolidated Industries Inc. The purchase of White amounted to SEK 5,400 million. In order to finance the acquisition an additional SEK 1,946 million were raised through bonds, and another SEK 1,500 million through divestment of subsidiaries and assets.

17.3.3. Balance Sheet Aspects

In the late 1970s, Electrolux had equity/asset ratios around 30 %. Those figures were down to around 20 percent at the turn of the decade, but were to increase during the first half of the 1980s, due to high profitability and divestment of assets. The ratio by the end of 1985 was 28 %. This was still very low and did not include the financially weak Zanussi. The consolidation of Zanussi in 1986 would decrease this figure by an additional 7 percentage points. Although divestment of assets during the year increased the ratio, the purchase of White reduced the figure to 20 %.

The low equity ratio limited future financing in a market facing increasing competition. A public offer was therefore necessary to strengthen the balance sheet and make expansion possible. By the end of 1986, with White and Zanussi included, the equity to total asset ratio of Electrolux was down to 24 %.

17.4. Company History

17.4.1. The Axel Wenner-Gren Era

In 1912, Elektromekaniska AB, a producer of vacuum cleaner motors and Lux, a stagnating producer of kerosene lamps, decided to merge. They hired Axel Wenner-Gren as Managing Director, a former salesman in vacuum cleaners. Due to high demand, Mr. Wenner-Gren went abroad. He received licenses to sell vacuum cleaners in Germany, France, and the United Kingdom.

Seven years later AB Electrolux was founded, with Mr. Wenner-Gren as chairman and major shareholder. A period of rapid expansion took place as a result of attractive styling and efficient marketing. Mr. Wenner-Gren used a door-to-door sales-technique.

Even when it came to advertising, he was ahead of his time. In the 1920s vacuum cleaner shaped cars could be seen on the streets of London, Berlin and Stockholm. Mr. Wenner-Gren himself enjoyed being out in the field selling vacuum cleaners. His charismatic leadership was perhaps the most important reason behind the company's success.

Already in 1928 the company had 5 manufacturing plants, 350 worldwide offices, 20 subsidiaries and a sales record of SEK 70 million. The fast growth made the company look into other fields of business. In 1925, diversification began with the acquisition of Artic, a refrigerator producer. The first mass production of household refrigerators in the world was started. Since then, vacuum cleaners and refrigerators were the core businesses of the company.

Fast growth and payment by instalment made Electrolux short of funds. As a result, the company went public in 1928 in London. Due to the stock market crash, the flotation in Stockholm was delayed until 1930. B-shares with a voting power of 0.001 votes per share were issued. This entitled Mr. Wenner-Gren, in spite of a low capital share, to maintain control over the company.

The company survived the 1930s through heavy investment in R & D and in its well-known marketing. In 1939, Electrolux sales amounted to SEK 80 million. Mr. Wenner-Gren resigned in 1939. His ideas of how to run the company continued to be very influential. In the 1940s Electrolux went into kitchen appliances, outboard motors and washing machines and in 1959, the first dishwasher was introduced. Expansion had to a large degree been a result of internal growth. Expansion into other business areas was always closely related to the old ones.

In the 1950s the market growth began to deteriorate. The market suffered from overcapacity with mostly medium-sized companies. It was important for the participants to realise whether they were niche players or market leaders. A serious price competition took place with the most efficient companies ending as survivors. Size and rationalisation in production and distribution were essential. This meant economies of scale and necessitated international expansion. A globalisation of Electrolux' market began.

17.4.2. The Hans Werthèn Era

In 1967, a new phase of the company history began when Hans Werthèn was elected President. He realised that Electrolux was neither a niche player or market leader in its different branches of business. With the strategy to be either one, a phase of rapid expansion through acquisitions began. In 20 years it increased sales from SEK 1,070 million in 1967 to SEK 67,000 million in 1987. Fifty percent of this increase was due to internal growth while the remaining part was due to acquisitions. During this period of time, some 350 companies were acquired.

In order to follow this "do-or-die" strategy, Mr. Werthèn decided to withdraw from the US market in 1967. Electrolux sold its brand name, but when it later returned the company competed against its own name. The expansion began in the Nordic market, mainly within existing activities. When market leadership was reached, continued expansion through strategic acquisitions in Europe and the United States followed. The motive was always to either dominate the niche or the entire market.

17.4.3. The Acquisition Strategy

For the company, acquisitions were either a diversification to make Electrolux less sensitive to business cycles, or a consolidation to strengthen its existing market position. A precondition to a diversification was that management had knowledge about the acquired company's market or how to manage it. The acquired company should benefit Electrolux in production or distribution, enabling rationalisation in these areas. The price had to be right, meaning that Electrolux only bought "sick", inexpensive companies, which were turned around very quickly. According to Mr. Werthèn, good, expensive companies could not be afforded. Sick companies accumulated losses were also useful for tax deduction reasons.

Most acquisitions were self-financed since Electrolux was able to divest assets that did not fit in with its core businesses. In the cases of Zanussi and White, the management did however decide to raise funds through public offers. This decision came as a result of the financial size of the acquisitions in combination with the high share prices of Electrolux stock due to its prosperous outlook.

With the acquisition of Zanussi (1984), an Italian white goods producer, Electrolux's market share in Europe increased from 10 to 20 %. White Consolidated (1986), one of the largest American white goods producers, gave Electrolux a good stronghold on the US market. Those two were the most significant acquisitions in the 1980s. Other important acquisitions, organised by geographic area, were as follows.

Important Acquisitions in Sweden:
- Asab Serviceföretaget AB, a commercial cleaning-service, with internationally expanding business.
- Husqvarna AB, a household appliances producer, that contributed new products, such as sewing machines and chainsaws, to the Electrolux product range.
- Gränges, a large metal producer.

Important Acquisitions in Europe (outside Sweden):
- Usines et Arthur Martin S.A., a manufacturer of cookers, washing machines and dishwashers in France and Belgium.
- Tornado S.A. a French vacuum cleaner producer.
- Therma AG, a Swiss producer of cookers and heating appliances.
- Zanker Gmbh, which produced washing machines and driers in Germany.

Important Acquisitions in the United States:
- National Union Electric Corporation, a vacuum cleaner producer with a leading position in the U.S. market.
- The Tappan Company, a producer of cookers, microwave ovens and kitchen cabinets.
- The Duo-Therm Company, a producer of air conditioning and air heating for mobile homes and caravans.
- Diamond Cabinet, a kitchen furniture producer.

In 1986, after nearly 70 years of existence, Electrolux had grown from a single product, all-European, company into an international group of 500 companies, covering 46 countries, and employing 140,500 people.

Exhibit 17.3: Ownership Structure Before and After the Euroequity Issue.
(as of February each year)

Shareholder	Percent of capital		Percent of votes	
	1986	1987	1986	1987
ASEA AB (Wallenberg	12.7	10.2	49.0	48.6
The Wallenberg Group of which	5.5	3.2	45.9	45.7
AB Investor	3.1	2.5	33.5	35.4
AB Providentia	0.7	0.6	7.6	9.9
4th National Insurance Fund	5.7	4.4	0.2	0.2

17.5. Ownership Situation

Electrolux had been controlled by the Wallenberg family since 1956 when Mr. Wenner-Gren's A-shares were bought. At the time of the issue, this gave the Wallenbergs control over 95 % of the voting rights even though they only controlled 18 % of the equity. (See Exhibit 17.3) This was the result of dual shares as regards voting power, A- and B-shares. The A-shares entitled the owner to one vote per share while the B-shares entitled to 0.001 vote per share. Electrolux was one of six companies on the Stockholm Stock Exchange that had such a low voting percentage for their B-shares.

The Wallenberg group was composed of a number of companies, foundations and funds, that had major interests in Swedish industry. This ownership situation was very beneficial for Electrolux since the Wallenberg family's international financial network made it easy to get access to overseas funding, a necessity for rapid expansion. The family also protected the company from hostile takeovers, which gave management the possibility to emphasise a long-term perspective in running the company. Electrolux was also protected from foreign owners due to Swedish regulations, as explained in Chapter 2.

Although the 1986 issue corresponded to 13 % of total equity, the power structure was unchanged. Exhibit 17.3 shows the main shareholders before and after the 1986 equity issue. When the issue was settled, 23 % of Electrolux's shares were owned by foreigners.

17.6. Organization

At the time of the issue Electrolux was organised into six business areas: Household appliances, Commercial appliances, Commercial services,

Outdoor products, Industrial products and Building components. The business areas comprised 24 product lines, each consisting of several companies. Responsibility for the operations of a product was shared between the executives of the appropriate company and the product line manager. Units, which only operated one product line, were known as single-product-companies and reported to the product line manager. Multiproduct line companies reported primarily to the group management.

17.7. Product-Market Data

17.7.1. Market Conditions

Around the time of the 1986 issue, the world market for household appliances was divided into two major markets, the United States and European markets. These accounted for 40 % each of the world market.

The restructuring of the US market over the previous 30 years had left four major actors with a total market share of over 90 %. The economies of scale these companies enjoyed can be seen in productivity figures and profit margins that were substantially higher than their European counterparts'. (See Exhibits 17.4 and 17.5).

In Europe the four largest competitors had a total market share of 50 %. The profit margins were lower, which was a result of small domestic producers that ran fierce price competition. The Eastern Europe producers also offered low prices as a result of government subsidies. A restructuring of the market had just begun with Electrolux as a driving force. Exhibit 17.4 shows major competitors and Exhibit 17.5 shows market shares.

17.7.2. Sales

Exhibit 17.6 presents sales broken down by product division. The exhibit brackets 1986, the year of the equity issue. Note the heavy reliance on household appliances (Exhibit 17.6). Exhibit 17.7 shows that the geographical dispersion of sales was fairly evenly balanced between the Nordic region, rest of Europe, and the United States. The increase in the U.S. share of sales reflected the purchase of White Consolidated.

Exhibit 17.4: Major Competitors in the Area of Household Appliances (1987).

Company	Sales 87 (SEKm)	Increase in sales 83-87 (%)	Operating income after depr 87 (SEKm)	Increase in income 83-87 (%)	Margin 87 (%)	Margin average 83-87 (%)	Number of employees 83-87	Income per employee (SEK)
Electrolux	67,400	20.0	4,200	11.5	6.0	7.5	140,500	30,000
Household appliances	38,500	24.0	2,100	5.0	5.5	8.0	–	
General Electric (USA)	257,100	11.0	24,100	11.0	12.0	11.0	302,000	80,000
Household appliances	31,000	10.0	2,600	8.0	8.5	12.0	–	–
Siemens (W.Germany)	182,000	7.0	9,200	12.5	5.0	5.0	359,000	25,600
Household appliances	13,800	–	–	–	–	–	15,600	–
Philips (Holland)	165,000	3.5	7,600	-3.0	4.5	5.5	337,000	22,500
Household appliances	19,801	–	1,000	–	5.0	–	–	–
Whirpool (USA)	26,000	12.0	1,600		6.0	8.5	30,000	54,000
Maytag (USA)	12,000	5.0	1,600	6.0	14.0	13.0	13,100	120,300
Chicago Pacific (USA)	9,000	–	800	–	8.0	8.5	22,000	39,000
Average	–	10.0	–	6.0	8.0	8.5	–	50,000

Source: Affärsvärlden No. 32, 1988.

Exhibit 17.5: Market Shares (%).

US market		European market	
Competitors	Market share	Competitors	Market share
Whirpool	32.7	Electrolux	20.5
General Electric	5.5	Whirpool	11.5
Electrolux	18.4	Bosch/Siemens	11.0
Maytag	14.8	Merloni	10.0
Others	8.7	Others	47.0

Source: Veckans Affärer, No 23, 1990.

Exhibit 17.6: Sales by Product Division.

	Sales by product division	
(percentage)	1985	1986
Household appliance	50,9	61,5
Commercial appliance	8,4	8,0
Commercial service	5,7	4,7
Outdoor products	7,5	5,5
Industrial products	6,0	8,2
Building components (Gränges)	21,5	12,1

Source: Electrolux, Annual Report 1986.

Exhibit 17.7: Sales by Geographical Division.

	Sales by geographical area	
(percentage)	1985	1986
Nordic region	35,2	26,0
Europe (excl Nordic region)	33,0	33,2
USA	21,9	31,1
Rest of the world	9,9	9,7

Source: Electrolux, Annual Report 1986.

17.8. Financial Data

17.8.1. Implications of the Issue on Capital Structure

Regarding capital structure, one implication of a stock issue is an increase in shareholders' equity. Exhibit 17.8 shows the capital structure during 1984-1987. In the case of Electrolux, shareholders' equity increased from SEK 6,903 million in 1985 to SEK 11,659 million by the end of 1986. Out of this SEK 4,756 (68.9 %) million increase, SEK 2,224 million (32.2 %) came from the new issue. The effect on Electrolux's equity of the SEK 2,224 million issue was that capital stock increased by SEK 200 million (13.7%) and the remaining SEK 2,024 million was placed in restricted reserves. The transaction cost of SEK 204 million reduced unrestricted reserves.

Although the new issue increased the shareholder's equity, total indebtedness did not decrease. Instead, liabilities actually increased due to high activity in the international credit market. In 1986, Electrolux sold four bond issues and two other corporate securities for a total of SEK 4,446 million. Electrolux also established a program to sell medium-term notes totalling SEK 2,040 million.

17.8.2. Profits

The profits of the Electrolux Group showed constant growth during the years 1983-1989. Increases for 1985 and 1986, were, however, very low as shown in Exhibit 17.9.

Exhibit 17.8: Capital Structure 1984-1987.

	1984	1985	1986	1987
Total liabilities/Total assets (%)	73.7	71.9	75.8	75.4
	(66.7)	(64.7)	(71.5)	(70.7)
Total assets (SEK million)	26,281	29,524	48,181	48,470
Adj shareholder's equity acc to SAS (SEK million)	6,903	8,306	11,659	11,941
Net assets per share (SEK)	115	131	161	164

The consolidated financial statements are made in conformity with Swedish Accounting Standards (SAS), which differ in certain ways from International Accounting Standards (IAS). According to SAS, 50 percent of untaxed reserves belongs to liabilities and the other 50 percent belongs to shareholders' equity. But in accordance with IAS, a company can't make appropriations to untaxed reserves. This means that total reserves should be included in shareholders' equity. Figures in brackets show liabilities as a percentage of total assets in accordance with IAS. The unbracketed percentages are according to SAS. *Source:* Electrolux, Annual Reports 1983-1987.

Exhibit 17.9: Profit and Loss Account 1983-1989.

	1983	1984	1985	1986	1987	1988	1989
Income after financial items (SEKm)	1,763	2,470	2,576	2,583	3,060	3,727	3,608
Net earnings per share (SEK)	11.80	22.20	22.20	24.80	25.00	28.60	31.20

Source: Electrolux, Annual Report 1991

17.9. Preparations for the Euroequity Issue

The Electrolux Group had followed the strategy that growth should be reached mainly through continuous acquisitions of other companies. In the past Electrolux borrowed short-term both domestically and internationally to finance its expansion program, but this time the company partly financed the acquisition of White by issuing new shares.

The Company intended to list the new shares on multiple stock exchanges. The Central Bank of Sweden had granted Electrolux a dispensation from the requirement that the new shares should be purchased with currency obtained from sale of other Swedish securities under the precondition that no parts of the new issue were placed in Sweden.

The new shares were offered to specific banks, brokers and dealers for sale to investors in particular regions specified by Electrolux. The regions included a great number of countries with the exception of the United States, which was excluded due to exceptionally high sensitivity and volatility. It was unusual for an Euroequity issue to exclude both the home market (Sweden) and the United States.

17.10. Stock Market Reaction

17.10.1. Analysts View

The *Financial Times* published an article prior to the stock issue, in which Enskilda Securities, the issue coordinator, claimed "...it was confident about the timing of the issue despite the looming threat of widespread industrial conflict in the Swedish labour market. It hopes that equity markets will be buyoed by the current strength of activity on Wall Street."[1]

In the case of Electrolux's acquisition of White, Swedish periodicals published evaluations on aspects such as the new investment strategic

1.   *The Financial Times* 01.06.86

position, the management's ability to integrate White with Electrolux, and the historical and future performance of the Electrolux stock. These evaluations provided the basis for evaluating the issue price. The price had to be low enough to attract buyers and high enough to keep the owners satisfied.

The issue price was set at SEK 278. Considering that the stock sold for SEK 50-60 in 1982, *Affärsvärlden*, a Swedish weekly business magazine, argued that stockholders hardly could accuse the management of diluting the stock. They further said that since the stock was not under any pressure it was a golden opportunity for Electrolux to conduct a stock issue "....the foreign investors will be standing in line to participate in the issue..."[2] One week earlier Affärsvärlden presented another analysis, in which the periodical argued that Electrolux had the same characteristics today (1986) as in 1982. It had the same management and the same capital. Instead, what had changed was the investors' expectations in listed Swedish companies in general and in Electrolux in particular. "It is then both correct and easy to make a stock issue."[3]

Veckans Affärer, another Swedish business magazine, shared the same opinion and recommended Electrolux as a long-term investment.[4] It considered the White acquisition to be strategically in line with Electrolux's previous engagement in the United States, since both White's product lines complemented each other very well. They also believed that there could be economies of scale when coordination between the European and the U.S. production plants was completed. The above mentioned reasons, in combination with Electrolux's well known ability to turn around low performing units into high performing entities, would make the stock a good buy in the long run. They therefore forecasted a continued high demand for the stock, which would result in a successful stock issue.

17.10.2. Short-term Reaction

Exhibit 17.10 shows the stock markets' reaction to the 1986 Euroequity issue. Both Electrolux and the stock market as a whole showed an increase in the following days. The Electrolux B-share declined about 10 % during the trading week preceding the issue. However, in the three days following the issue it regained the entire decline. As is shown in Exhibit 17.11, a

2. *Affärsvärlden*, No 13-14, 1986 (author's translation)
3. *Affärsvärlden*, No 12, 1986 (author's translation)
4. *Veckans Affärer*, No 16, 1986

Exhibit 17.10: The Development of the Electrolux Share Price Compared to Market Index.

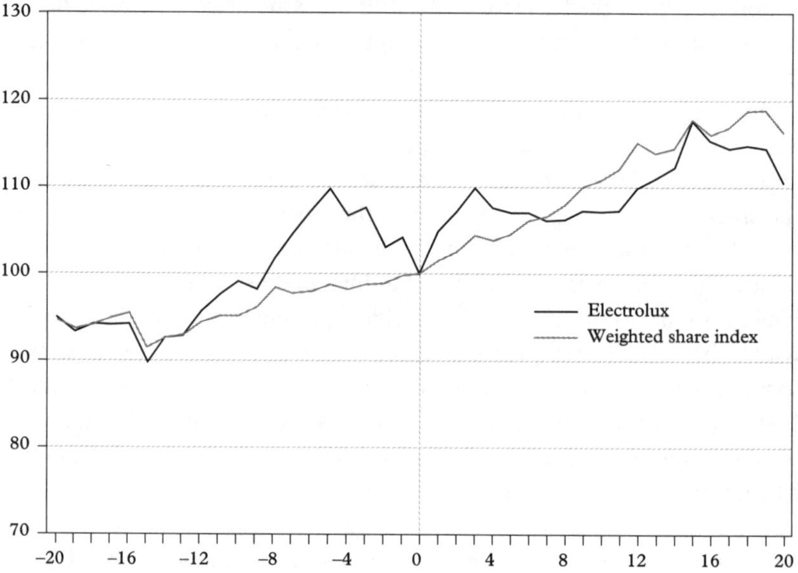

Note: The X-axis shows the number of days before and after the event day (day 0).

Exhibit 17.11: Daily Abnormal Returns around the date of Announcement of the Euroequity Issue.

Date	Abnormal return %
March 13	1.0
March 14	−1.8
March 17	−0.3
March 18	−4.5
March 19	−0.4
March 20, date for the release of information.	−4.2
March 21	2.0
March 24	0.7
March 25	−0.4
March 26	−1.5
March 27	−1.7

Note: The abnormal return on a particular day is the excess return after having considered the riskiness of the share and the general stock market development that very day. See also Chapter 4.

risk-adjusted decline of 4.2 % occurred the day of the announcement. This was typical for an unsegmented market and for a company that had already earned an international cost of capital and was being priced by global standards as explained in Chapter 4. Although there was a positive abnormal return during the two trading days following the issue, the cumulative

Exhibit 17.12: The Long Term Development of the Electrolux Share Price.

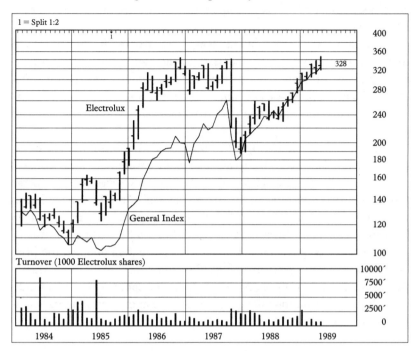

abnormal return for the six days following the announcement was a negative 5.1 %. On the other hand, there was no significant flowback of shares to Sweden.

17.10.3. Long-term Performance

As is shown in Exhibit 17.12 the Electrolux share underperformed the Swedish stock market in the 18 months following the issue. The underperformance continued again in the early 1990s.

17.11. The Aftermath to the Euroequity Issue of 1986

17.11.1. Further Acquisitions

After the issue, Electrolux continued its policy of gaining market shares through buying competitors, although none of these acquisitions amounted to the same large figures as Zanussi and White. Examples were the U.S. companies Poulan/Weed Eater in late 1986, Roper in 1988, and the household appliance division of the British manufacturer, Thorn EMI, in 1987.

In addition to Poulan/Weed Eater, Electrolux at the time also attempted to buy other manufacturers in the highly successful business area "Outdoor Products". Electrolux was continuously looking for suitable candidates to purchase and since the United States is the largest market for gardening products, the Group has naturally concentrated its effort in this market.

In 1988, Electrolux attempted to buy the U.S. lawnmower manufacturer, Murrey. However, due to fierce resistance from both local management and workers, Electrolux found that the price was not worth the effort. The affair ended when the British company, Tomkins, appeared as a "white knight" and offered US $56 per share, four dollars more than Electrolux's final bid. Electrolux was forced to sell its holdings in Murrey but made a capital gain, since Tomkin's bid more than doubled the price Electrolux originally paid. Although Electrolux lost some "face" due to the unsuccessful acquisition, Anders Scharp, the company president indicated that the purchasing policy was fixed and that there were more acquisitions to come.[5]

17.11.2. Financial Situation

The aggressive purchasing policy and extensive investment programs in Italy and the United States, together with poor development in several of Electrolux's core markets, strained Electrolux's financial strength. The acquisitions just after the large stock issue in 1986 were financed through a combination of retained earnings, new loans, and divestment of assets. Various factors strained Electrolux in the late 1980s. The downturning market decreased the earnings. The poor development of the price of Electrolux stock limited opportunities for a further stock issue. In the late 1980s, management had to embark on an extensive reconstruction program. This meant a close down of several plants to cut costs. Parts of the group were also for sale. First out for divestment was the Commercial Services Division. As of 1990, Electrolux had sold 70 percent of this business area, with gains amounting to approximately SEK 800 million in bookvalue.

5. Dagens Industri, July 7,1988

In conclusion, due to its early (1928) first crosslisting, the Electrolux share price was already at an international level at the time of the Euroequity issue of 1986. However, in practice the proceeds from that large issue helped to reduce short-term indebtedness caused by the acquisitions of White Consolidated and Zanussi. The improved liquidity enabled Electrolux to maintain its favourable international cost of capital.

About the Contributors

Lars Oxelheim is a Professor of International Business and Finance at the Institute of Economic Research, Lund University and Senior Researcher at the Research Institute of Industrial Economics (IUI) in Stockholm. He is chairman of the Swedish network for EU-research in Economics and Management. He is the author or co-author of some 20 books and a number of articles. His current research interest is in the area of corporate decision-making in an increasingly integrated world economy. Professor Oxelheim received his Ph.D. from Lund University (Sweden).

Arthur I. Stonehill is a visiting Professor of Finance and International Business at the University of Hawaii at Manoa (1991-present). He has held teaching and research appointments at Copenhagen Business School (Denmark) (1991-96), and Oregon State University (1966-93). He is past President of the Academy of International Business. He has authored or co-authored eight books and twenty-five other publications. His current research is focused on internationalisation of the cost of capital. Professor Stonehill received his B.A. in history from Yale University (1953), MBA from Harvard Business School (1957) and Ph.D. from University of California, Berkley (1965). He received honorary doctorates from the Aarhus School Of Business (1989) and the Copenhagen Business School (1992).

Trond Randøy is an Associate Professor of International Business at Agder College, Kristiansand, Norway. He also holds a Research Directorship at the Centre for International Economics and Shipping, Agder Research Foundation. Randøy has a Ph.D. from the Norwegian School of Economics and Business Administration, Bergen, Norway. He has produced a number of publications on issues related to foreign direct investments and the behaviour of multinational firms.

Kåre B. Dullum is partner/president of Gudme Raaschou Bankaktiesel-skab, an independent Danish investment bank. He served as the chief financial officer of Novo Industri A/S 1974-1984. Prior to this he taught Management Accounting at the Copenhagen Business School 1967-1974 and chained his department. He holds a MBA-degree from University of Wisconsin, Madison and a cand.polit.-degree from University of Copenhagen. He is adjunct professor of the Copenhagen Business School and a member of the board of directors of the Scandinavian International Management Institute. Kåre B. Dullum has authored or co-authored seven books and twelve other publications.

Kaisa Vikkula is the Senior Vice President of Investor Relations and Corporate Communications at Partek, a major Finnish industrial corporation. She holds a Ph.D. from the Finnish School of Economics and Business Administration. Her research has been focused on strategic choice and performance.

Karl-Markus Modén holds a Ph.D. in Economics from the University of Pennsylvania. He is currently a Researcher at the Industrial Institute of Economic and Social Research (IUI) in Stockholm. Modén's main research interests focuses on the internationalisation of businesses and the related public policy issues.

Eva Liljeblom is an Associate Professor in Finance at the Swedish School of Economics and Business Administration, Helsinki, Finland. She is the Prefect of the Department of Finance at her school, and the director of the Graduate School of Finance and Financial Accounting (GSFFA), a joint Ph.D. program also involving the departments of Finance at the Helsinki School of Economics and at the University of Vaasa. She has produced a number of publications on issues related to asset pricing and corporate finance.

Anders Löflund (Ph.D.) is an Assistant Professor in Finance at the Swedish School of Economics and Business Administration, Helsinki, Finland. He has published a number of articles on empirical asset pricing which continues to be a key area on his current research agenda.

Svante Krofors has a masters degree from the Swedish School of Economics and Business Administration, Helsinki, Finland. He is a financial analyst at Evli Fondkomission, Helsinki, Finland.

Index